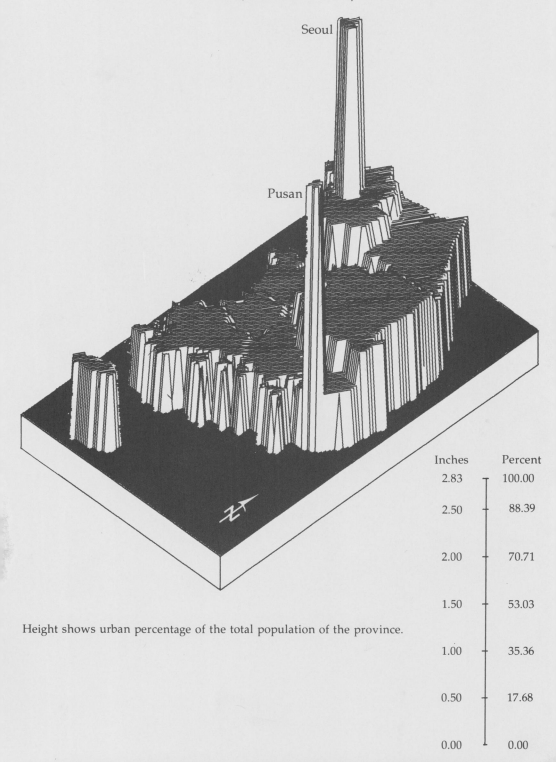

The Urban Population of Korea by Province, 1975
A Computer-Generated Map

Seoul

Pusan

W9-AUS-748

Inches	Percent
2.83	100.00
2.50	88.39
2.00	70.71
1.50	53.03
1.00	35.36
0.50	17.68
0.00	0.00

Height shows urban percentage of the total population of the province.

KOREA

Problems and Issues in a Rapidly Growing Economy

A WORLD BANK COUNTRY ECONOMIC REPORT

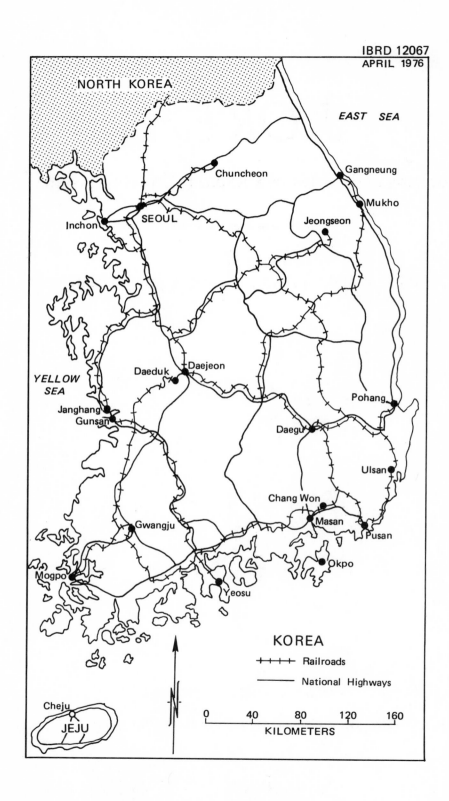

IBRD 12067
APRIL 1976

NORTH KOREA

EAST SEA

Chuncheon

Gangneung

Mukho

Inchon

SEOUL

Jeongseon

YELLOW
SEA

Daeduk

Daejeon

Pohang

Janghang
Gunsan

Daegu

Ulsan

Chang Won

Gwangju

Masan

Pusan

Okpo

Mogpo

Yeosu

KOREA

+ + + + Railroads

National Highways

0   40   80   120   160
KILOMETERS

Cheju

JEJU

KOREA

Problems and Issues in a Rapidly Growing Economy

Parvez Hasan

Published for the World Bank

THE JOHNS HOPKINS UNIVERSITY PRESS • *Baltimore and London*

'3101.34

*330.9519
H344*

Note

The currency unit of Korea is the won (W).
W485 = US$1.00
The fiscal year is January 1 to December 31.

Copyright © 1976 by the International Bank for
Reconstruction and Development / The World Bank
1818 H Street, N.W., Washington, D.C. 20433, U.S.A.
All rights reserved.
The views and interpretations in this book are
those of the authors and should not be attributed
to the World Bank, to its affiliated organizations,
or to any individual acting in their behalf.

Library of Congress Cataloging in Publication Data

Hasan, Parvez.
   Korea: problems and issues in a rapidly growing economy.
   (A World Bank country economic report)
   Includes index.
   1. Korea—Economic conditions—1945–   2. Korea—Commerce.
I. International Bank for Reconstruction and Development. II. Title.
III. Series: World Bank country economic reports.
HC467.H37   330.9′519′043   76-17238
ISBN 0-8018-1864-8

RIDER COLLEGE LIBRARY

Foreword

THIS IS THE TWELFTH IN THE CURRENT SERIES OF World Bank country economic reports, all of which are listed on the following page. They are published, in response to a desire expressed by scholars and practitioners in the field of economic and social development, to aid and encourage research and the interchange of knowledge.

Economic reports on borrowing countries are prepared regularly by the Bank in support of its own operations. These surveys provide a basis for discussions with the governments and for decisions on Bank policy and operations. Many of these reports are also used by the governments themselves as an aid to their economic planning and by consortia and consultative groups of governments and institutions providing assistance in development. All Bank country reports are subject to the agreement of—and several have been published by—the governments concerned.

HOLLIS CHENERY
Vice President for Development Policy
The World Bank

Washington, D. C.
June 1976

v

WORLD BANK COUNTRY ECONOMIC REPORTS

Published for the Bank by The Johns Hopkins University Press

Korea: Problems and Issues in a Rapidly Growing Economy
Kenya: Into the Second Decade
Yugoslavia: Development with Decentralization
Nigeria: Options of Long-Term Development
Economic Growth of Colombia

Published by the World Bank

The Philippines: Priorities and Prospects for Development
Lesotho: A Development Challenge
Turkey: Prospects and Problems of an Expanding Economy
Senegal: Tradition, Diversification, and Economic Development
  (also published in French)
Chad: Development Potential and Constraints (also published
  in French as *Le Développement du Tchad: Possibilités
  et Limites*)
Current Economic Position and Prospects of Peru
Current Economic Position and Prospects of Ecuador
Employment in Trinidad and Tobago

Contents

Foreword   v
Preface   xiii

Summary and Conclusions   3
   Growth and Structural Change   4
   Resource Management Problems   6
   Recent Developments   8
   Long-term Strategy   9
   Resource Requirements   11
   Export Growth versus Import Substitution   13
   External Capital Requirements   15
   Domestic Saving Needs   17
   Industrial Plans   19
   Resource Allocation   21
   Distribution of Growth Benefits   22
   Social Goals   23

1. Historical Background and the Origins of Growth   25
   Historical Setting   25
   Origins of Rapid Growth   29
   Infrastructure Development   30

2. Problems of Rapid Growth: 1963–72   37
   Overall Trends   38
   Resource Management   41
   Distribution of Growth Benefits   45
   Export Incentives   56

3. Recent Economic Developments and New Economic Challenges   59
   Upsurge during 1973   60
   Export Boom   62
   Debt Service   65
   Industrial Growth   66

New Economic Challenges   69
Government Policy Response   73
An Overview of the Adjustment Process   79

4. *Long-term Strategy and Development Issues*   81
Major Issues   82
Export Prospects   84
Resource Requirements   95
Social Goals   107

5. *Long-term Industrial Plans*   115
Deepening of Industrial Structure   117
New Factors Influencing Strategy   120
Industrial Financing Needs   122
Framework for Industrial Planning   124
Research and Development   126
Problems and Prospects of Major Industries   127

6. *Agricultural Development: Past Performance and Future Plans*   139
Production Prospects   143
Grain Self-Sufficiency   144
Foreign Trade   146
Development of Land and Water Resources   146
Farm Mechanization and Labor Productivity   147
Investment Projections and Priorities   148

Appendix A. Long-term Employment Projections   151

Appendix B. The Sae Maeul Movement   159

Appendix C. The Textile Industry   165
Cotton Textiles   167
Knitting Industry   170
Garment Industry   171
Synthetic Fibers   172

Appendix D. The Electronics Industry   177
Structure and Performance   177
Development Plans and Issues   182
Marketing Development   186

Appendix E. The Shipbuilding Industry   187
Recent Developments   188
Export Market   190
Domestic Market   191

Statistical Appendix   195
Index   269

Tables

1. Rates of Growth of GNP by Sector 27
2. Growth of Industrial Production 28
3. Expansion of Social Overhead Capital 31
4. Share of Traffic by Mode of Transport 31
5. Rate of Increase in Transport Service by Mode 32
6. Housing Construction, 1962–73 33
7. Improvement in Communications Facilities 33
8. Major Exports 38
9. Principal Indicators of Structural Change in the Economy 40
10. Shares of Gross Savings in GNP, 1965–72 42
11. Government Revenue and Expenditure 43
12. The Terms of Trade of Agriculture 46
13. Aggregate Trends in Sectoral Output and Employment, 1963–72 48
14. Labor Force and Employment, 1963–74 49
15. Manufacturing and Agricultural Wages 50
16. Comparison of Incomes of Rural and Urban Households 52
17. Number and Cropland Area of Farm Households, 1971 54
18. Saving and Investment Trends 61
19. Geographical Concentration of Exports 64
20. Private Direct Foreign Investment: Net Inflows 65
21. Gross Disbursements on Medium- and Long-term External Loans 65
22. Debt Outstanding and Debt Burden 66
23. Manufacturing Growth and Investment 67
24. Composition and Growth of the Manufacturing Sector, 1960–74 68
25. Manufacturing Concentration 70
26. Demand and Supply of Total Energy 71
27. Pattern of Imports 72
28. Public Sector Savings and Investment 75
29. Monetary Survey, 1970–74 77
30. Export Targets 90
31. Adjusted Real Effective Exchange Rate on Exports 94
32. Incremental Capital-Output Ratios, Unlagged 96
33. The Overall Resource Position 97
34. Uses and Sources of Foreign Exchange 102
35. Summary Balance of Payments, 1972–81 104
36. Desirable Growth of Urban and Rural Incomes 109
37. Farm Household Labor Employed Outside Agriculture 111

38. Population and Employment by Farm and Nonfarm
    Households and Sectors   *112*
39. Composition of Manufacturing Output   *116*
40. Manufacturing Investment, 1973–81   *117*
41. The Planned Expansion of Manufacturing Capacity   *118*
42. Exports as a Percentage of Total Demand   *119*
43. Total Manufacturing Investment   *122*
44. Food-Grain Production   *140*
45. Annual Growth Rates of Principal Subsectors in Agriculture *142*
46. Grains: Per Capita Disappearance and Share of Total Supply
    Imported   *145*
47. Exports of Agricultural Products   *146*
48. Investment Projections for Agriculture, Forestry, and
    Fisheries   *149*
A1. Population and Age Distribution, 1966–81   *152*
A2. Availability of Labor Force, 1966–81   *153*
A3. Economically Active Population and School Attendance   *155*
A4. Trends in Employment   *155*
A5. Employment, Gross Value Added, and Employment-Income
    Elasticities   *156*
B1. Physical Achievements of the Sae Maeul Movement, 1971–74   *160*
B2. Gross Investment under the Sae Maeul Movement, 1971–74   *161*
C1. Production of Yarns   *166*
C2. Production of Fabrics   *166*
C3. Structure of the Textile Industry, 1972   *166*
C4. Textile Exports   *168*
C5. Supply and Demand for Cotton Yarn and Cloth   *169*
C6. Consumption of Synthetic Fibers   *173*
C7. Domestic Production of Synthetic Fibers   *173*
D1. Growth of Electronics Industry Production   *178*
D2. Exports by Investor   *178*
D3. Composition of the Electronics Industry   *180*
D4. Korean Electronics Industry Supply and Demand Projection   *183*
D5. Projected Exports of Consumer Electronics   *184*
D6. U.S. Imports and Consumption of Electronic Consumer Goods *185*
E1. Launchings by Major Shipbuilding Countries of Ships 100
    Gross Tons and Over   *188*
E2. Ship Export Contracts on Hand, August 1974   *189*
E3. Ship Construction, Import, and Export, 1965–72   *193*

Statistical Appendix

SA1. Total Population Trends and Projections, 1960–81   *195*
SA2. Selected Economic Indicators, 1962–74   *196*
SA3. Expenditure on Gross National Product, 1965–74, at Current Market Prices   *200*
SA4. Expenditure on Gross National Product, 1965–74, at Constant 1970 Market Prices   *201*
SA5. Industrial Origin of Gross National Product, 1965–74, at Current Market Prices   *202*
SA6. Industrial Origin of Gross National Product, 1965–74, at 1970 Constant Market Prices   *203*
SA7. Industrial Share of Gross National Product, 1965–74   *204*
SA8. Aggregate Distribution of the National Income, 1965–74   *206*
SA9. Percentage Distribution of the National Income, 1965–74   *207*
SA10. Gross Domestic Fixed Capital Formation, 1965–74: Amount by Sector   *208*
SA11. Gross Domestic Fixed Capital Formation, 1965–74: Percentage by Sector   *210*
SA12. Balance of Payments: Consolidated Account, 1965–74   *212*
SA13. Balance of Payments: Goods and Services Account, 1965–74   *213*
SA14. Commodity Composition of Exports, 1965–74   *214*
SA15. Destination of Exports, 1965–74   *216*
SA16. Imports by Funding Source, 1962–73   *216*
SA17. Imports by Country of Origin, 1965–74   *217*
SA18. Commodity Composition of Imports, 1964–74   *218*
SA19. External Public Debt Outstanding as of December 31, 1974, Repayable in Foreign Currency   *220*
SA20. Foreign Trade Quantum and Unit Value Indexes and Terms of Trade, 1965–74   *222*
SA21. Total Medium- and Long-term Loans from Official Sources, 1962–74   *223*
SA22. Total Medium- and Long-term Loans to the Banking System, 1968–74   *223*
SA23. Total Medium- and Long-term Loans from Commercial Sources, 1962–74   *224*
SA24. Medium-term Trade Finance of One- to Three-year Maturities, 1966–74   *224*
SA25. Total Medium- and Long-term External Debt, 1962–74   *225*
SA26. External Borrowing and Terms, 1966–72   *226*
SA27. Official Loans Classified by Terms, 1959–74   *227*
SA28. Commercial Loans Classified by Terms, 1962–74   *228*
SA29. Public Revenues and Expenditures, 1970–74   *230*

SA30. Central and Local Government Tax Revenues, 1965–74   233
SA31. Public Investment Program (Development Budget), 1974–75 *234*
SA32. Selected Annual Interest Rates on Loans and Discounts
        of the Bank of Korea, 1965–72   236
SA33. Selected Annual Interest Rates on Loans and Discounts
        of Commercial Banks, 1965–74   236
SA34. Deposit Interest Rates of Banking Institutions, 1965–74 237
SA35. Production of Agricultural Crops, 1965–74   238
SA36. Yield per Hectare of Major Crops, 1965–74   239
SA37. Utilization of Cultivated Land, 1965–74   240
SA38. Number of Livestock and Output of Livestock Products,
        1965–74   *241*
SA39. Paddy Area Classified by Irrigation Facilities, 1965–74 242
SA40. Growth of Industrial Production, 1967–74   242
SA41. Number and Tonnage of Fishing Vessels, 1965–74   243
SA42. Index of Industrial Production, 1962–74   244
SA43. Gross Output and Value Added of the Manufacturing
        Sector by Economic Activity, 1973   246
SA44. Structure of the Manufacturing Sector, 1970–72   248
SA45. Summary of Mining and Manufacturing Survey, 1972   249
SA46. Financial Indicators of the Manufacturing Sector, 1968–73 250
SA47. Foreign Investment, 1962–June 30, 1973   251
SA48. Imports of Raw Materials for Manufactures, 1966–74:
        Dollar Value   252
SA49. Imports of Raw Materials for Manufactures, 1966–74:
        Percentage Distribution   253
SA50. Average Monthly Earnings of Regular Employees in
        Mining and Manufacturing, 1970–74   254
SA51. Annual Changes in Price Deflators, 1954–74   255
SA52. Changes in the Price of Food Grains, 1969–73   256
SA53. Family Income Distribution in All Cities, 1965–71   257
SA54. Price Trends, 1966–74   *258*
SA55. Pattern of Consumption of Electric Power, 1965–74   259
SA56. Growth of Power Demand by Industry, 1968–72   260
SA57. Power Generation and Fuel Use, 1965–74   262
SA58. Number of Registered Vehicles at Year's End, 1964–74   262
SA59. Korean National Railroads: Equipment and Revenues,
        1964–74   263
SA60. Growth of Domestic Traffic, 1962–73   264
SA61. Mode of Transport of Major Commodities, 1967–74   *266*
SA62. Status of Harbor Facilities, December 31, 1973   267
SA63. Public Roads, 1962–73   267
SA64. Hospital Beds per Population Unit, 1960–72   *268*

Preface

As this book goes to press, the third five-year plan (1972–76) of the Republic of Korea is successfully drawing to a close with many of the original targets exceeded, and the government is completing the fourth plan which will be launched at the beginning of 1977. The impressive economic success of Korea during the last decade has attracted worldwide attention and is of special interest to the developing nations. This report does not dwell on the factors underlying the rapid growth, however, but rather concentrates on the problems which the country has faced and is likely to face in sustaining a high rate of economic expansion while bringing about structural changes in the economy and ensuring a reasonable distribution of the benefits of growth. The issues of resource mobilization, resource allocation, and rural-urban income disparities, which have been dominant concerns of government policy in the past and will remain the focus of attention in the near future, are the main subjects of this report.

Problems of resource management have been particularly difficult since Korea entered the 1960s with a heavy reliance on foreign inflows. Definite progress was made in 1972–73 in reducing the dependence on external capital through a high rate of export expansion, but there was a sharp setback in 1974–75. The terms of trade deteriorated seriously, mainly but not entirely because of the steep rise in oil prices, and export growth slowed considerably as a result of the deep international recession. Resource availability has therefore reemerged as the major constraint on growth, and the issues of resource mobilization and allocation are likely to figure prominently in the fourth plan.

This report is the product of the economic work done in the World Bank on the Republic of Korea over the last several years. Initially an economic mission went to Korea in the fall of 1973, in response to a request by the government, to focus on the long-term development strategy and planning goals set for 1981.[1] A further substantial review of the Korean economic plans, policies, and prospects became necessary in the light of international developments and was undertaken during several subsequent visits. The final text of this report was prepared in the summer of 1975 and generally takes account of information available as of June of that year. On a selective basis, however, it has been possible to update information until the end of 1975.

I would like to express my deep appreciation to the members of the 1973 economic mission who helped me prepare the original report. I am also grateful to Richard Dosik who headed the updating mission in January 1975 and to Frederick T. Moore who led the industrial sector mission to Korea in late 1974, on whose work I have drawn heavily in bringing the analysis up-to-date.

In preparing the final version I have benefited from detailed comments from Larry E. Westphal and been ably assisted by Shahid Yusuf, who helped greatly to clarify my thinking. George Kalu was particularly helpful in updating the statistical annex. Gregory B. Votaw, David Loos, and D. C. Rao made useful comments on the entire manuscript, and Mr. Loos was kind enough to provide a draft of the chapter on the historical background.

It would not have been possible to prepare this report without the active cooperation and support of the Korean government, particularly the senior officials of the Korean Economic Planning Board. My special thanks are due to His Excellency Duck Woo Nam, Deputy Prime Minister; Suk Joon Suh, Minister for Planning; and Jae Ik Kim, Director of the Bureau of Economic Planning, for many hours of helpful discussion and for their very useful comments on the final draft. I am also grateful to Mahn Je Kim, Director of the Korean Development Institute, for his helpful comments.

1. The members of the September 1973 economic mission were: Parvez Hasan, chief of mission; Bahman Abadian, general economist; George Kalu, general economist; Raymond Christensen, agricultural economist; Guenter Reif, general economist; James Langley, industrial economist; Nestor Santiago, industrial economist; and Azucena Zorrilla, secretary.

My thanks go also to my secretary, Gracita R. Clavecillas, who not only typed the successive versions of the report but also, on occasion, served as a valuable research assistant. Jane Carroll edited the final manuscript, and John Sifton prepared the index.

PARVEZ HASAN

Washington, D. C.
June 1976

KOREA

Problems and Issues in a Rapidly Growing Economy

Summary and Conclusions

THE ECONOMIC PROGRESS of the Republic of Korea during the last decade or so has been phenomenal. From a position uncomfortably close to the bottom of the international income scale and without the benefit of significant natural resources, Korea embarked on a course of industrial growth that became one of the outstanding success stories in international development. During 1963–74 the real gross national product (GNP) more than trebled, growing at 10 percent a year; per capita GNP reached an estimated $470 in 1974, well over double the level of ten years earlier. Though this rapid growth has clearly been the result of a number of interacting economic, political, and social factors which are not easy to quantify or rank by importance, export expansion and outward-looking strategy have played a key role in Korean development. Indeed, manufactured exports can be called the engine of growth. They rose from less than $10 million in the early sixties to well over $4 billion[1] in 1974, indicating a real growth rate of 55 percent a year. According to rough estimates, manufactured exports accounted for about one-third of the incremental output of the dynamic manufacturing sector which expanded, in value added terms, at an average annual rate of 19 percent during 1963–74.

1. Dollar amounts are U.S. dollar equivalents; "billion" is used in the American sense of a thousand million.

Growth and Structural Change

Structural changes in the economy have transformed Korea from a largely agricultural society into a semi-industrialized country in a relatively short time. Highlighting these changes, the share of manufacturing in gross national product rose from 13 percent in 1961 to 28 percent in 1974 with a corresponding decline in the share of agriculture from 40 percent to 25 percent over the same period. Total employment in agriculture, forestry, and fisheries is at present only marginally higher than it was in the early sixties, and the share of these sectors in total employment has declined from 63 percent in 1963 to 48 percent in 1974. Manufacturing employment over this period has increased threefold, indicating an annual growth rate of about 10 percent, and its share of total employment has increased from 9 to 18 percent. Generally speaking, industry has provided at least one job out of every three created during the last several years. These developments have been related to Korea's concentration, at least so far, on labor-intensive industries such as textiles, clothing, electronics, wigs, and plywood. The capital-output ratios in manufacturing have been low with a tendency to decline further from 1.7 in 1963–67 to 1.4 in 1968–72. The significant improvement in the employment situation is indicated by a decline in the open unemployment rate from 8.2 percent in 1963 to 4.1 percent in 1974 and a substantial annual rise in real wages that averaged 11 and 8 percent respectively in manufacturing and farm sectors during 1967–72.

Korea is more industrialized than other countries at comparable levels of income and population as suggested by the relatively high shares of manufacturing employment and output in the total employment and GNP and by the fact that manufactured goods now account for nearly 90 percent of total exports. It can be argued that Korea was driven by necessity to export-oriented industrial growth as a consequence of its poor natural resources and an extremely low ratio of exports to GNP, 2 to 3 percent in the early sixties. Nevertheless the development of an industrial output base which is larger than any other developing country in Asia with the exception of India and mainland China is impressive. Some aspects of its industrial and export structure, however, are viewed with concern. For instance, Korean exports have shown a relatively heavy concentration of markets and products. Japan and the United States have accounted for about 70 percent of Korean exports in recent years. Similarly a few labor-intensive products have continued to account for over 60 percent of total manufactured exports. Furthermore there is a heavy dependence on imports which is reflected in the relatively low domestic value added in exports. Though progress has definitely been made in deepening the industrial structure through development of backward and forward linkages, most notably through development of steel, petrochemicals, and shipyard industries, the import content of exports remains at a high level of around 50 percent.

The impression of vulnerability given by the pattern of Korean industrial output and exports can, however, be easily exaggerated. While the share of textiles and clothing in total exports has remained at about one-third since 1967, the relative importance of plywood and wigs has decreased markedly from nearly 20 percent in 1967 to a little over 5 percent in 1974. At the same time the share of electronics increased from less than 3 percent to nearly 11 percent. In 1974 Korea began sizable exports of iron and steel products, ships, and other transport equipment. Inasmuch as important shifts in the structure of exports have been taking place in response to changing demand conditions, future expansion of exports might be influenced less by the present structure and more by Korea's ability to make the right judgments about trends in international trade and its own comparative advantage.

The commodity and market concentration of Korean exports has not, at least till recently, caused a great deal of economic instability. GNP growth rates during 1963–74 fluctuated rather widely from year to year, between a low of 6.1 in 1965 and a high of 16.5 percent in 1973, but these fluctuations were more often related to changes in the level of investment rather than to exports. Between 1967 and 1972 real exports expanded at an average annual rate of 38 percent and never at less than 28 percent. This was partly because growth rates of exports to Japan and the United States generally differed rather widely from year to year. During the last three years, however, the Korean economy has experienced an unprecedented boom as well as a record slackening of growth related largely to the movement in exports. Led by a real export expansion of over 55 percent, growth rates of GNP, investment, and savings reached new peaks in 1973. During 1974–75, however, the annual growth rate of exports dropped to 14 percent, and there was a net deterioration in the terms of trade of around 25 percent between 1973 and 1975, reflecting mainly the steep rise in prices of imports (including oil).

Therefore the purchasing power of exports grew very little over the period. Notwithstanding this setback in trade the GNP growth rate during 1974 and 1975 averaged 8 percent a year, partly because of earlier government efforts to cushion the recession. The combination of international circumstances which produced this relatively large fall in the growth rate of Korean exports has of course been exceptional. But quite apart from the economic difficulties since early 1974, the financial position of Korean manufacturing enterprises has been sensitive to modest changes in the profitability of exports because of the relatively high debt-equity ratio which averaged 3:1 during 1968–73.

Resource Management Problems

The Korean economy as a whole has also been faced with serious problems of resource management during the last decade. The heavy investments required to sustain rapid economic growth have been well beyond Korea's own saving capabilities. The saving-investment gap has been persistently large and tended to widen considerably at least during the second half of the sixties. With a sixfold growth in real investment and a rise in the ratio of investment to GNP from 12 to 25 percent between 1960–62 and 1970–72, the dependence on external resources expanded enormously. This was not the result of a failure of the domestic saving effort as such, and there is no evidence that large external inflows weakened the domestic mobilization of resources. In fact the ratio of national savings to GNP made an impressive rise from a little over 2 percent in 1960–62 to over 15 percent in 1970–72.

The basic problem is that Korea entered the period of rapid growth with a very low rate of savings; in the early sixties the bulk of investment was financed from abroad, principally by U.S. assistance in the form of grants. Despite a high marginal saving rate during the last decade of around 25 percent, the initial low level of savings and the rapidly growing need for investment have prevented a reduction in the reliance on foreign savings. Defined as the deficit on goods and services account in the balance of payments, foreign savings[2] averaged over 10 percent of GNP during

---

2. They essentially measure the net inflow of foreign transfers (grants), external loan capital, direct foreign investments, and use of international reserves. The gross disbursement of foreign capital and transfers is obviously much larger.

1960–62, rose to the high level of 11 percent in 1969, and remained close to 9 percent of GNP during 1970–72. The problems of resource management inherent in the need for such large external inflows were compounded by a shift in the type of foreign assistance from grants to loans. Net transfers from abroad (grants) declined steadily from 5.8 percent of GNP in 1966 to less than 2 percent in 1972, and the balance of payments deficits had to be financed mainly from external borrowings since foreign investments were also relatively small. Korean medium- and long-term debt which was negligible before 1965 expanded by over $2.5 billion during 1965–72. Debt service payments rose from $20 million to $400 million in the same period, and the ratio of debt service to exports of goods and nonfactor services averaged nearly 22 percent during 1970–72, although it has declined sharply since then. The steep rise in debt burden was at least partly because of excessive reliance on suppliers' credits.

As for domestic resources, the sharp rise in government savings provided 40 to 45 percent of the total increment in national savings in the sixties while private savings were stimulated by policies which assured high real interest rates to savers. Nevertheless, the reliance on credit creation for mobilizing private sector savings was unduly high; credit to the private sector expanded around 45 percent a year during 1965–72 and the annual inflation rate during 1965–72 averaged 13 percent. The inadequate institutionalization of the saving effort and the low level of corporate savings were also reflected in the high debt-equity ratio of business enterprises mentioned above. Not surprisingly, therefore, the concern of government policies during 1970–72 was mainly to slow down the rate of increase of investment, to curb the expansion of foreign capital requirements, and generally to improve the balance of payments. These policies included substantial adjustments of exchange rates, restrictions on suppliers' credits, increased efforts toward obtaining official foreign assistance, and curbs on the expansion of domestic credit. Real investment stagnated during 1970–72, and the ratio of fixed investment to GNP dropped sharply from 27 percent in 1969 to 20 percent in 1972. Consequently, even with a continued high annual rate of export expansion (38 percent) the GNP growth averaged only 8 percent a year during 1970–72 compared with nearly 12 percent in the preceding three years. The general economic slowdown did not lead to greater financial stability, however, and the national saving rate actually tended to fall as business profits were squeezed and efforts were made to transfer larger incomes to rural areas. The government therefore took further measures in August 1972 to improve the financial position of business enterprises, change the inflationary psychology, and help revive private savings and investment. These measures had a considerable influence on prices as well as on business attitudes. But above all a further dramatic rise in Korean exports during 1973 helped mitigate the financial strains of the previous few years.

These strains were partly the inevitable result of the process of rapid economic growth and partly attributable to the fact that the growth rate outran expectations. The actual growth rates of GNP, investment, and exports substantially exceeded the targets of both the first (1962–66) and second (1967–71) five-year plans. For instance, the 1966 target of $40 million for manufactured exports was exceeded by nearly 300 percent as a result of aggressive action by private entrepreneurs. This suggests that the rapid economic expansion has not been altogether planned. As a result of economic opportunities and growth continually outstripping expectations and goals, there has been a persistent shortage of resources for development. The reliance on external debt of relatively short maturity and the inflationary financing of investment outlays in the late sixties were both consequences of an investment boom which was larger than anticipated. The inflationary pressures in turn made it difficult to maintain export competitiveness and necessitated increased export subsidies and major adjustments of the exchange rate. The rapid rise in the domestic price level prior to 1970 also frustrated the government efforts to improve the terms of trade for the agricultural sector through high support prices. These developments combined with growing international monetary disequilibrium in 1971 produced a cautious attitude toward high rates of growth. The third plan (1972–76), completed in 1971, aimed at a relatively moderate annual growth of 8.6 percent and stressed "harmony in growth, stabilization and a balanced economy."

Recent Developments

We expect that the original growth target of the third plan will be exceeded because of the exceptional economic performance during 1973, and that the annual growth rate of GNP during 1972–76 will be around 9 percent. The stabilization of the domestic price level has not been feasible, however, largely because of the steep rise in the prices of imports such as oil, food grains, and raw materials during 1973–74. The GNP deflator, which rose by 12 percent a year during 1972 and 1973, jumped by 27 percent during 1974 and showed a further increase of 25 percent during 1975. Similarly the deterioration in the Korean terms of trade resulting from higher prices of imported food and fuel has impeded progress toward reducing the reliance on foreign savings. We estimate that during 1974–75 foreign saving will be about 12 percent of GNP, substantially higher than the average level of 10 percent of GNP in 1968–72. The current balance of payments deficit averaged around $2 billion annually during 1974–75 and has undoubtedly been affected by the deep international recession which had serious repercussions on Korean exports. On the whole, however, the downward trend of the Korean terms of trade has had a more serious impact on the balance of payments. The terms of trade declined by 18 percent in 1974, a loss equivalent to a reduction in gross national income of 5 percent or in gross national savings of 25 percent. In 1975 there was a further deterioration in terms of trade of 8 to 9 percent as export prices declined. Inasmuch as exports have a high import component, say 50 percent, a 20 percent reduction in export growth may be only half as serious as the same magnitude of reduction in the purchasing power of exports through a deterioration in the terms of trade. To the extent that the reduction in exports has been due to cyclical factors a fairly sharp recovery in the near future can be expected. A large part of the overall terms of trade loss must be considered permanent, however, since a major reduction in the real price of oil is not anticipated. Apart from the cyclical and other factors which distort the levels of national savings and domestic investments, it appears that the underlying gap to be filled by foreign savings narrowed markedly during 1972–73 but has widened substantially during 1974–75. Korea will thus continue to face problems related to the management and financing of a large gap in external resources.

Long-term Strategy

The reemergence of a serious resource problem, uncertainty about the future trends in international trade, and downward revision of the long-term growth prospects of the Japanese economy have made it necessary for Korea to reassess its plans for the second half of the seventies and review its development strategy. The long-term economic goals were set by President Park in late 1972 and involved the attainment of a per capita income of US$1,000 and exports of US$10 billion by 1981; these figures were in current prices but assumed only a modest annual rate of inflation of 5 percent.[3] To achieve these targets in real terms, average annual growth rates of GNP and exports of 10.5 percent and 18 percent were required during 1973–81. The strategy for attaining these objectives called for major shifts in production and exports through the expansion of heavy and chemical industries, notably steel, shipbuilding, and electronics. The macroeconomic framework for 1972–81 prepared by the Economic Planning Board also projected the almost complete elimination of dependence on foreign savings by 1981.

The upsurge in exports, investment, and GNP that took place in 1973 appeared for a while to give momentum to Korean growth, and most of the original targets seemed feasible. But this favorable thrust has since been more than offset by the adverse changes in Korea's external circumstances noted above. Some reduction in the Korean growth rate during the second half of the seventies will thus be unavoidable from the past several years' annual average of 10 percent. The Korean government's preliminary reassessment of the long-term prospects now under way shows full awareness of this. The guidelines for the fourth five-year plan (1977–81) issued in mid-1975 suggest a tentative growth target of 9 percent a year for 1977–81 as against the target of 11 percent for the same period implied in the long-term framework. Considerably more work will have to be done before some of the key targets for the fourth plan can be firmed up. It is already clear, however, that the Korean government is not abandoning the goal of high growth which it has pursued during the last decade.

It will be a major economic challenge for Korea to sustain an annual growth rate of, say, 8 to 9 percent during the next decade, especially if the external circumstances remain distinctly less favorable than during the last decade. Nevertheless, the continuation of a high growth rate appears essential not only to raise living

3. These targets in fact superseded the original goals of the third plan (1972–76) and provided a preliminary outline of the fourth plan (1977–81). The original target for GNP growth in 1972–76 was set at 8.6 percent a year and revised to 9.5 percent a year in the macroeconomic framework for 1972–81.

standards rapidly but also to achieve the Korean government's goals of greater viability of the balance of payments, expanded employment opportunities, and more even distribution of growth benefits. In the Korean context, rapid growth itself has been the most important source of generating foreign exchange and domestic savings and improving income and employment opportunities for the poor. Similarly structural changes in the economy to which the Korean government is attaching increasing importance—notably diversifying industry and increasing the value added content of exports—will also probably be facilitated by rapid growth.

Resource Requirements

The investment requirements will be sizable for a growth rate of 8 to 9 percent a year, although by Korean standards this might appear to be a relatively modest target. The rate of gross investment, which averaged around 26 percent of GNP during 1968–72 and will be over 27 percent of GNP during 1973–76, will have to rise during 1977–81. The overall incremental capital-output ratio has already increased from 2.6:1 in 1968–72 to around 3.0:1 during 1973–75, slightly higher than the original official estimates. This reflects the increased capital intensity of manufacturing as well as increased emphasis on housing and rural infrastructure which were relatively neglected earlier. Further increases in the capital-output ratios during 1977–81 will be likely, particularly if the capital-intensive investments in the fields of energy, food grains, and intermediate products for industry are emphasized. But even if there is no further increase in the capital intensity of production and the government consciously limits commitments on projects that are capital intensive and have a long gestation period, it will take a massive effort to mobilize the resources required. In the short run the major constraint on resources is the shortage of foreign exchange, but as the balance of payments deficit is reduced through sustained export expansion, domestic savings will become more crucial. Theoretically a part of the domestic savings shortage could be overcome by foreign borrowings over and above what is necessary to meet the need for foreign exchange. But Korea's external requirements are already large enough to preclude this as a serious option for any extended period. Even with a decline in the external deficit as a percentage of GNP, the total gross inflows required will be sizable and their mobilization in itself will be a major challenge. Furthermore, although it is no longer practical to eliminate dependence on foreign savings by 1981, the government's desire not to rely on external flows more than necessary will tend to limit balance of payments deficits.

Given both the desirability and feasibility of a gradual reduction in the deficit on goods and services account in the balance of payments to, say, 3 percent of GNP by 1981, from the estimated level of 12 percent in 1974–75, the mobilization of domestic resources will become a major concern. Foreign saving needs having been determined largely exogenously, the marginal saving rate required during 1975–81 will depend almost entirely on the growth target and the incremental capital-output ratio. If a growth target of 8 percent a year for 1977–81 and only a slight increase in the capital-output ratio is assumed, a marginal saving rate of close to 30 percent will be necessary during the next five or six years. If, however, a growth rate of 9 percent is projected and an increase in the marginal capital-output ratio to 3.2:1 is allowed for, the required marginal savings rate jumps to over 35 percent.

In the recent past the marginal saving rate has never been above 25 percent for any sustained length of time, but even this historical rate may be difficult to achieve in the future. Savings might suffer as a larger share of income is acquired by rural groups whose earnings are relatively low. Indeed, the setback in savings during 1970–72 may have been due in part to a shift in the terms of trade in favor of agriculture. In the past savings have grown faster in real terms than in current prices because of the relatively slow rise in the price of investment goods. Now these prices are expected to grow as fast as the GNP deflator, under the pressure of worldwide inflation and the realistic pricing of foreign exchange. In addition, the government has hitherto mobilized a substantial portion of the increment of savings, but in the future it is likely to play a less active role which could hamper the overall growth of savings inasmuch as private savings institutions are underdeveloped. Finally, interest and profit remittances are expected to increase faster than GNP with a rise in foreign loans and investments, and the domestic savings available for domestic investment will thus be reduced. It must again be stressed, however, that the national savings rate, which averaged around 17 percent of GNP during 1974–75 (if partial allowance is made for statistical discrepancy), probably understates the saving potential because savings during this period were constrained by foreign exchange shortages.

Export Growth versus Import Substitution

In order to overcome or minimize the resource constraint, the government of Korea will have to give special attention to policy measures to promote domestic savings. At the same time the decisions on the pattern of growth will have implications for the resource position that should be closely scrutinized; there might be important trade-offs between the program to deepen the industrial structure and the effort to maintain high growth rates.

An immediate issue for the fourth five-year plan (1977–81) is the role of export expansion versus import substitution, particularly the possibilities of import substitution in the key areas of food grains, energy, and industrial machinery. We believe that in the near future it would be both desirable and necessary for Korean exports to continue to grow faster than GNP. The long-term goal of eliminating the current account deficit in the balance of payments will require not only an increase in the ratio of exports to GNP but also a reduction in import ratio because the present trade gap is so large. The argument that Korea's dependence on exports is excessive does not appear valid because with value added exports accounted for only 13 percent of GNP in Korea during 1974. For relatively small and specialized countries such as Malaysia, Belgium, Norway, and the Netherlands the comparable ratio is about one-third. In any case, since capital scarcity is likely to loom large, the continued promotion of labor-intensive exports and relative restraint on capital-intensive import substitution activities appears to be indicated.

The export growth rate of 13 to 16 percent a year during 1977–81 projected in fourth plan guidelines is regarded as feasible and deserving high priority. Real exports of manufactured goods from developing countries are expected to grow 12 to 15 percent a year during 1975–80 depending on the growth in OECD countries (Organisation for Economic Co-operation and Development). Thus Korea has merely to maintain its share among other developing countries to achieve its export goals. In any case the country enjoys the advantages of a head start, special links with the Japanese market, and wages that are still quite low.

The main problem in the export field is the diversification of markets and products. The macroeconomic framework for 1972–81 originally placed excessive emphasis on the export of heavy manufactures, notably steel, ships, and passenger cars, and the export goals for 1981 for these products are likely to be trimmed down substantially. In contrast, exports of light manufactured goods are likely to do better than originally envisaged. Given a realistic exchange rate and reasonable export incentives, electronics and textiles are likely to dominate the export scene even in 1980, but growth in the export of miscellaneous manufactures in recent years has also been encouraging. Similar progress is being made in the geographical dispersal of exports. In 1974 exports to markets other than the United States and Japan expanded by 40 percent in real terms, and their share in total Korean exports increased from an average of 27 percent in 1970–72 to 33 percent. During 1975 the share of exports to U.S. and Japanese markets declined further to less than 60 percent of the total.

On the whole, a significant overall reduction in the ratio of imports to GNP during the next few years is probably not consistent with an economic use of scarce resources. The official export targets and the goal of a gradual reduction in relative foreign inflows also imply more or less unchanged overall dependence on imports till 1981. There are two main reasons for this. First, the export sector itself will be growing rapidly and is fairly dependent on imports. There will undoubtedly be some import substitution in raw materials and intermediate products required for export production, but this is likely to be offset by a shift in the export pattern to clearly more import-intensive exports such as electronics. Second, in many areas of the economy, notably food grains and energy, the trend has been toward a growing relative reliance on imports in spite of greater efforts at import replacement. A dramatic decline in the ratio of imports to domestic demand in the next few years will therefore not be feasible for structural reasons alone. This does not mean that careful planning for a substantial investment in import substitution industries will not be required or should not be undertaken. It merely suggests that import substitution should not be attempted at the sacrifice of essential export goals.

External Capital Requirements

Korea's requirements of medium- and long-term loans during 1976–81 are projected at $14 billion on the assumptions that real merchandise export growth will be about 14 to 15 percent a year, real import growth will be limited to 10 to 11 percent a year, there will be some improvement in the terms of trade, and international inflation will slow down considerably. The current account balance of payments deficit is expected to decline from around $1.9 billion in 1975 to $0.9 billion by 1981, averaging $1.25 billion annually during 1976–81. The decline in current account deficit will, however, be more than offset by the growing requirements of amortization payments and the need to ensure reasonable additions to foreign exchange reserves. Thus the gross disbursements of medium- and long-term loans will have to rise steadily, averaging $2.4 billion annually during 1976–81. These are large inflows, particularly compared with the actual average disbursements of only $700 million a year during 1970–73. But it must be stressed that although the current account deficit will increase from an average of $530 million in 1970–73 to $1.25 billion in 1976–81, nearly two-thirds of this increase is due to the rise in international prices. The balance is entirely attributable to the sharp and sudden loss in terms of trade. If the foreign resources required to compensate the terms of trade loss are excluded, the real external inflows assumed above are in fact substantially less than was actually achieved during 1970–73. In other words Korea will not be transferring to the external sources of capital the main burden of its adjustments to the changed situation.

The mobilization of the required capital inflows will nevertheless pose a considerable challenge, particularly in the early years, because of the lag between commitments and disbursements. To achieve the high level of foreign loan disbursements in the early years, a substantial part of the 1976–77 commitments should take the form of nonproject assistance that can be quickly disbursed.

Fortunately the debt servicing capacity of Korea has increased markedly during the last few years as evidenced by the sharp drop in its debt service ratio from an average of 22 percent during 1970–72 to less than 13 percent during 1974–75. This improvement is related in large part to continued high real growth in exports, but it also reflects the high rate of international inflation which has reduced the real burden of external debt. Nevertheless Korea will need to obtain at least half its large borrowing requirement during 1976–81 from concessionary or semiconcessionary sources and seek an average term of ten years for loans from private sources in order to maintain its debt burden within prudent limits.

Concessionary assistance to Korea in recent years has not been large, was mainly from the United States and Japan, and was expected to be eliminated by 1976. To adjust to the new circumstances, however, the Korean government has modified its earlier goal of not requiring official development assistance beyond 1976. Nonetheless the great bulk of future borrowing from official sources will have to be from multilateral agencies, notably the World Bank, the Asian Development Bank, and the Organization of Petroleum Exporting Countries. If the recommended mix of private credits and public assistance can be attained, however, the debt service ratio will rise only moderately from about 13 percent in 1975 to 15 percent by 1981 and not exceed this level in the first half of the eighties. Total debt service payments will no doubt quadruple from about $700 million in 1975 to $2.5 billion in 1981, but at the same time the export of goods and nonfactor services, in current prices, will rise by over 20 percent a year from $5.7 billion in 1975 to $17.5 billion in 1981. Korea's total debt outstanding will rise from around $6 billion at the end of 1975 to about $14 billion at the end of 1981, but it will decline somewhat as a percentage of annual exports of goods and nonfactor services. The rise in the debt service ratio over the period will thus be entirely due to some hardening of the average terms.

Because of the number of assumptions involved, our estimates of the balance of payments provide only a rough framework for a discussion of external capital needs and indicate essentially the order of magnitude. The estimates of capital requirements are in current U.S. dollars and are particularly sensitive to assumptions about the rate of international inflation, which has been extremely high during the last couple of years but is expected to be considerably more moderate in the second half of the seventies. If the annual rate of international inflation is more than the 5 to 6 percent assumed, the need for external capital inflows will increase correspondingly. What will happen if Korea is not able to obtain external flows on the scale required, notwithstanding good creditworthiness and sustained growth in exports? The major burden of this adjustment will probably fall on the growth rate. A relatively small reduction in GNP growth of, say, one or two percent a year could in the long run be sufficient to overcome a substantial shortfall in external resources. But in the short run flexibility is limited because of the structural balance of payments problem caused by the terms of trade loss. Thus in the next few years when the dominant constraint on growth will be the availability of foreign exchange, a sharp reduction in net real inflows would not only reduce investment and growth but could also considerably slow down progress toward closing the balance of payments gap.

Domestic Saving Needs

The task of arranging the required external capital inflows from foreign sources over the next six years will not be at all easy. But, as mentioned earlier, the task of mobilizing requisite domestic savings could prove even more difficult. Even with continued care in the allocation of scarce capital resources, Korea will need to save about 30 percent of the increment in income during the next several years if the growth rate of GNP is not to fall below 8 percent a year. With only a moderate increase in capital-output ratio and a growth rate of 9 percent, the marginal saving will be above 35 percent. This will involve a growth in real savings of 16 percent a year, nearly double the rate of GNP growth. To stimulate this growth the government will need to take positive measures regarding interest rates, taxation, public expenditures, and subsidies.

Public savings which averaged 6 percent of GNP during 1968–72 became negligible during 1974 as a result of a combination of circumstances. The principal factors responsible were the stagnation of the budgetary current account surplus and the rapid rise in the extrabudgetary deficit. The former reflects a weakness in Korea's public finances which has been apparent for some years. The ratio of central government taxes to GNP reached a peak of 15.4 percent in 1971 but declined sharply in the ensuing two years and recovered to only 15.1 percent in 1974. Notwithstanding recent tax measures related to the need for increased defense spending, the ratio of central government taxes will rise at best only modestly during 1975 and 1976. While real government revenues may grow faster than GNP, increased consideration of national security may make it difficult to limit the growth in current expenditures as in the recent past.

The ratio of current surplus in the general budget to GNP dropped from slightly above 4 percent in 1970 to about 3 percent in 1974. To raise this ratio an early reduction of the deficit on the extrabudgetary accounts is necessary. This deficit, which will be well over 2 percent of GNP during 1975, is mainly from grain and fertilizer subsidies. The government's commitment to a step-by-step elimination of these subsidies over the next few years will involve resisting farm pressures to raise the procurement price of rice to the full extent of domestic inflation. The terms of trade for agriculture were relatively favorable in 1973 and 1974, and any attempt to freeze them at that level could be a drain on public resources. In view of government concern to improve rural incomes, however, a major change in the agricultural terms of trade will not be politically acceptable. Indeed, as discussed elsewhere, in order to attain its rural income goals the government is counting on an improvement of over 2 percent a year in the agricultural terms of trade during 1974–81.

The policy on interest rates is as urgent an issue as that on agricultural prices. As mentioned earlier, during the sixties Korea relied heavily and successfully on high interest rates to mobilize domestic savings and ensure efficient use of investment resources. Concern about the continued high rate of inflation, the development of inflationary psychology, and the financial position of enterprises, however, led in August 1972 to measures that included a substantial reduction in nominal interest rates. The hope at that time was that inflation would be brought to a 3 percent annual rate, but international developments have resulted in the reemergence of strong inflationary pressures. As a result, the real interest rates for loans were substantially negative in 1975, though the rates for savings and time deposits have been increased and the spread has disappeared. The negative real interest rates have thus been accompanied by interest rate subsidies and increased reliance on direct allocations of credit. The government has been reluctant to increase interest rates on grounds that this would add to inflationary pressures and might accentuate expectations about the rate of future inflation. A further cause for reluctance is the recurrence of financial difficulties of enterprises in the wake of the recession. Unless inflationary pressures abate considerably in 1976, it will appear most desirable to review thoroughly the level and structure of interest rates so as not to discourage savings and create undesirable effects on the pattern of investment.

Industrial Plans

The long-term plans for industrial expansion originally called for a massive shift toward heavy and chemical industries during 1973–81 as well as the maintenance of a high manufacturing growth rate of 17 percent a year, roughly the same level as in the past decade. Notwithstanding its relatively sluggish performance in 1974–75, manufacturing growth during 1973–76 will be close to the target, mainly because it expanded well over 30 percent in 1973. The target for manufacturing growth in the fourth plan period (1977–81) has been tentatively revised downward to 12 to 15 percent a year, however. This reflects not only the reduction in the overall growth rate but also the increased attention to infrastructure investment in the light of social concerns such as housing, and the greater priority of food grains and energy. Thus manufacturing investment during 1976–81 might be as much as 35 percent below the $15 billion estimate, in 1970 prices, contained in the macroeconomic framework.

Of even greater significance will be the changes in the composition of manufacturing investment. A reassessment of the original plans is now made necessary by recent events, notably the sharp rise in energy costs, increased scarcity of foreign exchange and capital resources, growing uncertainty about Korean access to the Japanese market, and last but not least the sharp rise in the price of imported machinery and equipment. Heavy and chemical industries originally accounted for about two-thirds of the planned total investment in manufacturing for 1973–81, but plans for steel, shipbuilding, petrochemicals, and nonferrous metals must now be subjected to close scrutiny. As a general principle low priority should be given projects which are extremely capital and energy intensive and heavily dependent on foreign investment, foreign markets, and imported raw material.

The government fully recognizes the need to prune the plans for heavy and chemical industries. The plan for the second steel plant has already been postponed, and the program for shipyard construction and expansion of shipbuilding capacity is now being reviewed in the light of the changed pattern and level of international demand for ships. Plans for the petrochemical industry will now focus chiefly on domestic demand with attention on optimum scale. Similarly export plans for aluminum, lead, and copper will be reexamined to take account of financial requirements, comparative cost advantage, and pollution problems.

The extent to which original plans for heavy industrial projects might need adjustment has probably not yet been fully realized. It seems neither feasible nor desirable, however, to reduce the planned investment in light manufacturing industries because their output and export potential was seriously underestimated earlier. Protection of the investment in light manufacturing, which originally accounted for only one-third the total, will mean that the entire cut will fall on the heavy and chemical industries. In effect this will imply reducing the program for the latter by half. In the long run the industrial structure will require a relatively greater emphasis on the manufacture of intermediate and capital goods to sustain rapid industrial growth, but the government should ensure that heavy industry does not preempt a disproportionate share of resources and result in a major squeeze on light manufacturing.

The task of ensuring a balance between import substitution and export production and between light and heavy industries will rest on trade policies and incentives on the one hand and the framework of industrial planning on the other. In the past, although the government's direct support and guidance to industry have been important, responses to new opportunities and market incentives have come mainly from the private sector. Inasmuch as planning is always an imperfect exercise, it should be decentralized to a certain extent so that Korean entrepreneurs can take advantage of domestic and overseas business opportunities that might not always be apparent to the economic planners. With the change in the structure of industry, however, centralized programming of investment is becoming more important. Even though the program for heavy and chemical industries for 1977–81 will be substantially reduced, the role and responsibility of the central authorities in determining the direction of industrial growth will inevitably expand with the multiplication of capital-intensive projects that require long gestation periods. The excellent macroeconomic planning will have to be related even more closely than in the past to development plans for individual sectors and subsectors and even to the timing of key projects. At the same time, the government should guard against the tendency to regard large and lumpy projects as dominant in the process of developing backward linkages. Small and medium firms have a particularly important role to play in the field of industrial machinery and can contribute significantly to deepening the industrial structure and increasing import substitution.

Resource Allocation

Contrary to the impressions of some observers, Korea's rapid industrial growth has not generally been associated with excessive protection of domestic industry or unduly large incentives for exports. Korea has relied heavily on a variety of export incentives, but they were largely needed to compensate for the lag in the adjustment of the exchange rate to changes in purchasing power parity. The subsidies (in Korean won) per dollar of exports rose sharply between 1964 and 1970 and in the latter year amounted to 32 percent of export value. Analysis shows, however, that this sharp rise in subsidies merely offset a much faster rise in Korea's price level compared with that of its major trade partners while the official exchange rate remained relatively stable. During 1970–72 a substantial adjustment was made in the exchange rate, amounting to about 24 percent on the basis of a weighted average. This strengthened the competitiveness of Korean exports and reduced the need for subsidies, which were further lowered in 1973.

Of greater relevance to the allocation of resources is the effective rate of subsidy on exports. For the international comparison of prices, exemptions from duties and indirect taxes should not be treated as export subsidies. A recent study suggests that the effective rate of subsidy on total exports of manufactured goods in the late 1960s was in the range of 9 to 12 percent. The main effect of the subsidies was to make intermediate products available to Korea's export sector at international prices. This does not mean, however, that the rate of export subsidy was not in some cases excessive. The same study further indicates that on the average the domestic sale of manufactured goods received negative protection, which thus created a bias in favor of exports. In particular the domestic production of capital goods has been discriminated against because long-term credit at reasonable interest rates has not been available for domestic purchases of machinery. To a considerable extent this has recently been remedied, and import substitution of capital goods has been encouraged. Nevertheless the policy tilt in favor of export production should be maintained since export expansion will remain the most dynamic element in Korean growth during the next few years. A realistic rate of exchange will continue to be the key to adequate export incentives.

Distribution of Growth Benefits

Income distribution in Korea is generally more equitable than in comparable developing countries. But, at least in the sixties, the benefits of economic growth were not shared evenly. The absolute gap in incomes between urban and rural areas, where nearly half of the population still lives, was widening until 1970, despite a massive migration to urban centers. Most of the emigrants went to Seoul and Pusan which together absorbed nearly 60 percent of the total growth in population in the sixties. Labor productivity in agriculture (excluding fisheries) grew at only about half the rate of that in other sectors.

The government attempted to bring about a sharp rise in rural incomes through a massive increase in price supports for rice and barley amounting to 122 and 112 percent respectively during 1968–72. Between 1970 and 1972 the terms of trade for the agricultural sector improved by 13 percent, and the gap in rural-urban incomes was reduced significantly. The official index that relates average rural household incomes to wages and salaries in urban areas stood at 83 in 1972 compared with the low of 60 in 1967. During 1973–74 the relative position of rural areas advanced further—in part because of continuing improvement in agricultural terms of trade and a high growth rate in agriculture—and the gap in income was eliminated. It must be stressed, however, that the index understates the extent of the disparity because rural households are substantially larger than those in urban areas and contain more workers. Even after allowing for underemployment in agriculture, the average urban worker appears to earn considerably more than the average rural worker. Nonetheless there is little doubt that in absolute terms there has been substantial improvement in the living standard of all rural groups since 1967.

There has also been considerable improvement in the employment situation during the last ten years. Reflecting the rapid growth in nonagricultural employment, the overall employment growth of 2.5 percent a year during 1969–72 exceeded the corresponding growth in the labor force (2.2 percent), and there was a noticeable reduction in open unemployment. Evidence of concrete improvement in the employment situation is also provided by the growth in real wages during 1963–72 of 7.5 and 6.5 percent a year respectively in the manufacturing and rural sectors. The rise in rural wages particularly helped small farmers who supplement their incomes by working for wages. The proportion of rural incomes obtained off the farm was only 18 percent in 1972, however, which is low compared with 55 percent for Taiwan and 68 percent for Japan. The lack of opportunities for nonfarm employment in rural areas in Korea is in turn related to the heavy concentration of industry in Seoul, Inchon, and Pusan.

Social Goals

A major objective of the long-term plan is to bring about a much wider dispersal of benefits than in the sixties. With rapid economic growth, a continued improvement in the overall employment situation and a sustained rise in real wages will be assured during the seventies. But the past experience of lagging rural income and excessive migration to urban areas has underscored the need for a comprehensive strategy to deal with the economic imbalance of rural and urban areas. The Sae Maeul (New Community) movement initiated in late 1971 by President Park is a concrete expression of this strategy. As a nationwide self-help program to improve the rural standard of living, the Sae Maeul movement obviously has economic as well as social and political objectives. The economic goal is to maintain the parity between the incomes of farm and urban households which was achieved during 1974. To accomplish this, farm household incomes must rise by an average annual rate of over 15 percent in current prices. The plan calls for an increase in both net income from farming operations and off-farm income, especially wages from nonagricultural employment.

The maintenance of full parity in rural and urban incomes over the next decade may prove to be difficult because of the optimistic assumptions implicit in a 6 percent annual growth of labor productivity in agriculture and a trebling of off-farm jobs in rural areas. Furthermore it might be difficult to achieve the planned steady improvement in the terms of trade of the agricultural sector of over 2 percent a year without putting a major burden on the budget. The basic emphasis of the government policies appears, however, to be fully justified. Without increased job opportunities in rural areas and the rapid improvement of agricultural productivity the drift of the population to urban areas will continue, and the task of narrowing rural-urban income differences will be hampered.

1

Historical Background and the Origins of Growth

THE NAME KOREA IS DERIVED from that of an old dynasty, Koryo, which may be translated as "the land of high mountains and sparkling streams." French Catholic priests who were among the first visitors to Korea from the Western world described the land as resembling "a sea in a heavy gale." These are apt epitomizations of the topography and geophysical features of the Korean peninsula, which is for the most part a succession of hills and valleys. The total area of the peninsula is about 220,000 square kilometers.

Historical Setting

The twentieth century has been a period of travail in Chosun, "the land of the morning calm," another descriptive phrase applied to Korea. The struggle for supremacy of the peninsula, which stands at the crossroads of civilization, began soon after Korea was opened up in 1882. The first two protagonists were Japan and China. Chinese designs to convert Korea into a protectorate were challenged by Japan in the Sino-Japanese War (1894–95). This was followed by the Russo-Japanese War (1904–05) which culminated in the Japanese military occupation of Korea in 1905 and outright annexation in 1910.

The thirty-five years of Japanese rule significantly influenced Korean culture and society, although only limited segments of Korean life were affected. Japanese influence was most evident in the administrative and legal fields. Substantial inflows of Japanese capital and administrators brought changes to Korea's economic structure, particularly through the introduction of new agricultural practices and the development of a fairly significant industrial base. The impact of the Japanese was limited, however, by the restrictions placed on Korean participation in economic and political planning and management, and the customs and structure of Korean society as a whole were not deeply affected.

Korea regained its independence in 1945, but this did not bring surcease from political and economic problems; in fact, the first years after independence were extraordinarily difficult and influenced the pattern of subsequent political and economic events. There were increasingly bitter power struggles in the South and an almost complete breakdown in the economic, political, and social order. But the separation of the nation into two states had the most far-reaching effect.

The geophysical characteristics of the Korean peninsula make it an economically interrelated unit with the large mineral deposits and hydroelectric facilities in the North complementing the predominantly agricultural economy of the South. The division of the country destroyed this interdependency of the economy. It gave the South less than half the land, about three-fifths of the population, most of the agriculture, and very little of the industry.

With the establishment of the Republic of Korea in 1948 the internal political difficulties seemed to subside, and considerable economic progress was made in the first two years of the new republic. Perhaps the most significant development in this period was the implementation of a land reform program. This important and popular measure redistributed about three-fourths of the cultivable land and benefited over half of the rural households.

The new republic's efforts to achieve economic stability, supported by massive economic assistance from the United States, appeared to be bearing fruit when the Korean War erupted in June 1950. Spared from fighting on its soil during World War II, Korea became the scene of bloody battles which devastated the whole country except for the southeastern area around Pusan. Three-fifths of the cultivated land was laid to waste, and the rich rice fields, forests, and mining areas were rendered unproductive. Property damage was estimated at some $3 billion; most of the nation's industrial capacity was demolished and agricultural production declined markedly. The extent of human suffering and social upheaval during the conflict is indicated by the fact that over a quarter of the population roamed the country as refugees, and the death toll on both sides was estimated at over 3 million.

The war left a legacy of horrendous proportions. In the immediate postwar period an estimated ten million, including two million children, were without homes, adequate food, and medical care; approximately five million were on relief. The Neutral Nations Inspection Committee reported: "The country is dead . . . there is no activity . . . the cities are completely destroyed."

The social and economic upheaval caused by the war combined with Korea's poor economic endowment forced greater reliance on foreign assistance. In December 1953 the Korea–U.S. Joint Economic Committee for Economic Rehabilitation and Stability was established to set up guidelines for economic assistance and reconstruction. The United Nations Korean Relief Agreement on Economic Matters signed in May 1954 was intended to supplement the efforts to stabilize and rehabilitate the war-torn Korean economy. Foreign aid totaling some $2.3 billion was provided in the 1953–61 period.

With financial assistance flowing in from abroad, the process of reconstruction was taken in hand and the foundations of the industrial sector were laid. During the next few years the economy notched a fairly respectable rate of growth with much of the impetus coming from the expansion of industry. Tables 1 and 2 present numerical evidence of this growth but also suggest a

Table 1. Rates of Growth of GNP by Sector

	Average rates of growth		
Industrial group	*1954–58*	*1959–62*	*1954–62*
Agriculture, forestry, and fisheries	3.9	0.9	2.6
Mining and manufacturing	13.4	9.5	11.6
Social overhead[a]	13.5	11.0	12.4
Other services[b]	3.3	3.6	3.5
Total	4.8	3.4	4.2

a. Includes construction, transportation, storage, communication, electricity, water, and sanitary services.
b. Includes trade, banking, insurance, real estate, ownership of dwellings, public administration, defense, and other services.
Source: Bank of Korea, *National Income Statistics Yearbook, 1973*, based on GNP series in 1970 constant market prices.

Table 2. Growth of Industrial Production

Year	Growth rate
1957	15.7
1958	10.3
1959	14.7
1960	8.9
1961	5.7

Source: Tae Wan-Son, *The Economic Development of Korea* (Seoul: Economic Planning Board, 1973).

slowdown, particularly of industrial growth, in the late 1950s and early 1960s, reflecting among other factors political instability. The economy grew steadily at an average rate of 5.5 percent during 1954–58 but slowed to a rate of 3.6 percent a year during 1959–62, and the earlier economic momentum was not regained until the mid-sixties.

As the Rhee regime became more autocratic, the resistance to its policies became ever more pronounced and culminated in the student revolt of 1960 which finally toppled the government. Rhee resigned on April 26, 1960, and in July of the same year the Democratic Republican party was elected into office. But this did not put an end to the political turmoil within the country. Factional struggles within the party and the insistent demands of students and intellectuals made effective policymaking well-nigh impossible and paved the way for a military takeover. The forces that brought General Park Chung Hee to power were in part a reflection of the slackened pace in the industrial sector in 1961.

The situation at the end of the fifties was such that Korea could hardly have been expected to achieve one of the outstanding development records of the First Development Decade. The republic entered the sixties with one of the lowest income levels in the world; it had little experience participating in international trade; and its potential for rapid economic progress was not evident.

One serious handicap has been the lack of natural resources. Only about a quarter of Korea's 10 million hectares of land is cultivable, and the average holding of cultivated land is about one-tenth a hectare. The country's geophysical features seriously limit the possibility of increasing the cultivated area and have principally determined the pattern of Korea's agricultural development. There is a paucity of mineral resources; although anthracite coal is found in various parts of the country its poor quality limits its use primarily to domestic heating. Despite considerable exploration no petroleum or new sources of mineral deposits has been discovered.

Origins of Rapid Growth

Korea's achievement in overcoming its considerable handicaps to make outstanding economic gains must be attributed to the interaction of several factors whose relative importance cannot be easily determined. Despite limited natural resources Korea is well endowed with the human capability for economic success. Its labor force is unusually well educated, vigorous, and industrious. Labor's acceptance, until recent years, of wages that lagged behind productivity, its adaptability to exacting industrial discipline, and an absence of labor militancy have all been conducive to rapid industrialization. The social environment of Korea has probably also been conducive to rapid economic change. For various historical and cultural reasons the society of postwar Korea was more fluid and less structured than in most other parts of Asia. There are no strong regional or religious differences, no deeply entrenched class or caste structure. Consequently the pursuit of economic opportunity was less inhibited by tradition and class, and the mobility and adaptability of labor was relatively unrestricted by social limitations.

Economic development in Korea has been supported in no small measure by an unusual degree of acceptance of the identity between the interests of groups and national economic advancement. This adds the strength of patriotic sanction to the motive of private gain as an underlying force in the economy. This association of individual economic objectives with national aspirations has undoubtedly been conducive to the unusually close, cooperative, and mutually dependent relationship between the Korean government and private business in the conduct of economic affairs. It also helps explain the apparent paradox that the Korean economy depends in large measure on private enterprise operating under highly centralized government guidance. In Korea the government's role is considerably more direct than that of merely setting the broad rules of the game and influencing the economy indirectly through market forces. In fact, the government seems to be a participant and often the determining influence in nearly all business decisions. This arrangement is generally acceptable to the private sector presumably because the success of business enterprises depends on government protection and support in various forms, including in some instances substantial subsidies.

Another factor underlying Korea's rapid economic growth appears to have been the availability of considerable entrepreneurial talent, nurtured during the decade of the fifties. This commercial florescence was at least partly rooted in government policies which created strong incentives for undertaking industrial investments. Not only did the state provide finance at concessional rates but it also secured monopolistic advantages for the new enterprises by erecting tariff barriers to the flow of foreign goods. This may not have provided the firmest basis for sustained economic progress, but it did create experience for a group of entrepreneurs whose capabilities and resourcefulness under subsequently more demanding conditions of development have been amply demonstrated.

The choices of economic policy and development strategy must also be accorded credit for Korea's rapid development. In its pursuit of industrialization Korea avoided the pattern common in the early sixties and chose not to depend on import substitution behind high protection to the neglect of export production. Manufacture for export was made the spearhead of Korean development strategy. This was probably partly in imitation of the nearby successful example of Japan and partly because there were few traditional exports which would support even a minimum rate of politically acceptable growth. It was probably also necessary because of large foreign deficits. In the absence of domestic primary resources for export, Korea clearly recognized the need to develop a substantial import capability based on the export of manufactures.

Infrastructure Development

Korea is a highly urbanized nation with more than 50 percent of its population living in cities and towns of over 20,000 persons. Furthermore, among the ranks of developing countries Korea is industrially one of the most advanced. The process of urbanization dates back to the Korean War, but the industrial spurt is more recent in origin. The growing demand of the industrial sector for particular services has precipitated the massive drive to develop

Table 3. Expansion of Social Overhead Capital

Item	Unit	1961	1972	Percentage increase
Electric power-generating facilities	Thousand kilowatts	367	3,871	1050
Freight cars	Number	9,435	16,808	180
Highways	Kilometers	—	655	—
Port loading and unloading facilities	Thousand metric tons	9,020	22,185	240
Railroads	Kilometers	4,630	5,507	120

— Not applicable.
Source: Economic Planning Board.

the country's social overhead capital. An encapsulated account of the expansion of infrastructure between 1961 and 1972 is contained in Table 3.

At the beginning of this period the lack of adequate transport facilities was one of the serious bottlenecks to growth in the Korean economy. Much effort has since been expended in enlarging these essential facilities. The railway network has been modernized and expanded, but the development of roads and coastal shipping has been even more rapid and led to a substantial redistribution of passenger and freight traffic away from the railroads. Tables 4 and 5 summarize the major developments in the transport sector.

Although the investment in transport facilities has been heavy, other infrastructural needs have not been ignored. The electricity generating capacity which was just 434,000 kilowatts in 1962 has now reached 4 million with over a million kilowatts of additional capacity in reserve. The growth in power demand since 1968 has been at an average annual rate of 20 percent.

Table 4. Share of Traffic by Mode of Transport
(percentage of total passenger kilometers and ton kilometers)

Year	Domestic passenger traffic				Domestic freight traffic		
	Railroads	Highways	Shipping	Airways	Railroads	Highways	Shipping
1961	52.9	45.6	1.3	0.2	88.2	8.1	3.7
1966	42.5	56.2	1.0	0.3	81.5	8.4	10.1
1969	39.3	59.2	0.9	0.6	68.2	12.2	19.6
1972	27.2	71.1	0.8	0.9	53.1	18.3	28.6

Source: Ministry of Transportation.

Table 5. Rate of Increase in Transport Service by Mode
(percentage of million passenger kilometers and million ton kilometers)

Mode of transport	1962–66	1967–71	1962–72
Domestic passenger traffic			
Railroads	10.5	0.7	6.4
Highways	20.8	15.1	17.7
Shipping	7.8	5.9	7.8
Airways	34.9	44.4	36.3
Total	15.4	9.7	12.8
Domestic freight traffic			
Railroads	9.4	7.6	8.5
Highways	11.8	28.4	20.1
Shipping	45.2	90.2	47.7
Total	11.2	18.5	14.8

Source: Tae Wan-Son, *The Economic Development of Korea.*

It appears that Korea has more or less fully exploited its hydro-electric potential, and new investment will be largely concentrated in expanding thermal power capacity. The country has also embarked on a nuclear power program in response to the massive increase in oil prices, and one nuclear power station is already under construction with another planned.

There is probably no country in the world which can claim to possess an adequate supply of housing units. The demand always seems to outstrip supply in the face of rapidly growing populations and incomes. Korea is no exception even though the government is making an effort to alleviate the shortage. Nearly a million units were constructed between 1962 and 1972, and given its political significance no let-up in the housing program is expected in the near future (see Table 6). There are some six million family units in the country, and with the population increasing at the rate of approximately 2 percent a year the demand for new housing is in excess of 120,000 units. The figures for new dwellings therefore suggest that only during the last year or two has the annual increment in housing been enough to satisfy the needs of the growing population, without making much of a dent in the backlog of demand that has been accumulating over the years.

The upgrading of communications has not been limited to transport alone. The number of postal stations has more than doubled while telephone and telegraph facilities have grown even faster (see Table 7).

Table 6. Housing Construction, 1962–73
(*dwelling units*)

Year	Total	Public	Private
1962	49,492	8,776	40,716
1963	58,507	6,232	52,275
1964	54,150	4,820	49,330
1965	70,465	7,953	62,512
1966	93,321	12,134	81,187
1967	94,568	9,559	85,009
1968	96,225	6,745	89,480
1969	104,545	25,258	79,287
1970	115,000	12,382	102,618
1971	130,000	15,669	114,331
1972	110,000	16,800	93,200
1973[a]	180,000	41,500	138,500

a. Provisional.
Source: Ministry of Construction.

Traditionally Korean society has placed a high value on education as a cultural and social asset. After the Japanese occupation there was a considerable expansion of schooling facilities especially at the primary level. By 1941, however, only 5 percent of Korean children were going beyond primary school, and a mere 304 students were enrolled in the country's single university. After 1945 primary education was made universal and study at both the secondary and collegiate level was greatly encouraged. As a result formal education in Korea as early as the mid-1950s was comparable to that of countries enjoying income levels thrice as high.

By 1965 the literacy rate was 80 percent as compared with 22 percent in 1945, and today virtually all age groups below fifty

Table 7. Improvement in Communications Facilities
(*units*)

Item	1961 (A)	1966 (B)	1972 (C)	B/A (percent)	C/A (percent)
Postal stations	804	1,728	1,884	215	234
Intracity telephones	123,154	313,331	719,790	254	584
Long-distance telephones	1,177	2,522	9,054	214	769
Telegraph	265	635	1,475	240	557

Source: Ministry of Communication.

years are literate. Even more impressive was the thirteenfold increase in secondary school enrollment and the eighteenfold jump in college enrollment during 1945–65. In the last decade secondary school and college enrollments have continued to grow at an average rate of 10 percent.

The government has accorded educational expenditures high priority. Over the last nine years, for example, the central government's outlay on education has risen at about the same rate as its budget, approximately 28 percent a year. Total educational expenditures in 1973 reached just over W200 billion (about $0.5 billion equivalent). Per capita public expenditure on education is around $11 a year, higher than that of other countries at a similar stage of development:[1] Philippines, $6.3; Thailand, $8.0; Turkey, $9.0. The investment already made in the education system provides a sound foundation for its further development and adaptation to meet the country's future manpower needs.

Primary education now reaches 97 percent of the six-to-eleven year age group, and roughly 92 percent of the students entering it complete the six-year cycle. The 5.7 million enrollment in 1973 is expected to decline slightly over the next six years because the population growth rate has dropped since the sixties. There is some evidence, however, that the official estimate of 1.6 percent a year underestimates the population growth. Primary education appears to be of adequate quality. The curriculum is sufficiently broad, textbooks are easily obtainable, and virtually all of the teachers meet the qualifications for their jobs, though the student-teacher ratios are rather high.

Nearly 70 percent of the eligible students attend the country's 1,920 middle schools. The standard of education is fairly good, and almost all the teachers are university graduates. Over 800,000 students, representing some 32 percent of the relevant age group, received education at the senior secondary level (grades ten to twelve) in 1973. About 40 percent of the students were in general high schools; the rest, over 400,000 pupils, received vocational education in a variety of institutions offering technical, agricultural, fishery, and commercial subjects, including about 2,000 hours of practical work for each student over three years.

The technical training system administered by the Ministry of Education is fairly efficient, although some adjustment of curricula is required, especially for teacher training. The Office of

1. Private education expenditures are higher in the Philippines and Thailand.

Labor Affairs operates a well-equipped and well-staffed Central Vocational Training Institute (CVTI) at Inchon under a United Nations Development Programme/International Labour Organisation project. Four hundred and thirty students attend the two-year regular course for instructors and about 210 graduate each year. The training standard in skills is high, and graduates are qualified to become shop instructors. The total enrollment at CVTI is about 8,000, including 6,800 students in correspondence courses. Another well-equipped and well-staffed training institute administered by the Office of Labor Affairs is in Pusan.

2

Problems of Rapid Growth:
1963–72

KOREA'S ECONOMIC RECORD during 1963–72 was one of the most impressive among the developing countries. The growth in gross national product (GNP) averaged 9.5 percent a year, and average per capita income in 1972 was around US$310, in real terms more than double the level of ten years before.[1] The rapid increase in per capita income was due mainly to the large gains in output, but it was also facilitated by a sharp decline in the rate of population growth from nearly 3 percent in the early sixties to less than 2 percent at present. By international comparison,[2] only Taiwan has had a higher sustained growth in output per head in the recent past. But the pace of industrialization—led by the expansion of manufactured exports—has been as dramatic in Korea as in Taiwan. The average annual manufacturing growth rate during the past decade was about 18 percent, compared with 16 to 17 percent in Taiwan. Manufactured exports from Korea rose from less than $10 million in 1962 to about $1,365 million in 1972 and were the key element in the expansion of the dynamic industrial sector. Generally speaking, manufactured exports have increased in the past decade more than twice as fast as industrial production.

1. Comparisons in real terms are in 1970 prices throughout the book.
2. Oil countries, Hong Kong, and Singapore are excluded from comparison.

Overall Trends

According to rough estimates, industrial exports accounted for about 30 percent of the increment of industrial output during 1963–72, and the value added in manufactured exports constituted about 30 percent of the value added in manufacturing in 1972. Manufactured exports[3] which by 1972 already accounted for nearly 85 percent of merchandise exports have thus, in a very real sense, been the engine of growth. Though the export pattern is being slowly diversified, labor-intensive light manufactured goods, notably textiles, garments, footwear, wigs, electronics, and plywood, still predominate and account for about 75 percent of total manufactured exports. As Table 8 shows, the major shifts in the structure of industrial exports during 1965–72 were the decline in the relative importance of textiles and plywood and an increase in the share of clothing, electronics, and footwear. Korean exports still concentrate heavily on four major export commodities which accounted for over two-thirds of total manufactured exports in 1972. In addition, there is great dependence on two principal markets, Japan and the United States, which together have accounted for 70 to 75 percent of total Korean exports in re-

Table 8. Major Exports
(million U.S. dollars)

Item	1965	1968	1972	Annual growth (percent) 1965–72
Clothing	20.7	112.2	442.2	56.0
Electrical machinery	1.9	18.9	125.2	88.5
Footwear	4.1	11.0	55.4	48.8
Iron and steel	12.7	1.2	92.8	102.0
Plywood	18.0	65.6	153.6	30.8
Textiles	26.3	61.2	176.6	31.1
Wigs and false beards	6.8	35.5	73.8	49.4
Other manufactured goods	16.3	32.6	245.1	39.0
Total manufactured goods	106.8	338.2	1,364.7	44.2
Other exports	68.3	117.2	259.4	4.7
Total	175.1	455.4	1,624.1	36.3

3. The analysis in this section takes into account developments until 1972 only; more recent developments are discussed in the next chapter.

cent years. The impression of vulnerability given by this pattern of exports is, however, somewhat misleading because Korea has rather deliberately concentrated on developing exports in areas such as clothing and wigs where international demand in general and U.S. demand in particular were growing very rapidly. The present structure of exports will probably have less effect on sustained future expansion than will Korea's continuing ability to evaluate its own comparative advantage and interpret correctly the trends in international trade.

So far, at least, an important aspect of Korea's industrial success has been its concentration on industries where capital requirements were low relative to output. Investment in manufacturing has absorbed in the past less than 20 percent of total fixed investment in Korea compared with nearly one-third in Taiwan,[4] although the overall ratios of fixed investment to GNP in the two countries have been roughly the same.[5] The capital-output ratios in Korean manufacturing have not only been low but also shown a tendency to decline further, in part because of the marked expansion in electronics and clothing. The incremental capital-output ratios in manufacturing at constant (1970) market prices, with a one-year lag, are as follows:

1954–62	2.3
1963–67	1.7
1968–72	1.4

At the same time, the value added per worker in manufacturing, around US$1,600 in 1972, compared favorably with other developing East Asian countries.

The real fixed investment increased at double the rate of GNP during the last ten years. A large portion of this was directed toward a massive public investment program in infrastructure in the second half of the sixties. Widespread improvements in transport, power, and communications were designed essentially to remove bottlenecks in the country's infrastructure that emerged

4. The comparison is affected, however, by the fact that a portion of the infrastructure investment in Taiwan is undertaken by the productive sectors. The overall incremental capital-output ratios have been somewhat more favorable in Taiwan than in Korea, reflecting perhaps more adequate investment in social overhead capital in Korea.

5. The ratio of fixed investment to GNP in Korea averaged 24 percent during 1967–72 compared with 26 percent in Taiwan.

with the expansion of the manufacturing sector. The investment program that resulted strongly supported overall economic expansion.

The structural changes in the economy highlighted by the sharp rise in the ratio of manufacturing output, exports, and fixed investment to GNP are summarized in Table 9. The share of agriculture in GNP fell dramatically from 41 percent in 1962 to 25 percent in 1972, and the contribution of manufacturing to output then exceeded that of agriculture for the first time. In itself the agricultural growth rate of 4.0 percent a year was quite high during the last decade, but the manufacturing sector was expanding more than four times as fast as agriculture. Under the impetus of the sharp rise in the export of manufactured goods, the ratio of exports to GNP rose steadily to 21 percent in 1972 from less than 4 percent a decade earlier. At the same time the ratio of fixed capital formation to GNP rose from around 12 percent during 1960–62 to an average of above 23 percent during 1970–72, reflecting the rapid growth in real investment.

The process of rapid growth which transformed the Korean economy from the sluggish agricultural-rural pattern of the post-Korean war years to the dynamic semi-industrialized urban pattern of the present has not been without problems. Three key issues have been causing serious concern to the Korean planners

Table 9. **Principal Indicators of Structural Change in the Economy**
(*percent*)

Indicator	1960	1965	1969	1972
The proportion of GNP[a] from:				
Agriculture	41	39	30	25
Manufacturing	11	14	20	26
Gross domestic product[a]				
Consumption	99	91	83	84
Gross fixed captial formation	9	13	27	22
Export of goods and services	2	5	13	21
Import of goods and services	10	10	24	27
Investment saving gap[b]	10	7	12	6
Ratio of gross investment to GNP	11	15	30	21
Rate of national saving to GNP	1	8	18	15
Debt service ratio[c]	n.a.	3	13	18

n.a.: Not available.
a. In constant 1970 prices.
b. In current prices.
c. Debt of one-year maturities and above.

since the end of the sixties. First is the considerable problem of resource management. The heavy investments required to sustain Korea's rapid economic growth have been well beyond Korea's own saving capabilities. The large saving-investment gap has not only persisted but also widened considerably during the second half of the sixties. Second, the disparities between rural and urban areas increased, and at least till the late sixties there was not much improvement in the living standard of the rural population. Third, the cost of export incentives rose sharply during the late sixties and, though subsequent examination shows that effective export subsidies have hardly been excessive, they appeared so at the time.

Resource Management

The reliance on foreign savings (including current transfers) increased from an average of 7.3 percent of GNP during 1964–66 to around 11 percent during 1968–70. Net current transfers from abroad which were very large in the early sixties declined steadily from 5.9 percent of GNP in 1966 to less than 2.0 percent in 1972, due mainly to the elimination of official grants. The growing deficits on goods and services accounts therefore had to be financed by large external borrowings. Korean medium- and long-term debt was negligible before 1965 but expanded by about $2 billion during 1965–71. The debt service payments rose from less than $20 million in 1966 to over $360 million in 1971, and the debt service ratio jumped from 3.7 percent to 24.6 percent over the period notwithstanding the remarkable expansion in export earnings. The steep rise in debt burden was due in part to an excessive reliance on suppliers' credits; official flows provided for less than 30 percent of gross disbursements during 1966–71.

The emergence of a debt problem threatened to become a serious constraint on growth during 1970–71. The resource problems were not, however, the result of any failure of the domestic saving effort as such, nor did the large external inflows weaken the domestic mobilization of resources. Indeed the rise in the ratio of national savings to GNP from about 2 percent in the early sixties to 15 percent in 1972 has been quite impressive (see Table 10). The basic problem is that at the beginning of the period of rapid growth Korea's domestic savings were negligible. In the early sixties the investment rate of about 12.5 percent of GNP

Table 10. Shares of Gross Savings in GNP, 1965–72
(percentage at current prices)

Savings	1965	1966	1967	1968	1969	1970	1971	1972
Corporate sector	4.0	4.0	4.1	4.7	4.6	4.0	3.7	5.1
Noncorporate sector	1.8	5.0	3.8	2.7	6.7	5.4	4.8	6.0
Total private	5.8	9.0	7.9	7.4	11.3	9.4	8.5	11.1
Government	1.7	2.8	4.1	6.3	6.2	7.0	6.0	3.9
Total national savings	7.5	11.8	12.0	13.7	17.5	16.3	14.5	15.0

was financed mainly by resource inflows from abroad, principally in the form of U.S. aid. Even though the real marginal saving rate during the last decade has been around 25 percent, the initial level of savings made it impossible to reduce reliance on external resources,[6] mainly because investment was also growing very rapidly. The mobilization of domestic resources also created financial strains because of the unduly high reliance on credit expansion (over 35 percent a year during 1962–72) and an average inflation rate during 1965–72 of 13 percent a year. The saving effort was not adequately institutionalized, corporate savings remained relatively small with high debt-equity ratios, and the financial position of business enterprises became extremely vulnerable toward the end of the sixties.

Indeed the major factor sustaining domestic savings was the sharp rise in government savings which provided 40 to 45 percent of the total increment in national savings during the sixties. The ratio of public savings to GNP—negative in the early 1960s—climbed to the high level of 6.4 percent during 1969–71, though it suffered a temporary setback during 1972.

The improved fiscal performance was brought about by a sustained tax effort and a restraint on current expenditures. Government revenues rose from around 8 percent of GNP in 1960 to over 15 percent by 1971, though they dropped to 14 percent by 1972. In the latter half of the sixties, current revenues grew in real terms by about 25 percent a year. This impressive fiscal effort resulted from the rapid growth of income and the general expansion of economic activity in the period as well as from increased levels of taxation and improved tax administration. In

6. The ratio of foreign saving to GNP dropped to 6 percent in 1972 from 11 percent in 1971, but this was almost entirely due to the reduction in the investment ratio.

1971–72, however, there was a distinct slowdown in the growth of revenues to less than 2 percent a year in real terms, largely because of a drop in government enterprise income and the transfer of funds from abroad and also a slower growth in tax receipts. Whereas revenues grew at an impressive rate in the latter part of the sixties, the government was able to restrain the growth in current expenditures to about 16 percent a year in real terms. Current public savings in current prices had risen to W198 billion in 1971 compared with W46 billion in 1965 (see Table 11).

Private savings also experienced a sharp upsurge during the late sixties although the saving rate fluctuated rather widely from year to year. The banking system was an important instrument in the mobilization of private savings, and it is quite probable that some of the incentive for higher savings came from the government policy which served to maintain real interest rates at a fairly high level.

The problems of financial management became particularly pressing after 1969 when investment surged to nearly 30 percent of GNP, the economic growth rate reached a record of 15 percent, and net foreign borrowing increased to a peak of $556 million. During 1970–72 the government took a number of measures to reduce the rate of increase of investment, curb further expansion in foreign capital requirements, and generally improve the balance of payments. Following the massive devaluation of 1964, the exchange rate remained relatively stable for several years, but it was gradually adjusted down from around W300 per U.S. dollar in the beginning of 1970 to W400 per U.S. dollar by the middle of 1972. Restrictions were placed on suppliers' credits with relatively short maturities, and efforts were made to in-

Table 11. Government Revenue and Expenditure
(*billion won*)

Item	1967	1968	1969	1970	1971	1972	1973
Current revenue[a]	231.6	325.5	405.5	519.2	609.8	666.4	793.6
Current expenditure[a]	149.3	199.6	255.2	324.1	411.7	512.6	576.5
Savings on current account	82.3	125.9	150.3	195.1	197.8	153.8	217.1

a. In current prices.

crease the inflow of capital from official sources. Measures were also taken to limit the expansion of domestic credit with the result that the rate of credit creation dropped from around 85 percent a year during 1967–69 to 25 percent in 1970–71. These measures, combined with a reduction in government real investment and uncertainty in the Korean business community about export prospects (after the United States took steps in 1971 to strengthen its balance of payments), produced a definite slowdown in the Korean economy. The GNP growth averaged only 8 percent a year during 1970–72 compared with nearly 12 percent in the preceding three years. Real investment stagnated during 1970–72, and the ratio of fixed investment dropped sharply from 26.6 percent of GNP in 1969 to 20.2 percent in 1972. The general economic slowdown did not, however, result in an abatement of inflationary pressures, and price increases accelerated during 1971–72 partly as a result of higher procurement prices of rice and barley and partly because devaluation raised the prices of imported raw materials and the cost of debt service. An inflationary psychology also dampened savings, and the real marginal rate of savings was actually negative during 1970–72. This disappointing performance was related to the reduction in government savings, a larger relative transfer of incomes to rural areas, and the tight profit squeeze in the corporate private sector. The latter in turn points to the sharp deterioration in the financial structure of Korean business enterprises. Heavy reliance on borrowed capital during the 1968–69 investment boom had raised the debt-equity ratio of manufacturing enterprises from 2 : 1 in 1968 to 4 : 1 in 1971. Interest expenses rose from 5.9 percent of sales to 9.9 percent over the same period. Consequently, even with a small decline in operating profits[7] from 10.6 percent in 1968 to 8.4 percent in 1971, the return on equity decreased very sharply from 16.0 to 4.4 percent. The number of business failures associated with this state of affairs seriously undermined business confidence.

A presidential decree on August 3, 1972, instigated measures designed to improve the financial position and the structure of business enterprises and showed increased determination to tackle the inflationary problem. It aimed at reviving business confidence and indicated a definite shift toward giving higher priority to price stabilization. In order to achieve a more balanced financial structure of business enterprises, prime emphasis was placed

---

7. Ratio of payable interest and net profit to gross capital.

on mandatory rescheduling of their short-term borrowing from the unorganized private market, usually referred to as the curb market, and from commercial banks. An amount of W550 billion of debt was initially affected, or roughly 43 percent of the total liabilities of manufacturing enterprises. A substantial part of this debt was converted into eight-year loans (including three years' grace) at 8 percent rate of interest. At the same time the basic lending and time deposit rates of commercial banks were reduced from 19 to 15.5 percent and from 16.8 to 12 percent, respectively. The reduction in interest rates was intended not only to provide financial relief to enterprises but also to change the inflationary psychology. The direct attack on inflation was symbolized by the objective of limiting price increases to 3 percent a year, avoiding an increase in utility rates, and exercising maximum restraint on the 1973 government budget. These measures were supplemented by selective price controls, a much smaller increase in the government's purchase price of rice for the 1973 harvest, a series of tariff reductions, a lowering of the import deposit requirement, and some relaxation of import restrictions.

Distribution of Growth Benefits

The uneven distribution of the benefits of economic growth has been another important issue in Korea. The wide disparity between the agricultural and the manufacturing growth was accompanied until 1970 by a growing gap, in absolute terms, between the living standards of the rural and urban populations, despite a massive flight of rural people to urban centers. Notwithstanding the rapid rate of urbanization, heavily concentrated in Seoul and Pusan which together absorbed nearly 60 percent of the growth in population in the sixties, about half the population still lives in the rural areas. The Korean government has therefore been increasingly concerned with the dangerous political and social implications of a relatively neglected rural sector, particularly because the ruling Democratic Republican party has traditionally had its strongest support in the rural areas. Moreover, the armed forces, the other major pillar of support for the government of President Park, also view the relative neglect of the farming population with growing concern. A large and increasing number of middle and lower echelon officers come from rural areas and have maintained their close affinity with the rural population.

Table 12. The Terms of Trade of Agriculture

Year	Prices received by farmers			Prices paid by farmers	Terms of trade	Wholesale prices (index)
	All products (1,000.0)[a]	Rice (401.8)[a]	Barley and wheat (49.3)[a]			
1963	40.1	45.8	65.2	35.3	113.6	46.3
1964	50.2	57.0	84.3	44.8	112.1	62.3
1965	52.2	53.5	61.4	51.8	100.8	68.5
1966	55.4	56.5	58.1	58.1	95.4	74.6
1967	63.5	62.2	69.5	65.8	96.5	79.4
1968	74.3	73.2	75.9	78.8	94.3	85.8
1969	84.8	90.8	89.3	86.8	97.7	91.6
1970	100.0	100.0	100.0	100.0	100.0	100.0
1971	121.4	125.6	136.2	114.4	106.1	108.6
1972	147.9	159.5	176.7	130.5	113.3	123.8
1973	164.2	167.7	183.7	143.1	114.7	132.4
1974	215.6	242.8	238.5	192.5	114.1	188.2

a. Weight.

Because of the relatively depressed pay for public servants and military personnel, they feel that they are not receiving an equitable share of the general rise in incomes.

Since 1967 the government support prices for rice and barley have been a major instrument for raising farm incomes and at the same time providing incentives for accelerated production of food grain. But as Table 12 shows, it is only since 1970 that a noticeable improvement in the agricultural terms of trade has taken place. More recently the government has broadened its attack on unbalanced regional growth to remedy the overcentralization of industrial production and labor in a few highly congested centers. The Sae Maeul movement for rural community development,[8] initiated by President Park in late 1971, is to become a crucial instrument in lifting rural incomes and improving the quality of rural life. One important objective of these policies is to create more industrial jobs in the rural areas and thus expand off-farm employment opportunities.

EMPLOYMENT AND WAGE TRENDS

Even though rapid economic growth has not had a uniform impact on the income levels of the various sections of the popula-

8. See Appendix B.

tion, there has been a considerable improvement in the employment situation and a definite reduction in the absolute level of
rural poverty. As Table 13 shows, employment in industrial and
service sectors expanded by 8 to 9 percent and 5 percent a year
respectively during 1963–72, notwithstanding impressive annual
average gains in labor productivity in those sectors of 9 percent
and 5 percent respectively. Agricultural employment remained
roughly unchanged over the period, and its share in the total
dropped from around 63 percent in 1963 to about 50 percent in
1972. Nonetheless the overall employment growth of 2.5 percent
a year during 1964–72 exceeded the corresponding growth in the
labor force[9] (2.2 percent), and the rate of registered unemployment declined from 8.1 percent in 1963 to 4.5 percent in 1972 (see
Table 14). Official statistics indicate an average official unemployment rate in nonfarm households of 7.6 percent in 1972, but this
probably underestimates urban unemployment, which by unoffi-
cial estimates appears to be at least in the order of 10 to 11 percent.[10] Nevertheless a substantial improvement in the employment situation is evidenced by the rapid growth during 1967–72
in real wages in manufacturing of almost 11 percent a year as well
as by an annual 8 percent increase in real farm wages (see Table
15). During 1967–70, indeed, real wages in manufacturing rose by
a record average of 14.5 percent a year, outstripping productivity

9. Population data on the age group 14 years and over, the economically active, participation rates, employment, and registered unemployment are the result
of quarterly employment surveys. They exclude armed forces, national police, and
prisoners. There is some reason to believe that the surveys do not adequately take
into account recent changes in the age structure of the population. Between 1966
and 1970, for example, the survey data show an annual growth in the population
below 14 years of 2.4 percent and in the population aged 14 years and over of only
1.6 percent. Census data for 1966 and 1970 give an opposite trend: an annual
growth rate of only 1.0 percent in the population below 14 years and 2.46 percent
in the population 14 years and above. While the census data would support the
claim of a declining birth rate, the Economic Planning Board's data seem to con-
tradict it. If the population of working age is underestimated by the survey data,
then the actual unemployment rate would be higher than the official rate derived
from this data.

10. The official unemployment figures tend to be on the low side since they
include only those who are actively seeking jobs and have not worked at all during
the quarterly period prior to the sampling date. The extended family still provides
sufficient social security so that potential job seekers often prefer not to take jobs
outside the family. In addition, young men delay employment until after completion of their compulsory three-year military service. Another cultural factor is
that many Koreans tend to feel embarrassed to admit by registering as unem-
ployed that they had failed in finding jobs. (See also note 9 above.)

Table 13. Aggregate Trends in Sectoral Output and Employment, 1963–72

| | Employment and relative output per head | | | | | | Annual growth rate 1963–72 | | | Contribution to growth | |
| | 1963 | | | 1972 | | | | | | | |
Sector	Output[a]	Employ-ment	Produc-tivity	Output[a]	Employ-ment	Produc-tivity	Output[a]	Employ-ment	Produc-tivity	Output	Employ-ment
Agriculture, forestry, and fisheries	40.0	63.2	0.63	25.5	50.6	0.50	4.1	0.1	4.0	13.5	2.7
Agriculture and forestry	38.3	60.7	0.63	22.8	48.4	0.47	3.4	0.1	3.3	10.5	1.5
Mining and manufacturing	14.1	8.7	1.62	26.2	14.2	1.85	17.4	8.4	9.0	35.8	35.3
Social overhead capital and services	45.9	28.1	1.63	48.6	35.2	1.38	10.3	5.1	5.2	50.7	62.0
Total	100.0	100.0	1.00	100.0	100.0	1.00	9.6	2.53	7.0	100.0	100.0

a. Gross value added at constant 1970 market prices.

Table 14. Labor Force and Employment, 1963–74

Year	Population 14 years and over (thousands)	Participation rate (percent)			Total labor force (thousands)	Annual growth rates (percent)	Employed (thousands)	Annual growth rates (percent)	Official unemployment rate (percent)
		Average	Male	Female					
1963	15,085	55.3	76.4	36.3	8,343		7,662		8.1
						1963–67 2.7		1963–67 3.3	
1967	16,764	55.4	76.1	36.8	9,295		8,717		6.2
						1967–70 1.8		1967–70 3.8	
1970	18,253	55.9	75.1	38.5	10,199		9,745		4.5
						1970–72 2.4		1970–72 4.1	
1972	19,724	56.1	74.1	38.9	11,058		10,559		4.5
						1963–72 2.2		1963–72 3.6	
1973	20,438	56.8	73.9	40.8	11,600		11,139		4.0
						1972–73 4.9		1972–73 5.5	
1974	21,148	57.1	79.4	50.2	12,080		11,586		4.1
						1973–74 4.1		1973–74 4.0	

Source: Quarterly Official Employment Sample Survey in EPB, *Monthly Statistics of Korea.* various issues. The data represent annual averages of the quarterly sample figures.

Table 15. Manufacturing and Agricultural Wages
(1970 = 100)

Item	1963	1964	1965	1966	1967	1968	1969	1970ᵃ	1971	1972	Average annual change		
											1963–67	1967–72	1963–72
Manufacturing													
Nominal wages													
Index	21.8	26.6	32.5	38.3	46.9	59.4	79.6	100.0	119.1	138.1			
Annual change (percent)	14.4	22.0	18.6	17.8	22.5	26.7	34.0	25.6	19.1	16.0	20.3	24.6	22.7
Real wagesᵇ													
Index	56.6	54.0	55.7	58.6	64.7	73.7	89.7	100.0	104.9	108.9			
Annual change (percent)	−4.5	−4.6	4.4	5.2	10.4	13.9	21.7	11.5	4.9	3.8	3.9	10.7	7.5
Agriculture													
Nominal farm wages	27.2	36.6	40.2	46.0	53.8	65.7	80.5	100.0	119.5	142.7	21.7	21.4	21.5
Index of prices paid by households for household goods	38.4	49.5	55.1	61.8	69.6	80.3	87.6	100.0	112.3	125.3	16.1	12.5	14.8
Real wages	63.2	66.5	67.3	70.2	76.1	82.4	91.7	100.0	106.9	111.1	4.8	7.9	6.5
Annual change (percent)	3.5	13.5	1.2	4.3	2.4	8.1	11.3	9.1	6.9	3.9			

a. For 1970 and thereafter electricity has been excluded from manufacturing.
b. Real wage indexes are deflated by the All Cities Consumer Price Index, except for 1963 and 1964 where the Seoul Consumer Price Index was used.

growth. The increase in real wages as well as in manufacturing employment slowed down to 4 percent and 2 percent a year respectively during 1971–72, but this was attributable mainly to the excessive rise in labor costs in the preceding years rather than to any slackening in manufacturing growth. The temporary squeeze on industrial profits was probably a further factor restraining wage increases. Taken as a whole for 1963–72, real wages in manufacturing have not risen faster than labor productivity. The fact that during 1971–72 real wages in the farm sector rose faster than in manufacturing indicates some success of the government's policies in favor of agriculture.[11]

RURAL-URBAN DISPARITY

The government index of the parity between rural household income and wage and salary income in urban households is given in Table 16. The figures indicate a sharp deterioration in the relative position of farm households during 1963–67 when their annual income expanded by 12.5 percent compared with a corresponding growth of 33 percent for urban households. Indeed, with the rise in price of farm household goods, there was a 15 percent decline in real incomes in the farm sector over the 1963–67 period compared with a rise in real income of 80 percent for wage-earning households in urban areas. Consequently the parity ratio between rural and urban incomes was practically halved between 1963 and 1967. Although 1963 was no doubt a relatively favorable year for agriculture, the fact remains that the living standard in rural areas was not to reach this peak again until 1970. Meanwhile the income of the average wage-earning family in urban areas had more than doubled.

The absolute gap in rural-urban incomes was largest in 1970 but came down sharply during 1971 and 1972 and had disappeared by 1974. This relative improvement in the position of rural areas is due in part to the slow growth in real wages in urban areas mentioned above. The agricultural growth rate during the last few years has been only somewhat higher than the long-term trend of 4 percent a year.

---

11. The somewhat surprising jump of over 5 percent in agricultural employment during 1972, after a small but almost steady decline during the past several years, also represented in part a return to rural areas, especially of female labor, as job opportunities in manufacturing and related services became more scarce.

Table 16. Comparison of Incomes of Rural and Urban Households
(won)

Category	1963	1967	1968	1969	1970	1971	1972	1973	1974
Rural									
A. Household	93,179	149,470	178,959	217,874	255,804	356,382	429,394	480,711	674,500
B. Per capita	14,582	24,423	29,727	36,373	43,210	61,129	75,200	84,000	118,000
C. Per worker	29,209	47,907	59,653	73,606	87,905	122,049	144,092	164,000	218,000
Urban									
D. Household	80,160	248,640	285,960	333,600	381,240	451,920	517,440	550,200	644,520
E. Per capita	14,417	45,538	52,566	61,550	71,393	85,591	98,186	105,000	123,000
F. Per worker	67,361	192,744	219,969	254,656	286,647	339,789	394,992	405,000	476,000
Ratio									
A/D	116.3	60.1	62.6	65.3	67.1	78.9	83.0	87.4	104.7
B/E	101.1	53.6	56.6	59.1	60.5	71.4	76.6	80.0	96.0
C/F	43.4	24.9	27.1	28.9	30.7	35.9	36.5	41.0	46.0

Source: Economic Planning Board (EPB).

52

A major source of the sharp increase in real incomes of rural households of over 9 percent a year since 1967 has been the massive increases in the support prices of rice[12] and barley, amounting to 122 percent and 112 percent respectively during 1968–72.[13] By 1972 the domestic price of rice was around 60 percent above the international price. In the crop year 1973, however, a relatively modest growth in the support price, combined with a dramatic rise in the world price of rice, eliminated the difference almost entirely. On the assumption that 1970–72 world rice prices were equilibrium prices, protection afforded to domestic rice production would appear to be heavy. It did not lead to a serious misallocation of resources because of the physical constraints on expanding rice output. The growth in rice output was only 1.9 percent a year during 1967–72, and imports of rice grew substantially (see Chapter 6). But rice support prices have had important internal effects on the redistribution of income. It is interesting to note, however, that within the farm sector high supports tended to have a regressive influence on income distribution.

Although farms do not vary in size as widely in Korea as in many countries,[14] there are still substantial differences between the very small and the relatively big farmers in the average size of landholdings.

Table 17 shows that two-thirds of farm households have less than one hectare. These households constitute the bulk of the bottom 40 percent of income receivers. For households with a farm of less than one hectare, only 11 percent of the gross farm receipts (including noncash receipts but excluding changes in inventories) in 1971 was attributable to cash rice sales. This proportion rose steadily with the size of the farm to 30 percent for those exceeding two hectares. This is in part due to the fact that smaller farms derive a smaller proportion of their gross income from cash sales. But it is also significant that the sale of vegeta-

12. Rice now accounts for over 60 percent of the gross agricultural receipts of farm households.

13. As a complementary policy, the government during the same period kept prices of fertilizer and other farm inputs almost stable. Prices paid by farmers for fertilizers and pesticides are lower relative to those received for rice and other crops in Korea than in most other countries.

14. Since the land reform in the early 1950s most farms are operator owned and limited in size to three hectares of cultivated land per household, except in new upland areas recently developed for cultivation.

Table 17. Number and Cropland Area of Farm Households, 1971
(*percent*)

Size of farm (hectares)	Number	Cropland area
0–0.5	33.6	11.4
0.5–1.0	31.7	27.3
1.0–2.0	26.0	41.1
2.0–3.0	4.8	13.4
Over 3.0	1.5	6.8
Total	100.0	100.0

bles, fruit, livestock, and raw silk provides a much larger proportion of the cash income of the smaller farmers than does the sale of rice. Because the prices of these commodities rose somewhat less rapidly than those of grains, the improvement in the terms of trade for the smaller farmers was probably less pronounced than for rural households as a whole. But smaller farmers who supplement their income by working for wages on larger farms[15] gained from a relatively sharp increase in real farm wages averaging 8 percent a year during 1967–72.

Sufficient information is not available to judge the shift in the relative income position of the rural poor over the last decade. There is little doubt that in absolute terms the living standard of all rural groups has improved substantially since 1967 and the disparity between rural and urban areas has lessened. But the rural-urban income ratios in Table 16 need some qualification. The ratio of 83 percent in 1972 does not take into account the differences in the size of urban and rural households and the average number of workers in each. Traditionally farm households are larger than urban and include considerably more workers. Still, if comparison is made on the basis of income per worker, it would indicate that the average rural worker earned 50 percent less than the average urban wage and salary earner in 1974. This may be partly because of different statistical treatment of females in urban and rural households. But even if allowance is made for

15. About 15 percent of the average labor input on farms during 1971 was hired. For farms over 2 hectares hired labor accounted for over 30 percent of total labor input while for the farms less than 0.5 hectares the proportion was only 10 percent. About 84,000 farm households (out of 2.48 million) own no cropland and earn most of their living by working for other farms.

underemployment in agriculture, measured by the number of hours worked,[16] the ratio of rural to urban earnings is still $3:5$.

The basic problem is that the growth of productivity will almost always be more rapid in the dynamic industrial sector than in the agricultural, and if the real wages in both sectors grow as fast as productivity[17] the sectoral income differentials must widen. Under the circumstances, the increase in the relative prices of agricultural products can provide only a limited solution. Perhaps the main failure of government policies regarding the distribution of growth benefits has been that the proportion of nonfarm sources of rural income has not increased over time. In 1972 rural households in Korea derived 17 percent of their income off the farm, which compares unfavorably with the corresponding figure of 55 percent for Taiwan. The lack of opportunities for nonfarm employment in rural Korea is related to the heavy concentration of industry in Seoul, Inchon, and Pusan. This concentration has probably helped the export effort by making it relatively easy for the concerned government agencies to set up targets and monitor progress. This polarization of the economy was probably also unavoidable in the earlier periods of Korea's economic development because of the absence of adequate infrastructure outside the two major metropolitan areas that were also the country's major ports. Nevertheless the costly results of this concentration have been migration from rural areas, pressure on urban wages, serious urban housing shortages, and pressures for expanding urban infrastructures. Government efforts to disperse industry into the provinces are steps in the right direction and should bring about a more balanced growth of the economy. The continuing expansion of infrastructure will further assist industrial decentralization.

Given the practical difficulties of bringing about a more rapid increase in real earnings in rural areas relative to urban wages, the government's goals must be set realistically. Even if some widening of the rural-urban disparity takes place initially, the industrial urban sector may make a significant contribution to the

16. An average of 41 hours a week was worked in agriculture, forestry, and fishing during 1971 compared with 57 a week in nonagricultural activities.

17. The 4 percent growth in labor productivity in the agricultural sector during 1963–72 was quite impressive but considerably short of the corresponding rate of 9 percent for the secondary sector and still below the 5 percent rate for the tertiary.

welfare of the farm population by substantially reducing its dependence on the agricultural sector for income. This is precisely how the rapid industrial growth in the cities has had a favorable impact in Korea's rural areas. The disparity between rural and urban household incomes has probably not changed over the last decade, but at least the proportion of agricultural to total employment has dropped sharply and the absolute labor force in agriculture has not grown much since 1962.

Export Incentives

The economic and financial cost of promoting exports has been another major concern. Korea has relied heavily on a variety of incentives as well as on frequent adjustments of the exchange rate to encourage industrial exports. A major incentive has been tariff exemptions on the import of raw materials and capital goods. Other export subsidies were indirect tax exemptions, preferential interest rates for exporters, reduced business income tax rate on export income, and special accelerated depreciation. In addition to these rather standard incentives several other measures were instituted to increase the relative profitability of exports. The most important of these was the so-called wastage allowance.[18] In addition a limited export-import link system was set up to increase exports with low profit margins and develop new export markets. In both cases the exporter was given the temporary right to import duty free certain restricted popular items. A less important subsidy took the form of preferential rates for electricity and transportation. Last but not least, it has been argued, the heavily protected domestic market in Korea permitted high profits for many industries, which constituted an indirect subsidy by enabling those industries to accept the rigors and low margins of the export market. This rather complex system of incentives and subsidies has been workable mainly because of the close alliance

18. Exporters and suppliers of exporters were given the automatic right to duty-free imports of intermediate products up to stated limits. These limits were established in such a way that the wastage allowance for an input exceeded normal wastage through loss, damage, and other causes. The portion of the allowance not used in export production could be sold domestically, often at a high profit since the imports involved either had quantitative restrictions or were subject to import duties. There is evidence that this subsidy grew in importance and that the allowances to many industries increased in the late sixties.

between government and business in Korea, a pattern similar to that in Japan and Taiwan.

The question is whether these export incentives have been excessive. The quantifiable won subsidies per dollar of exports rose from W27.4 in 1964 to W99, or 32 percent of commodity exports, in 1970. This apparent sharp rise gives a misleading impression of the competitiveness of Korean exports, however. In actuality the growth in these subsidies was necessitated by the fact that Korea's price level rose much faster than that of its major trade partners while the official exchange rate remained relatively stable during 1965–70. According to Korean Development Institute estimates, the real effective exchange rate on exports (including tariff and indirect tax exemptions as well as direct tax and interest preferences and adjusted for relative changes in domestic and foreign price levels) in 1965 prices remained in the range of W300 to W315 per dollar. Without the increase in subsidies the real effective exchange rate on exports would have fallen over the 1968–70 period.

During 1970–72 the real exchange rate rose and probably further strengthened the Korean competitive position. The nominal exchange rate of W322 per U.S. dollar in early 1971 depreciated by 18 percent in relation to the U.S. dollar and 39 percent in relation to the Japanese yen by 1973. The weighted average exchange rate increased by about 24 percent from April 1971 to September 1973; this more than compensated for the somewhat higher rise in the domestic price level in Korea. With the improvement in the real exchange rate and the related reduction in import tariffs and the liberalization of imports, the need for export subsidies lessened. The wastage allowances were reduced; business income tax preference on export earnings was abolished; interest-rate subsidies came down because interest on export credits rose from 6 to 7 percent (and more recently to 9 percent) and, more importantly, the general level of interest rates on advances declined; and the incidence of duty exemptions reduced because of lower tariffs. Though precise estimates are not possible, the overall export subsidies now probably represent only 15 percent of the total export value compared with over 30 percent in 1970. (See Table 31.)

To evaluate the repercussions of export incentives on resource allocation, it is more relevant to consider the effective rate of subsidy on exports. For comparison with the international price level, exemptions from customs and indirect taxes ought not to be regarded as export subsidies. A recent study[19] suggests that the effective rate of subsidy on total exports was only about 7 to 9 percent in 1968 though for manufacturing exports it was in the range of 9 to 12 percent. This does not mean that the rates were not in some cases excessive. The subsidies on plywood exports, for example, were largely in the form of a liberal wastage allowance on imported roundwood; according to one estimate for a recent year half the total subsidy from the wastage allowance system was attributable to roundwood imports.

The same study suggests that the average rate of effective protection in Korea, around 10 percent in 1968, was quite low by international standards and indicates that the exchange rate policy has been realistic. Furthermore the average protection has been limited mainly to primary production. In manufacturing industries the average effective protection on domestic sales was indeed negative, mainly because of the high nominal protection accorded to inputs. In general, therefore, protection favored exports over domestic sales, mainly because the export sector was able to obtain its inputs at world market prices. But in a number of cases, notably fabrics, knit products, and electronic components, produced for both export and the home market, indirect subsidies were in effect given to exports by high rates of effective protection. On the whole, however, policies toward export promotion have been coherent and consistent, and protection of domestic industries is generally not excessive. Although there is little reason to be concerned about the general effect of the overall level of export subsidies on resource allocation, these subsidies should be reviewed in the interest of strengthening government revenues, achieving a more equitable distribution of income, and rationalizing specific industries.

19. Larry Westphal and Kwang Kim, "Industrial Policy and Development in Korea" (World Bank, restricted circulation draft, February 1974).

3

Recent Economic Developments
and New Economic Challenges

DURING 1973–75 THE KOREAN ECONOMIC situation was subject to sudden and sharp changes. Beginning the latter part of
1972, the Korean economy experienced an unprecedented boom
and in the course of 1973 set new records of growth in GNP, exports, and savings. These favorable economic developments were
interrupted, however, by external developments in 1974—the
sharp rise in the price of petroleum in late 1973, the recession in
the Japanese and U.S. economies, and the high price of food grains
and raw materials. Although the current account balance of payments deficit had narrowed substantially during 1972 and 1973, it
rose to a record level in 1974, both in absolute amount and as a
percentage of GNP, reflecting the much higher cost of imports
and a major slowdown in exports. These difficulties persisted
during most of 1975, although the growth rate of GNP showed
considerable resilience and remained above 7 percent.

The detailed analysis of recent developments in this chapter illustrates both the strengths and the weaknesses of the Korean
economy. Because of its export-oriented strategy, Korea was one
of the nations which benefited most from the boom conditions in
industrialized countries during 1972–73 and the related expansion in international trade—especially the exceptional growth in
Japanese imports in 1973. But the high ratio of merchandise exports to GNP (at present around 26 percent) and the relatively
heavy dependence on the Japanese and U.S. markets made Korea

particularly vulnerable to the deep recession in the U.S. and Japanese economies during 1974–75. Furthermore the impact of sharply higher prices for energy, raw materials, and food has been particularly severe on Korea because of its poor natural resources and dependence on imported food grains. These recent changes not only created serious problems of short-term economic adjustments but also contain implications for the path and pattern of future growth.

Upsurge during 1973

GNP grew by 16.5 percent in real terms during 1973 primarily because of increases in exports and fixed investment. Merchandise exports during 1973 in current dollars rose by over 90 percent, denoting an increase in real terms of over 55 percent. Real fixed investment which had shown very little increase during the previous three years increased by nearly one-third in 1973, most of it concentrated in private investment.

Given the export expansion, however, the upsurge in investment did not lead to a widening of the balance of payments deficits. Even with the unparalleled import growth of nearly 75 percent in 1973, reflecting the higher price of food grains, raw materials, and fuels and the import of much larger quantities of machinery and intermediate products, the current account deficit was somewhat smaller than in 1972. Foreign savings, measured by the deficit on goods and services account, amounted to only about 4 percent of GNP in 1973 and dropped to only 15 percent of gross investment. These figures represent a dramatic reduction in the relative reliance on external resources compared with 1968–71 when foreign savings averaged 11 percent of GNP and financed 35 to 40 percent of gross investment (see Table 18).

Underlying a more manageable balance of payments position was the apparent sharp improvement in domestic savings. The national saving rate, which had dropped to 15 percent of GNP during 1971–72, went up sharply in 1973 to a record level of 22 percent. The marginal saving rate was close to 50 percent in 1973 reflecting the pull of attractive investment opportunities, continued wage restraints, a sharp revival in industrial profits, and higher government savings notwithstanding the increased subsidies on food grains and some reduction in tariffs to limit the impact of rising import costs on the domestic price level. Part of the good savings performance must also be attributed to the time lag in consumption resulting from a higher disposable income.

Table 18. Saving and Investment Trends
(percent at current prices)

Item	1969	1970	1971	1972	1973	1974	1975
Gross domestic investment/GNP	29.8	27.2	25.6	20.9	26.2	31.4[a]	27.1
Gross national savings/GNP	17.5	16.3	14.5	15.0	22.1	19.2	18.1
Foreign savings/GNP	11.0	9.7	11.3	5.6	4.0	13.5	11.3
Statistical discrepancy	1.3	1.2	−0.2	0.3	0.1	−1.4	−2.3
Foreign savings/gross domestic investment	36.9	35.3	43.8	26.7	15.1	43.6	41.7

a. Including an unusually large increase in stocks equal to 5.5 percent of GNP.

The improvement in Korea's growth performance and financial balance was attributable in part to external factors, notably an unprecedented growth in international demand for Korean exports, and in part to government efforts to stabilize the economy. These measures greatly improved the competitiveness of Korean exports and provided generous assistance to industry as a whole. The 1973 investment boom and sharp increase in industrial profits were in no small measure due to the improved financial structure of business enterprises and a sharp reduction in their interest costs. The competitiveness of Korean exports was further strengthened by the 24 percent devaluation of the won between April 1971 and August 1973, considerably larger than the increase in the Korean price level over that of its major trade partners.

The government had only limited success, however, in containing inflationary pressures. According to official statistics, wholesale prices were about 15 percent higher in December 1973 than the previous year. But the official price indexes did not take account of the extensive price controls and understated the extent of price pressures. In addition, the price increases were accelerating toward the end of the year. Further government control over prices became unworkable with the upheaval in the world commodity markets and the acceleration of price increases in the United States and Japan, Korea's major trade partners. The overseas price developments could not have been forseen when the target of limiting price increases to 3 percent was adopted as part of the August 3, 1972, package.

The 1972–73 boom proved to be relatively short-lived, and its impact on the economy has been overshadowed by the effects of higher energy costs and the downturn in international economic activity. Nevertheless it is useful to examine in some detail the record export and industrial expansion which provided the foundation for this exceptional economic performance.

Export Boom

About one-fourth of the gain in the value of exports in 1973 was apparently due to the rise in prices caused by worldwide inflation and a further decline in the value of the U.S. dollar. But still the gain in export volume was over 55 percent. What special factors enabled Korea to expand its exports much faster than the apparent growth in world trade?

First and foremost was the sharp expansion in total Japanese imports. The peak Japanese trade surplus of 1971 did not represent an equilibrium position. The realignment of the exchange rates of major international currencies during 1972–73 and the consequent improvement in the relative competitiveness of imports in Japanese markets, combined with shifts in Japanese trade policy, resulted in a record growth in Japanese imports of nearly 70 percent in 1973. Korea especially benefited from this expansion because of its traditional trade links with Japan and its improved export competitiveness as a result of a substantial downward adjustment of exchange rates in relation to the Japanese yen. Also contributing to Korea's advantage were the measures it had taken to rationalize industry and the presence of excess capacity in manufacturing. All these factors considered, it is not altogether surprising that Korean exports to Japan in 1973 were, in current prices, about 200 percent higher than in 1972. Of the total increment in the value of Korean exports over this period, exports to Japan accounted for nearly 50 percent, and the share of the latter in total exports increased from 25 percent in 1972 to 38 percent in 1973 though it fell to 31 percent in 1974. Koren exports to Europe have also expanded rapidly since 1971, stimulated in part by the rapid economic expansion in the European Economic Community, but a much more important factor again has been Korea's greater competitiveness, particularly in relation to Japanese exports.

The high level of economic activity in the United States, which remains Korea's most important market, also helped export expansion, though even here Korea's ability to upgrade the value of exports and thus counter the effect of textile quotas, for instance, was especially impressive. The share of the United States in total Korean exports has continued to decline and came down to 32 percent in 1973 from 52 percent in 1968. Nevertheless nearly two-thirds of Korean exports still went to Japan and the United States during 1974, indicating a heavy concentration not only in commodities but also in markets. The dependency of individual exports on the U.S. and Japanese markets is brought out in Table 19. It should also be stressed that the two principal export markets for textiles are to a certain degree a single market. Korea supplies Japan with low-cost textiles for domestic consumption so that Japan can export her higher priced products to the United States.

Even though the growth in Korean exports from $1.1 billion in 1971 to $3.2 billion in 1973 seems somewhat amazing, it was in fact well founded. Apart from the general rise in prices the growth can be explained by structural shifts in world trade, the opening up of the Japanese market, increasing competitiveness of Korean exports, and the good planning and investment decisions of the past few years. The average real Korean export growth rate of 52 percent a year during 1972 and 1973 was substantially higher than the corresponding rate of 35 percent during 1967–71. Thus even if cyclical factors are considered, there was no apparent tendency for the long-run export growth rate to decline. The growth rate of exports slowed down considerably during 1974 and 1975 and will in the future no doubt stabilize at a lower level than in the past, but the 1973 performance was by no means an accident.

In addition to the rapid expansion of exports, there were other developments during 1972–73 which might have long-run significance for the balance of payments. Tourism revenues increased more than eightfold between 1971 and 1973 from $31 million to $264 million mainly because of the increase in the number of Japanese tourists. Although tourism revenues declined somewhat in 1974, the long-term forecast indicates a rise in the number of tourists from 371,000 in 1972 to 1.8 million in 1981.

There was also a substantial improvement in the inflows of direct private foreign investment during 1972–73 though again the extent to which this will be sustained is difficult to judge (see Table 20). Foreign equity investments totaled only $242 million at the end of 1972 and did not play a key role in the past decade in providing external resources, but the rate of net foreign investment inflows has gone up markedly since 1971–72. A large part of the recent inflow of foreign investment was related to Japanese

Table 19. Geographical Concentration of Exports
(percent)

Commodity	1971 United States	1971 Japan	1971 Total	1972 United States	1972 Japan	1972 Total	1973 United States	1973 Japan	1973 Total	1974 United States	1974 Japan	1974 Total
Electronics	35.0	37.0	72.0	34.2	35.5	69.7	38.4	39.7	78.1	32.4	43.9	76.3
Footwear	69.0	2.6	71.6	68.2	5.0	73.2	50.9	19.1	70.0	50.5	23.9	74.4
Plywood	88.4	2.6	91.0	84.0	9.8	93.8	55.6	34.4	90.0	59.2	25.0	84.2
Textiles	51.0	19.1	70.1	42.0	20.6	62.6	26.3	38.8	65.1	24.8	32.4	57.2
Wigs	71.0	17.6	88.5	77.4	8.0	85.4	72.7	9.3	82.0	65.3	12.0	77.3
Miscellaneous manufactures	66.0	19.2	85.2	66.4	12.6	79.0	54.5	21.8	76.3	44.0	25.0	69.0
Percent of total exports	50.0	25.0	75.0	47.0	25.0	72.0	32.0	38.0	70.0	33.5	30.9	64.4
Rate of increase (percent)	34.6	11.8	26.1	42.7	55.7	47.0	34.6	204.4	93.9	46.1	11.2	26.9

Source: Bank of Korea.

Table 20. Private Direct Foreign Investment: Net Inflows

Year	Million U.S. dollars
1968	19.2
1969	12.7
1970	66.1
1971	42.9
1972	78.8
1973	143.3
1974	124.1

sources; the major fields of foreign investment are textiles, electronics, tourism, and transport equipment.

Debt Service

Debt service payments, which had increased fivefold in the short period of three years from 1968 to 1971, grew relatively modestly during 1972 and 1973. The slower rise in debt service is due more to an improvement in the terms of the new debt (see Table 21) than to a reduction in the rate of growth of overall debt. If an improvement in the structure of debt had not taken place between 1970 and 1972, the debt service payment during 1973 would have been at least 25 percent larger than it actually was. The improvement in the debt structure represents a reduction in the relative reliance on suppliers' credits, lengthening of average

Table 21. Gross Disbursements on Medium- and Long-term External Loans
(*million U.S. dollars*)

Year	Official loans	To banking system	Over 3-year maturity	1-to-3-year maturity	Total[a]
			Commercial loans		
1968	70	40	268	167	545
1969	139	30	409	27	605
1970	115	25	367	31	538
1971	303	89	345	49	786
1972	324	20	326	47	718
1973	369	51	344	85	849

a. Gross disbursements of medium- and long-term loans in this table differ somewhat from the corresponding figures in Table 35, which incorporates more recent data for 1972 and 1973.

maturities of these credits, and a sharp increase in official assistance between 1968–70 and 1971–73.

The sharp reduction in the debt burden was signified by the drop in the ratio of debt service payments to exports of goods and nonfactor services from nearly 24 percent in 1970–71 to 18 percent in 1972 and further to 12 percent in 1974–75 (see Table 22). This improvement is related in large part to the huge expansion in foreign exchange earnings but has been assisted to some extent by inflationary forces. The devaluation of the dollar and the rapid growth in world prices have pushed up the current value of exports while debt obligations, mostly denominated in U.S. dollars, have remained fixed. Quite obviously the ability to borrow abroad on reasonable terms, which was causing major worries during 1970–71, has become a relatively less serious constraint. Despite a further substantial increase in debt during 1974–75, the debt service ratio remains fairly low.

The above discussion indicates that Korea's balance of payments was considerably strengthened during 1972–73 by the rapid growth in exports and tourism revenues, the prospect of larger foreign investment inflows, and the more balanced composition and terms of long-term capital inflows. As a result of these developments, Korea was in a stronger position to face the new difficulties which emerged.

Industrial Growth

The manufacturing growth rate, a rather depressed 15.7 percent in 1972, rose by 30.9 percent in 1973 to set a new record. The

Table 22. Debt Outstanding and Debt Burden
(million U.S. dollars)

Year	Medium- and long-term debt outstanding[a]	Debt service payments	Debt service ratio[b]
1970	1,931	286	23.4
1971	2,396	364	24.6
1972	2,978	374	18.0
1973	3,575	446	11.3
1974	4,435	610	11.8
1975	5,806	706	12.5

a. At the end of the year, including debts (amounting to about $400 million at the end of 1974) not guaranteed by the public sector.

b. Ratio of debt service payments to exports of goods and nonfactor services.

Table 23. Manufacturing Growth and Investment
(1970 prices)

Year	Fixed investment *(billion won)*	Growth rate of output *(percent)*
1968	111	27.0
1969	126	21.4
1970	129	18.4
1971	132	17.7
1972	129	15.7
1973	238	30.9
1974	195	17.5

sharp jump in industrial production led to substantial improvements in capacity utilization, labor productivity, and industrial profits. Utilization of industrial capacity was reported to be less than 70 percent during 1970, 1971, and the greater part of 1972. Fixed investment in industry began to rise during 1973, however, after remaining relatively stable for several years, and output has increased markedly (see Table 23). The rate of capacity utilization has therefore risen significantly, particularly in the major export industries, textiles, electronics, and plywood. At the same time wage restraint has continued, and real wages during 1973, as in 1971 and 1972, appear to have risen significantly less than the growth in labor productivity. These factors combined with the substantial reduction in the debt service burden resulted in a sharp improvement in the financial position of business enterprises compared with 1971. The ratio of net profits to net worth in the corporate manufacturing sector, which had dropped to the precariously low level of 4.5 percent in 1971, improved to 16.7 percent in 1972 and further to the all-time high of 30 percent in 1973.

As Table 24 shows, despite a decade of very rapid industrial growth, light manufacturing industries are still dominant in Korea. About 50 percent of the gross manufacturing output is attributable to two groups: food, beverages, and tobacco; and textiles, wearing apparel, and leather. Indeed the latter group has shown growth substantially more rapid than average during the last several years. Wearing apparel and leather products industries, though still rather small, have been growing particularly rapidly. At the same time chemicals, petroleum, iron and steel, cement, and electronics industries have also grown fast, but wood products, machinery, and fabricated metals were relatively

Table 24. Composition and Growth of the Manufacturing Sector, 1960–74
(percent)

Subsector	Composition					Annual growth rate[a]				
	1960	1965	1971	1972	1973	1960-65	1965-71	1972	1973	1974
Light manufactures										
Clothing, textiles, and footwear	27.8	22.4	22.3	25.8	28.0	7.1	20.5	36.2	39.8	16.4
Food and allied products	39.9	33.3	29.0	27.3	22.2	6.5	17.9	13.4	11.5	6.0
Other light manufactures[b]	16.9	19.8	18.9	17.8	23.5	15.4	19.8	13.6	61.3	48.1
Subtotal	84.6	75.5	70.2	70.8	63.7	7.7	19.2	19.9	35.3	15.4
Heavy manufactures										
Chemicals, coal, and petroleum	4.7	10.7	17.8	16.3	19.0	31.8	31.2	5.6	25.5	11.2
Machinery[c]	3.5	3.8	1.8	2.7	10.4	13.9	7.1	30.7	77.3	48.7
Metal (basic) and metal products	3.5	4.3	3.4	3.2	3.6	16.5	16.0	12.3	56.0	87.2
Transport equipment	2.4	4.0	4.3	3.9	d	24.0	21.9	-5.3	90.0	145.6
Subtotal	14.1	22.8	27.3	26.2	33.0	23.2	24.3	6.5	44.9	47.7
Other	1.3	1.7	2.5	3.0	3.3	17.3	29.1	25.9	13.0	15.4
Total	100.0	100.0	100.0	100.0	100.0	11.9	20.1	16.4	35.4	29.2

a. The 1972–74 data are based on an index of industrial production for those years; all other data are calculated on the basis of gross value added.
b. Includes wood products, furniture and fixtures, paper, printing and publishing, leather and rubber products, clay, glass, and stone products, electronics and plastic products.
c. Includes electrical machinery but excludes electronics.
d. Included in machinery, above.

68

sluggish, at least till 1971. Since 1970 over half the total industrial investment has been allocated to chemical, petroleum, and basic metal industries. The first major signs of the deepening of Korea's industrial structure were the opening of Korea's first steel plant at Pohang (one million tons capacity), a large shipyard at Ulsan (750,000 gross tons capacity), and the naphtha-cracking plant (100,000 tons) at the Ulsan oil refinery. There also appears to have been a tendency for the import content of Korea's two principal exports to fall slightly. In the case of textiles this reflects the use of domestically produced synthetic fibers, and in the case of plywood it results from upgrading the product and increasing productivity.

Another encouraging aspect of Korea's industrial development during 1972–73 was the increased contribution to exports made by small- and medium-size firms.[1] Such plants accounted for 36 percent of exports in 1972 and are particularly important in textiles, electronics, plastics, and metal products. The general measures to assist industry in the August 3, 1972, package, including debt rescheduling, lowering of interest rates, and the industrial rationalization fund, have particularly helped small- and medium-size industries. It should be stressed, however, that the 1966–71 period saw a considerable increase in the concentration of Korean industry. Whereas firms having more than 200 workers accounted for only 57.5 percent of value added and 39.8 percent of manufacturing employment in 1966, by 1971 these figures had grown to 72.0 percent and 53.8 percent respectively (see Table 25).

New Economic Challenges

Given the fact that the 1973 growth was helped by especially favorable factors affecting exports and investments, the pace of economic expansion would in any case have slowed down during 1974 and 1975. In fact there has been a rather dramatic reversal in the short-term economic trends, and uncertainties have been introduced into the long-term economic outlook for Korea. This was brought about by the sharp deterioration in terms of trade arising from higher import prices of food grains and petroleum, combined with the substantial slowdown in the rate of growth of

1. Firms with gross assets of less than W50 million and less than 200 employees.

Table 25. Manufacturing Concentration

Number of workers	Number of firms	Percentage of workers	Percentage of value added
1966			
5–49	21,013	39.44	24.88
50–199	1,326	20.81	17.64
200 and above	379	39.75	57.47
Total	22,718	100.00	100.00
1971			
5–49	21,045	27.86	12.83
50–199	1,605	18.32	15.15
200 and above	762	53.80	72.02
Total	23,412	100.00	100.00

exports. Reflecting mainly the recessionary tendencies in Japan and the United States, real export growth was limited to 14 percent a year during 1974–75. The higher costs of energy and food added over $1 billion to the Korean import bill between 1973 and 1974, and there was a further sharp increase in import prices in 1974–75 while export unit value rose only moderately. These international developments not only weakened the immediate balance of payments position but also clouded the future outlook for Korean exports to the extent that trends in world economic activity and trade have become uncertain. Korea is of course not unique in being adversely affected by the oil crisis; the entire world economy has felt the impact. It can, however, be easily demonstrated that Korea is among the countries most severely hit.

ENERGY SITUATION

Korea is extremely dependent on imported fuels. The bulk of the country's electricity generation is fueled by imported petroleum, and this proportion has been growing. Hydroelectric power is limited, and coal deposits though large are of low quality and difficult to extract. Coal production has stagnated at around 11 to 12 million tons annually for the last several years and until recently was deemed to have reached its limits under the constraints of deep-pit mining practices and the increase in production costs. Steam locomotives have been by and large phased out, and the number of diesels has grown rapidly during the last decade to account for nearly 75 percent of the railway power. In contrast there are comparatively few motor vehicles, especially passenger cars, in relation to the size of Korea's population and per capita income. At the end of 1972 there were only 36,000 private passenger cars or a little more than one car per 1,000 persons. The scope for possible economies in gasoline consumption is therefore quite small; only about 7 percent of total petroleum supplies takes the form of gasoline. Korea's heavy dependence on imported oil is thus largely linked to essential industrial and transportation uses. What is more, the growing demand for total energy was, before the sharp rise in oil prices, expected to increase import dependence from 52 percent in 1972 to 73 percent in 1981 (see Table 26).

TERMS OF TRADE LOSS

As Table 27 shows, the price of imported oil more than tripled in 1974; this, together with an almost 18 percent increase in the quantity of imports, raised the total cost of petroleum imports to $1,120 million compared with only about $296 million in 1973. The price increase alone served to inflate the fuel import bill by some $790 million. Important as the oil price increase was, however, it should not be allowed to overshadow the fact that Korea was also hard hit by the steep rise in price of other international commodities. The upward swing in the price of grains, already under way in 1973, accelerated further in 1974. Between 1972 and 1974 the threefold rise in the price of food grains increased foreign

Table 26. Demand and Supply of Total Energy
(percentage of thousand metric tons of coal equivalent)

Energy	1972	1973	1976[a]	1981[a]
Demand				
Coal	28.3	27.1	24.3	20.1
Hydroelectric power	1.5	1.2	1.8	6.1
Petroleum	52.2	57.5	64.5	68.7
Other	18.0	14.2	9.4	5.1
Total	100.0	100.0	100.0	100.0
Supply				
Domestic	48.0	42.5	33.0	27.0
Imported	52.0	57.5	67.0	73.0
Total	100.0	100.0	100.0	100.0

a. Original projections of the Economic Planning Board.

Table 27. Pattern of Imports
(current dollars, c.i.f.[a])

Import	1970	1971	1972	1973	1974
Petroleum and petroleum products					
Annual percent increase					
Quantity	16.7	29.3	2.3	14.2	17.9
Average price	5.8	13.1	6.5	22.2	354.2
Value					
Amount (million U.S. dollars)	133.0	187.0	218.0	296.0	1,120.0
Percent of total imports	7.2	8.5	9.8	7.0	16.0
Cereals					
Annual percent increase					
Quantity	−11.0	36.3	11.3	1.9	−16.0
Average price	13.2	−17.3	−12.1	32.6	105.9
Value					
Amount (million U.S. dollars)	245.0	304.0	283.0	444.0	613.0
Percent of total imports	12.3	12.7	11.2	10.5	8.8
Other consumer goods					
Annual percent increase					
Quantity	23.0	28.9	12.2	42.7	24.2
Average price	6.3	7.4	9.6	17.0	12.0
Value					
Amount (million U.S. dollars)	76.0	105.0	129.0	217.0	303.0
Percent of total imports	4.0	4.3	5.1	5.1	4.3
Raw materials and intermediate products					
Annual percent increase					
Quantity	8.7	9.9	13.9	26.9	−9.8
Average price	1.0	−2.0	−2.0	52.2	55.9
Value					
Amount (million U.S. dollars)	938.0	1,112.2	1,098.2	2,125.9	3,062.1
Percent of total imports	46.2	45.3	43.7	50.1	43.7
Capital goods					
Annual percent increase					
Quantity	7.0	7.7	1.4	27.7	39.0
Average price	7.0	8.2	9.4	15.0	16.0
Value					
Amount (million U.S. dollars)	589.5	685.4	761.8	1,157.0	1,902.0
Percent of total imports	30.8	29.8	31.4	27.3	27.2

a. Cost, insurance, and freight.

exchange requirements by $330 million despite a 14 percent decline in the volume of imports. A wide variety of raw materials and intermediate products which Korean industry must import also increased steeply in price.

The estimated 27 percent increase in Korean export prices in 1974 only partially offset the unprecedented rise in overall import costs. As a result, the terms of trade index showed a deterioration of over 18 percent during 1974. To put it roughly, a deterioration of this magnitude has meant a 5 percent reduction in gross national income and is equivalent to a decline in gross national savings of 20 to 25 percent. Some improvement in the terms of trade is likely by 1980 for commodities other than oil as prices revert to more normal levels; but since a major reduction in the real price of oil is not anticipated in the near future, a large part of the overall terms of trade loss must be considered as permanent. Actually, during 1975 the terms of trade deteriorated further by 8 percent, reflecting mainly a drop in the unit value of exports.

Notwithstanding this serious loss, the Korean economy might have been able to avoid a major slowdown except for a simultaneous setback to export growth. After reaching the peak of 52 percent a year during 1972–73, real export growth slowed down to 9 percent in 1974. In 1975 the growth in volume of exports recovered to about 20 percent but was partly offset by the fall in export prices. This sharp decline in export growth is attributable directly to the deep recession in the United States and Japan, Korea's major trade partners. In addition Japan's efforts to limit its overall current account deficit during 1974 in the face of a sharp rise in its oil import bill has seriously hurt the Korean balance of payments. The volume of Korean exports to Japan is estimated to have declined by about 6 percent during 1974, and Korea's trade deficit with Japan widened to $1.2 billion compared with $0.5 million in 1973. The volume of exports to the United States increased, however, even in 1974. There was also a marked real increase of 40 percent in Korean exports to countries other than the United States and Japan. If sustained, this considerable success will be credited to the effort toward market diversification.

Government Policy Response

Until the end of 1974, the government had not properly evaluated either the extent or the protracted nature of the downturn in its major overseas markets. Its policies were based on the premise that the country should remain poised to capitalize on the worldwide economic recovery which Korea expected to begin by early 1975. Thus the principal objectives of policy in 1974 were to ease the adjustment to higher prices for oil and other imports while cushioning the impact of the recession to avoid unduly slowing domestic investment and employment growth.

Imported inflation exerted sharp upward pressure on the domestic price level. In addition to the increased price of imported petroleum and food grains, the average unit value of other imports increased by 45 percent in 1974. Consequently the rate of domestic inflation accelerated, with consumer prices rising at an annual rate of 31 percent between December 1973 and June 1974 and wholesale prices increasing at double that rate. In the second half of 1974 the rate of domestic inflation slowed somewhat, reflecting seasonal factors, the slower increase in the price of imported goods, and the dampening effects of rising inventories of manufactured goods; for the calendar year 1974, consumer prices rose by about 26 percent and wholesale prices increased by about 45 percent. The provisional figures for 1975 indicate a further rise of around 25 percent in consumer prices and a slightly faster growth in wholesale prices.

In general the government has accepted the price adjustments made necessary by higher energy and other import costs; one major exception to this general policy was its unwillingness to place on consumers the full burden of higher import costs of basic foodstuffs. Of course there was still a dramatic increase in the consumer price of food grains, but the sale of wheat and rice was heavily subsidized. The extrabudgetary deficit attributed to grain and fertilizer subsidies rose from the equivalent of $148 million in 1973 to $445 million in 1974 and is expected, according to revised estimates, to exceed $550 million in 1975. To the extent that these are cash deficits and include provision for building up inventories, however, they tend to exaggerate the decline in public savings. Furthermore, complete avoidance of subsidies at a time of growing unemployment and declining real wages in manufacturing would have been inequitable. Nevertheless the government fully recognizes the distortions in the price structure resulting from these large subsidies and is greatly concerned about the virtual elimination of public savings (see Table 28) which has been an even more important consequence. Remodeling the price

Table 28. Public Sector Savings and Investment
(*billion won at 1970 prices*[a])

Item	1973	1974 (budget)	1975 (budget)
1. General budget, current surplus	96	111	108
Current revenue	435	513	523
Current expenditure	339	402	415
2. Special accounts, current surplus	51	26	33
3. Central government, current surplus (1 + 2)	147	137	141
4. Cash deficit on nonbudgetary accounts[b]	−43	−104	−137
Grains	36	88	82
Fertilizer	6	11	41
Procurement	1	5	14
5. Net public savings (3 − 4)	104	33	4
6. Public investment[c]	−178	−196	−241[d]
7. Public sector deficit (5 − 6)[e]	−70	−158	−226
8. Financing	70	158	226
Borrowing from Bank of Korea	43	103	151
Other domestic financing[f]	−40	15	14
Foreign financing	67	40	61

a. Adjusted by GNP price deflator; 20 percent price increase assumed for 1975.
b. To the extent that deficits were used to build up stocks, the negative savings are exaggerated.
c. Excluding National Investment Fund.
d. Includes W30 billion for Land Bank; excludes W20 billion of employment-creating investment added to budget.
e. Adjusted for net capital receipts of special accounts.
f. Includes bond sales, receipts from trust funds, and changes in cash balances.
Source: Economic Planning Board, Bureau of Budget.

structure is a major objective of the government, which has embarked on a two-year program to eliminate subsidies on grains and fertilizers step by step by 1977.

Selective credit measures to assist the most distressed industries were another element in the government's effort to cushion the impact of recession in 1974. At the end of 1973 a special credit program was developed which made available to industry a large volume of short-term financing for stocks of specified raw materials. Initially such credit was intended primarily to help industry adjust to higher import costs, but as time went on the program was extended to enable business to carry the excessive inventories of raw materials and finished goods that had resulted from the decline in export demand. A similar but smaller credit program was established to provide working capital loans to textile firms. Small- and medium-size firms which were particularly hard hit by the onset of the recession were assisted by a large credit program embracing both working capital and investment loans. These firms also benefited from a government-subsidized interest rate of 12 percent, 3 percent below the normal bank rate on such loans. Similarly, subsidized credit facilities were made available to the machinery industries and to export industries for new equipment.

All told, such programs provided credits totaling some W200 billion ($495 million), equivalent to over 20 percent of the increase in total credit to the private sector in 1974. Overall monetary policy though quite tight in the first half of the year was significantly eased after midyear. The increase in domestic credit in the second half of 1974 was more than double that in the January-June period, and over the year as a whole domestic credit expanded by about 50 percent compared with an increase of only about 30 percent in 1973. Owing to the contractionary influence of the external deficit, however, the money supply increased by only about 30 percent compared with 40 percent in 1973 (see Table 29).

In December 1974 the government introduced additional measures to offset the sluggish demand for exports and relieve the liquidity problems of exporters. It expanded the program of export financing, provided loans for stockpiling essential raw materials, and increased credits to exporters for the purchase of imported and domestic materials. On December 7, 1974, the currency was devalued by 20 percent to W485 per U.S. dollar. The devaluation was not expected to increase exports appreciably because of the depressed state of Korea's overseas markets, but like some of the other measures it was intended to improve the liquidity position of manufacturing enterprises. It was also expected to strengthen the competitive position of import substitution industries. But a negative result of devaluation was the continuation of inflationary pressures into 1975. To help the low income groups the government offered substantial income tax relief and a 30 percent increase in salaries of government employees and initiated public works projects, mainly in urban areas, to alleviate unemployment. The rural areas appear to have been hit less hard by domestic inflation. The terms of trade continued to be favorable for farmers during 1974 as the support price for rice was adjusted sharply upward to average $394 a metric ton for purchases from the 1974 crop compared with $485 for imports.

Table 29. Monetary Survey, 1970–74
(billion won)

Item	1970	1971	1972	1973	1974	1973 January–June	1973 July–December	1974 January–June	1974 July–December
Outstanding at end of period									
Net foreign assets	110.3	37.8	102.5	299.6	−179.6	57.0	140.1	−139.1	−340.1
Domestic credit	866.6	1,134.5	1,479.2	1,940.4	2,983.8	212.6	248.6	321.9	721.5
Net claims on government	−82.8	−98.7	−17.8	−2.4	101.3	28.9	−13.5	−26.2	129.9
Claims on official entities	30.0	32.0	34.0	43.0	20.0	7.0	2.0	−23.0	0.0
Claims on the private sector	919.4	1,201.2	1,463.0	1,899.8	2,862.5	176.7	260.1	371.0	591.7
Other items (net)	79.1	87.4	129.9	266.4	368.9	44.1	92.4	39.4	63.1
Total liquidity	897.8	1,084.9	1,451.8	1,973.6	2,435.3	225.5	296.3	143.4	318.3
Money	307.6	358.0	519.4	730.3	945.7	78.3	132.6	0.4	215.0
Quasi money	590.2	726.9	932.4	1,243.3	1,489.6	147.2	163.7	143.0	103.3
Percentage change from the end of the previous period									
Domestic credit	26.7	30.9	30.4	31.2	53.8	14.4	14.7	16.6	31.9
Total liquidity	27.4	20.8	33.8	35.9	23.4	15.5	17.7	7.3	15.0
Money	22.1	16.4	45.1	40.6	29.5	15.1	22.2	0.1	29.4
Quasi money	30.4	23.2	28.3	33.3	19.8	15.8	15.2	11.5	7.5
Change of each factor as a percentage of the change in total liquidity									
Total liquidity	100.0	100.0	100.0	100.0	100.0	100.0	100.0	100.0	100.0
Money	28.8	26.9	44.0	40.4	46.7	34.7	44.8	0.3	67.5
Quasi money	71.2	73.1	56.0	59.6	53.3	65.3	55.2	99.7	32.5
Net foreign assets	1.3	−38.8	17.6	37.8	−103.8	25.3	47.3	−97.0	−106.8
Domestic credit	94.5	143.2	94.0	88.4	226.0	94.3	83.9	224.5	226.7
Other items net	4.2	−4.4	−11.6	−26.2	−22.2	−19.6	−31.2	−27.5	−19.9

Source: Bank of Korea, *Monthly Economic Statistics.*

Largely because of the efforts to sustain the 1973 momentum of growth the real GNP rose in 1974 by more than 8 percent, and sizable gains were recorded in both consumption and investment. Notwithstanding government support, however, there was a sharp slowdown in industrial output, private fixed investment, and export sales in the second half of 1974. Furthermore the buildup of inventories of raw materials and export products (amounting to 5 percent of GNP during 1974) was proving extremely burdensome for businesses.

The impact of the adverse turn of events in 1974 was borne primarily by the balance of payments. The current account deficit widened from $0.3 billion in 1973 to $2 billion in 1974. It was provisionally estimated at $1.9 billion in 1975, which indicates a substantial improvement in the latter half of the year. The current account deficit in the first four months of 1975 alone amounted to $1.2 billion, but by April the decline in import letters of credit and the increase in export letters of credit had made them nearly equal. The financing of the 1974 deficit involved a large reduction ($760 million) in net international reserves (to $300 million), support from the International Monetary Fund (IMF) of $156 million net, and medium-term borrowing of a compensatory character from commercial banks of $274 million net. In 1975 the continued deficit meant further reduction in net international reserves which were already negative. The Korean short-term debt, which had been quite small in 1973, increased by about $1.6 billion during 1974 and 1975.

The ability to contain the balance of payments deficits in the short and medium run will depend partly on the speed of the recovery of exports and partly on the government's determination to narrow the fiscal deficit and reduce the rate of domestic credit creation. The latter in turn will hinge on the political acceptability of a further reduction in the growth rate of GNP, consumption, and investment. The official target of GNP growth for 1976 is 7 to 8 percent, but the economic planners are currently attaching a higher priority to narrowing the balance of payments deficit and stabilizing the price level than to achieving the growth target. Nevertheless substantial reduction in the current account deficit is likely to take several years unless there is a rapid and sharp upturn in the U.S., Japanese, and other markets of the Organisation for Economic Co-operation and Development in the years ahead.

An Overview of the Adjustment Process

The problem of economic adjustment in Korea stemming from the secular terms of trade deterioration of around 20 to 25 percent has been greatly complicated by the slower growth of exports during 1974–75, inflationary pressures exerted by increases in the prices of imports (including oil), and the inability of policymakers and economists everywhere to predict correctly the depth and duration of world business downturn. The fact that the growth rate of exports was slower than expected meant, on the one hand, reduced growth of GNP which thus limited the margin for adjustment in consumption growth and, on the other hand, reduced foreign exchange earnings which minimized the scope for narrowing the current account balance of payments deficit. Similarly the more than 50 percent rise in total import costs during 1974 exerted inflationary pressures that made it difficult for the government to restrain total consumption without further hurting the lower income groups which have borne the brunt of increased unemployment. To the extent that the government assumed a fairly quick international recovery, it did not begin to make the difficult choices about reducing the large balance of payments and fiscal deficits till the second quarter of 1975.

Under the circumstances the GNP, consumption, and investment growth were satisfactory during 1974–75. GNP grew by an average rate of 8 percent a year during this period, and consumption and fixed capital formation expanded respectively at annual rates of 6 and 12 percent between 1973 and 1975. Thus, as indicated earlier, the brunt of the adjustment has been borne by the current account balance of payments deficit. As a percent of GNP, foreign savings (defined as the deficit on goods and services account in the balance of payments) increased sharply from the average of 5 percent during 1972–73 to 12 percent during 1974–75. To some extent this comparison exaggerates the increased reliance on external flows. The average investment rate during 1972–73 (23 percent of GNP) was below that of the late 1960s and early 1970s, and the savings performance in 1973 was exceptional due in part to lags in consumption. In contrast, the investment rate during 1974–75 was unusually high because of excessive stockbuilding, and savings were depressed because of foreign exchange constraints. Moreover the growth in gross national income (as distinct from the growth in GNP) was only 4 to

5 percent a year during 1974–75 because of the terms of trade loss. But even if allowance is made for these factors which distort the levels of national savings and domestic investment, it would appear that the underlying gap to be filled by foreign savings had, after dropping temporarily during 1972–73, increased substantially during 1974–75. Korea is thus again facing a major resource constraint. As noted above, the external inflows as a percent of GNP have in the past often been at a level comparable to the present; foreign savings were about 11 percent of GNP during 1968–71. Still, the management and financing of the large resource gap have presented considerable difficulties in the past and will pose major challenges in the future. The adequate mobilization of resources, both domestic and foreign, will be the key determinant of Korea's ability to sustain high growth rates in the future. The next chapter discusses these problems and examines some of the policy issues involved in attaining a high rate of domestic savings and an orderly reduction in the dependence on external inflows.

4

Long-term Strategy and Development Issues

B EFORE RECENT INTERNATIONAL economic developments, Korea's long-term economic aspirations centered increasingly on achieving a per capita income of $1,000 and $10 billion worth of exports by 1981.[1] A good deal of the Korean planning effort during 1973 went into devising a strategy to reach these goals set by President Park in 1972. The Economic Planning Board (EPB) had prepared a macroeconomic framework[2] for 1972–81 which presented in some detail the growth strategy for the next decade. The long-term framework in fact superseded the third plan (1972–76) and provided an outline for the fourth plan (1977–81). The strategy envisaged was essentially an extension of the path to high growth that Korea has followed, on the whole successfully, in the past decade. The overall GNP growth rate of over 10 percent was to be maintained over the next ten years, as in the past decade, by a more rapid expansion of exports than of GNP. The ratio of merchandise exports to GNP was projected to rise to 30 percent by 1981 compared with less than 17 percent in 1972. The manufacturing sector was expected to provide the bulk of the increment of exports and 40 percent of the increment of total output between 1972 and 1981 (compared with about one-third during 1962–72)

1. These goals were expressed in current prices and provided for an inflation rate of 5 percent a year during 1972–81.

2. *Major Economic Indicators of the Korean Economy, 1972-81* (Seoul: Economic Planning Board, 1973), hereafter referred to as the long-term framework.

and was to absorb 40 percent of the total fixed investment (compared with about 20 percent in the past).

There were, however, several notable differences from the past pattern. The strategy aimed at major shifts in the structure of manufacturing output and exports with a great expansion of shipbuilding, steel, petrochemical, and electronic industries. The exports of these products, which amounted to less than $250 million in 1972—more than half of them in electronics—were expected to rise to about $5 billion by 1981. Another major difference was the aim to eliminate dependence on foreign savings[3] almost completely by 1981, a sharp contrast to recent trends. As mentioned earlier, during 1968–72 foreign savings provided for 35 to 40 percent of total investment. Another important feature of the long-term plan was its specific provision for parity of rural and urban household incomes by the early 1980s. This was to be achieved through the accelerated growth of labor productivity in agriculture and a massive increase in off-farm employment opportunities for the rural population by the regional dispersion of industry.

Major Issues

It is difficult not to be struck by the bold vision and imaginative approach of Korea's long-term strategy. The GNP growth and export targets for 1972–81 did not break with past trends, but they did present a fairly sharp change in the government's attitudes as expressed in the third plan. The GNP, exports, investment, and saving targets for 1976, the final year of the third plan, were all revised upward. The more aggressive growth strategy was also highlighted by the GNP growth target of 11.0 percent a year for 1977–81 compared with the original third plan goal of 8.6 percent[4] for 1972–76.

It must be stressed, however, that the long-term planning framework (1972–81) was devised before the upsurge in exports,

3. Foreign savings are defined as the deficit on goods and services account in the balance of payments.

4. According to World Bank estimates, GNP growth during the third plan, despite the setback in 1974–75, is likely to average about 9 percent a year, above the original goal of 8.6 percent but lower than the revised goal of 9.5 percent contained in the long-term framework.

investment, and GNP in 1973 could be fully foreseen and before the impact of energy-related developments on the world economy was known. As a result of the former circumstance the benchmark of production and exports was raised and thus a lower growth rate was required to attain the original targets of $1,000 per capita income and $10 billion worth of exports by the early 1980s. The effect of a more favorable starting point was, however, entirely offset by recent changes in Korea's external circumstances, notably the sharp deterioration in the terms of trade, the less buoyant outlook for growth in industrialized countries at least in the medium run, and the consequent slower growth expected in international trade. There is general agreement that these changes will mean downward adjustment in the Korean long-term growth rate in the second half of the 1970s compared with the past several years' average of around 10 percent a year. The Korean government's preliminary reassessment of the long-term prospects shows full awareness of this. The guidelines for the fourth five-year plan[5] issued in 1975 suggest a tentative growth target of 9 percent a year for 1977–81 as against 11 percent a year for the same period implied in the long-term framework. Considerably more work will have to be done before some of the key targets for the fourth plan can be firmed up. It is already clear, however, that the Korean government is not abandoning the high growth strategy on which it has been embarked during the last decade.

Sustaining an annual growth rate of, say, 8 to 9 percent during the next decade will no doubt pose a major economic challenge, especially if the external circumstances remain distinctly less favorable than during the last decade. Nevertheless the continuation of high growth rates appears essential not only for the rapid rise in living standards but also to achieve the government's goals of greater viability of the balance of payments, increased employment opportunities, and more even distribution of growth benefits. In the Korean context rapid growth itself has been primarily responsible for generating foreign exchange and domestic savings and improving income and employment opportunities for the poor. Similarly rapid growth will probably also facilitate the structural changes in the economy, notably the deepening of the

5. Economic Planning Board, "Guidelines for the Fourth Five-Year Economic Development Plan," June 1975.

industrial structure and the increase in the value added content of exports, to which the Korean government is attaching increasing importance.[6]

The broad issue of the feasibility of Korea's high growth strategy raises three fundamental questions: Can the export growth originally envisaged for the remainder of the seventies be more or less attained, and if so will it conflict with the goals of greater import substitution and deepening of industrial structure? Will it be possible to mobilize sufficient resources, both domestic and foreign, the lack of which has been a major constraint on growth in the past? Will the rapid growth be consistent with a more even distribution of growth benefits, especially the narrowing of the income gap between rural and urban areas which is also a key policy objective? These questions and related issues are examined below.

Export Prospects

According to the long-term framework, merchandise exports were expected to increase in current dollars from $1.7 billion in 1972 to well over $10 billion by 1981. The real rates of growth implied in these estimates were 22 percent and 15 percent a year during 1973–76 and 1977–81 respectively.[7] Nearly 95 percent of the expansion was expected from manufactured goods. Even though the exports of marine products were expected to rise fourfold over the period, the share of nonmanufactured goods was to drop from over 12 percent in 1972 to 6.5 percent in 1981. The main assumptions which underlay these ambitious export targets are:

1. During Korea's industrial development of the last decade, the basis of a modern industry was laid down, export markets were aggressively developed at an unusually high rate, and labor and entrepreneurial skills of a high order created. These accomplishments have demonstrated Korea's ability

---

6. This is not to deny that some structural change may itself be necessary for sustained high growth.

7. The strong international inflationary pressures caused a sharp rise in the unit values of Korean exports (averaging 26 percent a year during 1973–74) and have made somewhat meaningless the original current dollar targets of exports which assumed only 5 percent a year inflation.

to supply increasing quantities of consumer and capital goods to the domestic and export markets.

2. The skill, discipline, and application of Korean workers and the very low level of wages (at present one-sixth of that in Japan and not much higher than that in the Philippines, Malaysia, and Thailand) give Korea an important comparative advantage in labor-intensive industrial operations.

3. Pollution problems in other countries (particularly Japan, but to some extent the United States and Europe) will limit their rate of expansion of petrochemical production, metal smelting, and shipbuilding and provide an opportunity for Korea to expand in these areas. Korea has a number of regions, particularly in the south, where the population density is low and the prevailing winds and ocean currents combine with topographical characteristics to minimize the deleterious effects of industrial pollution.

4. Foreign investment, which has so far played only a limited role in Korea's industrial development, will be available in increasing quantities and will facilitate technology transfer and market development.

5. World trade in manufactured goods will continue to grow during the next decade at rates comparable to the recent past.

6. Korea can follow Japan's example and capture a substantial share of the world market in industries such as shipbuilding which are new to Korea.

Notwithstanding recent international developments, the general validity of most of these assumptions cannot be seriously questioned, and they therefore provide a reasonable basis for Korea's economic development strategy. The growth in the quantum of world trade during 1974–76 will no doubt be limited by the impact of international recession, but recovery to a growth rate of about 8 percent a year recorded during 1960–74 is expected during the latter part of this decade. Considerably more serious for Korea, however, is the prospect that the Japanese economy will grow much less rapidly than in the past. Before the energy crisis the general expectation in Japan was for the relatively high GNP growth rate of 9 to 10 percent a year in spite of increasing concerns with the pattern of growth and inflation. The sharp rise in the cost of energy and the current inflation have had a major impact on the trends of the Japanese economy. For 1974 and 1975 together the growth in GNP will probably be negative. At the same time a sharp curtailment in the rate of economic expansion during the remainder of the seventies, perhaps in the range of 6 to 7 percent a year, is now expected.

Fortunately for Korea, however, despite the recent setback in international trade and the stagnation in the Japanese economy during 1974–75, the real growth rate of exports for 1973–76 as a whole will be over 25 percent a year,[8] above the original long-term target of 22 percent for the period. As stressed earlier, this is entirely due to the remarkable performance during 1973 which more or less compensated for the relatively sluggish growth of exports during 1974–75. For the future the important question is whether the original target[9] for export growth of 15 percent during the period of the fourth plan can be achieved.

There is reason to be optimistic provided the growth in world trade during 1976–80 recovers more or less to the level of the past decade. About 90 percent of Korean exports now consist of manufactured goods, a proportion that is among the highest in the world. Trade in manufactured goods during the last fifteen years or so has expanded considerably faster than the growth in total world trade, reflecting essentially higher import elasticity of demand for manufactures than for primary products. Other factors have also contributed to the marked expansion in the trade of manufactured goods in relation to the growth in world output: a reduction in barriers to international trade; the growth of export industries in a number of relatively low-cost countries, which has resulted in a widespread decline in import prices in relation to domestic prices and the emergence of new sources of supply; and an increase in interindustry specialization in trade among the mature industrial economies. Between 1960 and 1973 the volume of world trade in manufactures grew by an average of 9.5 percent a year while trade in primary commodities expanded by 6.8 percent.[10] According to World Bank estimates, in the more recent 1965–73 period, total world trade in manufactures has grown in real terms by 12.5 percent a year while exports of manufactured goods from developing countries have expanded at the somewhat higher rate of about 15 percent. Since the export of manufactured goods from

8. This assumes growth in the volume of exports of about 20 percent during 1976.

9. The latest target in the "Guidelines for the Fourth Five-Year Economic Development Plan" is 13 to 16 percent a year.

10. Growth in total world trade average during this period was 7.7 percent a year.

Korea during 1965–73 expanded at an annual rate of 45 to 50 percent—admittedly from a very low base—Korea has steadily increased its share, estimated now at 12 percent, in the total market for manufactured exports from developing countries.

Prospects for manufactured goods exports from developing countries during 1976–80 will depend mainly on the rate of growth of GNP in the industrialized countries of the Organisation for Economic Co-operation and Development (OECD). If the rate of growth in the OECD countries in the second half of 1970s reverts to the historical growth rate of 4.9 percent a year attained during 1960–72, manufactured exports from developing countries in real terms could continue to increase at 15 percent a year. But if the OECD growth remains relatively sluggish, say 3.5 to 4 percent a year, manufactured exports from developing countries will be correspondingly lower. At present developing countries account for only 6 percent of the world trade in manufactured goods; but there is scope for further increasing exports of manufactures, particularly from those countries which follow an export-oriented strategy, if developed countries make some progress on import liberalization, especially regarding nontariff restrictions. Indeed, without special steps for expansion of manufactured exports, it will be difficult to resolve the serious balance of payments problem which most developing countries now face.

Given reasonable OECD growth and some further trade liberalization, manufactured exports from developing countries are expected to grow by 13 to 14 percent a year during the next several years. This means that Korea would only have to maintain its share among other developing countries in the field of manufactured exports to more or less achieve its original goal of 15 percent growth a year. This apparently is also the judgment of the government. The export growth target for the fourth five-year plan has been tentatively placed in the range of 13 to 16 percent. With a base of $4.5 billion in 1974 it will take growth of only 12 percent a year during 1975–81 to exceed exports of $10 billion in 1981 in 1974 dollars. The original current dollar export target for 1981 can thus be reinterpreted as the tentative revised target in 1974 dollars.[11]

---

11. The 55 percent overall price increase in unit value of exports assumed for 1972–81 was in fact exceeded in the first two years, 1973 and 1974. The reinterpreted 1974 target is therefore somewhat higher than the original export target in real terms.

EXPORT STRATEGY VERSUS IMPORT SUBSTITUTION

Notwithstanding the feasibility of rapid export expansion, there may be some question about the desirability of such a course for Korea. There has been some feeling that Korea's reliance on export growth has been excessive in the past, and a sharply rising ratio of exports to GNP might further increase the vulnerability of the economy. For instance, with 15 percent a year growth in exports over the next five years and about 8.5 percent growth in GNP, the ratio of merchandise exports to GNP will rise from 26 percent in 1973 to 34 percent in 1980. In the case of Korea, however, this ratio overstates the exposure to foreign markets. Since the value added in Korean exports is only about 50 percent of gross exports, the ratio of net value added in exports to GNP is at present only around 13 percent. The high ratio of gross exports to GNP in Korea merely reflects its poor natural endowments and consequent heavy dependence on imported raw materials.[12] But there are several relatively small and specialized countries like Malaysia, Belgium, Norway, and the Netherlands where the ratio of exports to GNP was in the range of 40 to 45 percent during 1973. Thus the projections of exports and GNP for Korea by 1980 signify a dependence on foreign trade that is by no means unique.

Of much more importance is the consideration that the long-term goal of eliminating the current account balance of payments deficit will be difficult to achieve without a substantial increase in the ratio of exports to GNP. While merchandise exports in current prices averaged 28 percent of GNP in 1974, imports were as high as 41 percent and the trade gap alone was equal to 13 percent of GNP.[13] The sharp rise in the ratio of imports to GNP resulting from the climb in prices of petroleum and food grains has of course heightened the need to examine possibilities for import substitution, but at the same time the widening trade gap has increased the urgency of export promotion. If in the final version of the fourth plan the Korean government does not raise the original

12. Bela Balassa, "Trade Policy and Planning in Korea," in Sung-Hwan Jo and Seong-Yawng Park (eds.), *Basic Documents and Selected Papers of Korea's Third Five-Year Economic Development Plan (1972–76)* (Seoul: Sogang University, 1972), pp. 163–74.

13. Total current account deficit as a percentage of GNP was only slightly higher because the net deficit on invisibles was largely offset by the net transfers.

export targets,[14] it will in a sense be recognizing the importance of import substitution.

The vulnerability of the Korean economy and the relative emphasis on export promotion as against import substitution and development of domestic market are nonetheless real issues that merit continuing attention.

DIVERSIFICATION OF EXPORTS

From the point of view of reducing vulnerability, a greater geographical dispersal of exports and a lesser commodity concentration appear desirable and are receiving priority attention by the government. As mentioned earlier, exports to markets other than Japan and the United States increased in real terms by 40 percent during 1974 and, according to provisional figures, showed a further increase of 35 to 40 percent in 1975. Thus the share of U.S. and Japanese markets in Korean exports, which had averaged 73 percent during 1970–73, declined to 64 percent in 1974 and to less than 60 percent in 1975. The most pronounced shift has been in exports to industrial European countries, which doubled in current dollar terms during 1974. Exports to oil-exporting countries (chiefly Iran, Saudi Arabia, and Indonesia) also more than doubled over the year though they are still only 3 percent of the total. Crucial to Korea's drive for diversification of markets will be its success in establishing a foothold in the oil-exporting countries and increasing its trade links with the European Economic Community which at present accounts for less than 12 percent of total Korean exports.

The heavy concentration of exports in a few labor-intensive commodities, notably textiles, clothing, footwear, electronics, plywood, and wigs, is also a matter of concern. Textiles, clothing, and footwear, which are especially sensitive to changes in economic activity in developed countries, still account for over 36 percent of all manufactured exports. These exports also face much stronger nontariff barriers in developed countries and therefore the outlook for their expansion is clouded. Taking into account the desirability of diversifying products, the long-term

14. The assumption being made here is that export markets are not a constraint.

framework provided for a massive shift toward exports of heavy manufacturers. As Table 30 indicates, the share of light manufactures in total manufactured exports was planned to fall from about 88 percent in 1972 to about 66 percent in 1981. This was to be accomplished by a large increase in exports of relatively new products such as steel, ships, nonelectrical machinery, and passenger cars. Starting absolutely from scratch, the export of ships was to exceed 3 million gross tons valued at over $1 billion by 1981, while steel exports were to approach 5 million tons by early 1980s. In real terms, with allowance for the 5 percent inflation built in the estimates, the exports of heavy manufactures were projected to grow by 33 percent a year and account for nearly 40 percent of the total increment in manufactured goods exports over the period. Nevertheless light manufactures were to rise in

Table 30. Export Targets
(million U.S. dollars)

Commodity	Actual			Projected[a]	
	1972	*1973*	*1974*	*1976*	*1981*
Heavy manufacturers					
Nonelectrical machinery	32	59	77	96	404
Ships	1	6	69	287	1,212
Steel and metal products	115	252	570	286	934
Transport equipment	14	24	121	60	471
Other	8	21	41	72	440
Subtotal	170	362	837	801	3,461
Light manufactures					
Electronics and electrical appliances	223	313	474	796	2,885
Footwear	55	106	180	165	256
Plastic products	7	14	15	82	259
Plywoods	154	273	163	182	215
Textiles and clothing	619	1,185	1,450	1,370	2,343
Other	241	576	818	589	829
Subtotal	1,299	2,467	3,180	3,184	6,787
Primary products	207	442	498	422	722
Total exports	1,676	3,271	4,515	4,407	10,970

a. These are original projections in the long-term framework and were stated in current dollars, allowing for 5 percent a year inflation during 1972–81. As discussed in the text, these can be reinterpreted as targets in 1974 dollars because the rise in export unit values during 1972–74 has already exceeded the original estimate for the entire 1972–81 period.

Source: 1972–74, Bank of Korea trade data (customs clearance basis); 1976 and 1981, Ministry of Commerce and Industry, adjusted projections.

constant prices by three and a half times, indicating an annual
growth rate of 15 percent. Within the light manufactures, the
share of textiles and synthetic fibers was to come down from
about half in 1972 to a little over one-third by 1981. This was to
be compensated largely by a rise in the share of electronics from
10 percent to about 35 percent over the period.

As the detailed discussion of industrial plans in the next
chapter suggests, we had reservations about the practicability of
many individual goals for heavy industrial exports even before
the ascent of energy costs and related changes in external circumstances. The goals for the export of ships and steel were particularly ambitious. In the light of recent events the government is
substantially revising the detailed industrial program for the
fourth plan. The second large steel plant has been indefinitely
postponed, and the program for large-scale shipyards is being reviewed. This will inevitably affect the targets for 1981. Meanwhile the breakdown of 1974 exports suggests a much larger contribution by textiles and other light manufactures than had been
envisaged before the 1973 boom. On the whole it seems almost
certain that the shift toward heavy manufactures will not materi-
alize to the extent originally planned. This need not be a source of
concern. Indeed the heavy industry plans in the long-term framework tended to confuse somewhat the need to diversify export
products with the desire to deepen the industrial structure. These
goals, though related, can be regarded as distinct. On the one hand
diversification of export products can be achieved by reducing the
present heavy reliance on textiles and clothing and introducing a
larger variety of light manufactures. On the other hand the development of heavy industrial exports does not necessarily deepen
the industrial structure if the value added in the new products is
not large. Purely from the viewpoint of export diversification, the
targets suggested under the long-term framework indicate too
much reliance on four commodity groups—textiles, electronics,
steel, and ships. The diversification achieved during the last two
years through the substantial development of steel and ship exports is no doubt impressive. In setting new targets, however, a
shift toward new heavy industrial exports should not be pro-
moted at the cost of reducing the value added in exports or the
economically viable but less capital-intensive light manufactures. In specific terms the export expansion of miscellaneous
manufactures and machinery, excluding electronics, deserves
more attention from the authorities than it has so far received.

KEY AREAS OF IMPORT SUBSTITUTION

Even though we believe that in the near future it would be both desirable and necessary for Korean exports to grow faster than GNP, the government is rightly stressing import substitution in key areas of food grains, energy, machinery, raw materials, and intermediate products for the export sector in order to establish a self-supporting growth structure and a viable balance of payments. The plan for import substitution will obviously be firmed up by the government only after detailed examination of the opportunities and the costs for each subsector. It is our strong impression, however, that the investment choices will be difficult because in many areas greater domestic reliance will require substantially higher unit costs of investment. Furthermore the gestation period of investments, particularly in energy and agriculture, may be quite long. Then too in many areas of the economy there has been a growing reliance on imports, so that even with greater efforts at import replacement, dramatic declines in the ratio of imports to domestic demand might not be feasible. This observation is particularly relevant in the energy field.

Petroleum consumption grew 18 percent annually from 1968–73, while GNP rose at a 10 percent rate during the same period. The apparent GNP elasticity of petroleum of 1.8 reflected in part the substitution of domestic coal by imports of petroleum. With the sharp rise in energy costs, the growth in energy demand in relation to GNP will drop probably close to unity. But because in the base period (1973–74) imported energy supplies accounted for well over half the total consumption, even with the rapid growth of domestic energy supplies it will be several years before the growth in petroleum imports begins to fall appreciably below the growth in GNP. Meanwhile the large investments needed to develop domestic energy resources will raise the requirements for imported capital goods.

Among food grains wheat constitutes nearly 60 percent of the total imports at present, and the possibilities for direct import substitution are negligible. Imports of rice and barley account for only 10 percent of the domestic supply, and self-sufficiency is likely to be reached over the next few years. But with a sharp increase expected in the import of feed corn and a modest rise in wheat imports, total imports of grain by 1980 are likely to remain at about the 1973–74 level of 3 million tons. Still, it may be possible to have a net saving in the share of imports in total food-grain supply. This analysis assumes, however, that domestic grain production, which has been fairly stable during the past decade, can increase during 1974–81 at an annual rate of 3 to 4 percent. Even if this level is attainable, it will in turn involve sizable investments in irrigation, the rearrangement of paddies, and farm mechanization.

Another potential avenue of import substitution is to increase the value added in exports by enlarging the domestic supply of raw materials. Overall progress in this area will depend to some extent, however, on the structure of exports. Net value added in clothing, textiles, wigs, and footwear is probably much higher than in electronics and possibly some of the new products such as steel and ships. Detailed studies of the domestic and foreign components of key domestic production and export sectors are much needed. These should analyze the machinery industry and its present role in meeting domestic demand for capital equipment, identify various bottlenecks to its development, and consider policy changes to spur the healthy growth of this vital industry. A dynamic machinery industry can contribute not only to foreign exchange savings but also in the long run to export diversification.

The overall prospects for substantial import substitution over the next several years cannot be considered to be excessively bright. This should not be taken to mean, however, that careful planning for and investment in import substitution industries will not be required. It merely suggests that for the next few years any reduction in the overall ratio of imports to GNP will be small, and a great part of the burden of reducing the balance of payments gap will fall on sustained export growth.

Trade policies

As discussed earlier, the incentive system for promoting Korean exports has been by and large reasonable and effective. Since the mid-sixties the effort has focused on the maintenance of realistic effective exchange rates for exports through frequent adjustments in response to changes in purchasing power parity and export subsidies to compensate for changes in real exchange rates. Even though the quantifiable export subsidies were at their peak in 1971 and accounted for over 30 percent of total exports, the overall rate of effective subsidy on manufactured exports was not much above 10 percent. In other words the main effect of the export subsidies was to make intermediate products available to the export sector at international prices. To the extent that the average effective protection afforded to manufacturing industries was small or negative, there has been a definite bias toward exports.

In January 1974 the duty-free import of machinery for the export sector was eliminated and replaced by a much more selective system of exemptions. In addition the preferential interest rate on short-term advances was raised from 7 to 9 percent. Foreign exchange loans for working capital, which previously carried the same interest rate as won financing to exporters, now carry a floating interest rate equal to the Eurodollar rate plus 2.5 percent a year. As a result of these changes and the devaluation in December 1974 the quantifiable export subsidies now account for only about 16 percent of total export sales. As Table 31 shows, however, the real effective exchange rate in June 1975 was less favorable than at any time since 1970. To maintain adequate export incentives government policy should try to restore

Table 31. Adjusted Real Effective Exchange Rate on Exports

Item	1970	1971	1972	1973	1974	1975[a]
Nominal exchange rate (r)	316.7	373.3	398.9	397.5	485.0	485.0
Incentive per dollar of exports						
Interest subsidy	17.2	18.6	9.6	9.6	6.9	9.0
Direct tax reduction[b]	6.9	8.3	5.6	5.2	5.7	5.9
Indirect tax exemption	21.9	26.9	21.0	12.5	12.5	11.9
Tariff exemption	42.6	57.7	53.5	40.3	42.2	54.5
Electricity discount	0.2	0.2	0.1	0.2	0.2	0.2
Railroad discount	0.1	0.1	0.1	0.0	0.0	0.0
Subtotal (s)[c]	89.1	111.7	89.9	66.6	67.7	81.6
Nominal effective exchange rate						
($r + s$)	405.7	484.9	488.8	465.1	552.7	566.6
Price indexes[d]						
Korea (P_d)	81.6	92.2	100.1	115.2	166.5	190.0
Japan (P_j)	99.7	98.6	104.5	134.8	157.7	156.0
United States (P_u)	92.6	96.3	102.5	118.3	143.0	144.9
Exchange rate index,						
Japan as against the United						
States (Z_j)[d]	84.2	95.7	99.7	107.5	100.0	101.6
Real effective exchange rate (R)[e]	436.6	500.7	505.5	537.3	501.9	454.7

a. As of June; all other data are for the end of the year.
b. Includes exemption from business activity tax.
c. Total may not reconcile due to rounding.
d. August 1972 = 100.
e. $R = \frac{r + s}{P_d} (.555\, P_j\, Z_j + .445\, P_u)$.
Source: Economic Planning Board, August 1975.

the real effective exchange rate to the level prevailing after the December 1974 devaluation.

Generally speaking Korea should also attempt to move toward a more uniform system of export incentives, inasmuch as the distinction between the export and the nonexport sectors is becoming somewhat blurred. At present about one-third of the total value added in manufacturing is exported. If the nontrade-competing manufacturing activities such as food, beverages, tobacco, printing and publishing, and furniture and fixtures are excluded, the export value added is close to half the total value added in manufacturing. With the dominance of exports in the total manufacturing sector, it may often be difficult and not very meaningful to assign incentives on the basis of whether industries are considered export oriented or not.

A number of policy changes made during the last two or three years have been prompted by the desire to stimulate greater use of domestically produced intermediate and capital goods. It is not easy, however, to judge the extent to which incentives to import substitution have been increased. While the structure of tariff rates and tariff collection as a percentage of the value of imports have moved downward,[15] import controls have been tightened—although possibly only as a temporary response to the world situation. There can be no doubt that an effort has been made to remove the bias against the domestic production of capital goods through improved access to longer term capital for the purchase of domestic machinery. These are changes in the right direction. But it seems desirable to review the level of effective protection for domestic machinery and intermediate goods before deciding on whether to continue import restrictions on capital goods and/or further increase tariffs on competing imports.

Resource Requirements

The continuation of a high growth rate during 1976–81 will require a massive effort to mobilize investment resources. According to the original Economic Planning Board projections in the long-term framework, the ratio of total investment to GNP was to increase from 22 percent in 1972 to nearly 32 percent in 1981 to sustain an average annual GNP growth of 10.4 percent

15. The actual average tariff rate was 6.7 percent in 1969 and declined to 4.5 percent by 1974.

Table 32. Incremental Capital-Output Ratios, Unlagged

Sector	Historical records			Official estimates		
	1954–62	*1963–67*	*1968–72*	*1973–76*	*1977–81*	*1973–81*
Agriculture	0.9	0.9	2.0	3.1	3.5	3.3
Manufacturing	2.1	1.7	1.4	2.0	2.0	2.0
Mining	1.3	1.5	5.5	5.0	5.0	5.0
Other	2.9	2.5	3.6	4.0	4.4	4.3
Overall	2.1	1.9	2.6	2.9	3.0	3.0

during 1973–81.[16] The overall investment ratio to GNP was projected to average 28.3 percent during 1973–81, rising from 25.7 percent in 1973–76 to 30.3 percent during 1977–81. Our estimate of growth for 1972–76 is 9.1 percent a year.[17] This, taken with the government's revised target of 9 percent a year during 1977–81, implies an average growth projection of around 9 percent for 1973–81 as a whole, compared with the original goal of 10.4 percent. This downward revision in the growth rate is not likely to change the investment rate requirements significantly, if at all. As Table 32 shows, the original estimates assumed a substantial increase in the incremental capital-output ratio from 2.6 in 1968–72 to 3.0 during 1973–81, reflecting the shift to more capital-intensive investments in industry and agriculture. In actuality the increase in incremental capital-output ratios during 1973–81 is likely to be even more pronounced. The government is stressing investments in social overhead capital, especially low-income housing and rural infrastructure. During 1973–75 the share of social overhead capital and other services in total fixed investment exceeded 63 percent, and during 1976–80 it is likely to be substantially higher than the earlier estimate of 52 percent. As might be expected, the incremental capital-output ratio for this sector has historically been much higher than the average. A second reason for the increase in the incremental capital-output ratio is that the increased priority of food-grain production and the development of domestic energy resources already mentioned are likely to raise the investment cost per unit of output sharply. In addition there may well be bunching of

16. These estimates were in 1970 constant prices and differed from current price estimates in that the prices of investment goods were estimated to rise less sharply than the GNP deflator.

17. Assuming a growth rate of 7 percent in 1976.

investments with relatively long gestation periods as new import substitution programs are developed and launched over the next few years.

We estimate that for the 1973–76 period the incremental capital-output ratio will be somewhat higher than the official estimate of 2.9, and a further increase to 3.2 or 3.3 during 1977–81 compared with the original projection of 3.0 cannot be ruled out. If about a 9 percent annual growth and a 3.2 incremental capital-output ratio are assumed for 1976–81, the gross investment will have to average about 28 percent of GNP during the period. Total investment will in this case increase between 1975 and 1981 at an average rate of 10 to 11 percent a year.

DOMESTIC SAVING NEEDS

Although the investment requirements are large, the overall resource position has become difficult, largely as a result of external developments. As Table 33 indicates, the ratio of gross investment during 1973–76 will be over 27 percent as against the original Economic Planning Board estimate of 25.7 percent. At the same time reliance on foreign savings has turned out to be substantially larger due to the deterioration in the terms of trade and slackening of export growth during 1974–75. The ratio of foreign savings[18] to GNP peaked at 13 percent in 1974 but remained at the high level of 11 percent during 1975. A grad-

Table 33. The Overall Resource Position
(percentage of GNP)

Period	Gross investments	National savings	Foreign savings
1968–72 (actual)[a]	25.8	17.0	8.8
Long-term framework[a]			
1973–76	25.7	20.1	5.6
1977–81	30.3	28.2	2.1
World Bank estimates[b]			
1973–76	27.5	18.8	8.7
1977–81[c]	28.4	22.4	6.0

a. In constant 1970 prices.
b. In constant 1973 prices.
c. Based on 9 percent growth and a capital-output ratio of 3.2:1.

18. Defined as the deficit on goods and services account in the balance of payments.

ual reduction in the current account balance of payments, both in absolute terms and as a percentage of GNP, is both desirable and feasible. As discussed in the next section, with the continued real expansion in exports of around 15 percent a year and definite progress toward import substitution, the foreign savings could come down to 3 percent of GNP by 1981. On the average, however, foreign savings equal to about 6 percent of GNP will be required during 1977–81. If external flows are taken as determined by foreign exchange need, national savings requirements can be estimated essentially as a residue. On this basis the ratio of national savings to GNP will have to rise markedly from the actual average of 18.8 percent during 1973–76 to 22.4 percent in 1977–81 in order to attain 9 percent growth a year, if the incremental capital-output ratio is assumed to be 3.2. The required rise in the average saving rate does not, however, fully convey the magnitude of the savings effort involved. That becomes clear only by looking at the implied marginal saving rate of over 35 percent during 1975–81. Even if a somewhat lower capital-output ratio of 3.1 is assumed, the marginal saving rate will still have to be around 33 percent.

As mentioned earlier, savings have shown considerable fluctuations in the past. The marginal saving rate exceeded 33 percent during the late sixties but declined to about 5 percent during 1970–72. The latter was to some extent an aberration that resulted from the slowdown of the economy and a financial squeeze on business enterprises. There was again a spurt in 1973 though it represented in part a lag in consumption. At best the experience in the recent past suggests a marginal saving rate of around 30 percent. As discussed earlier, there are many factors, however, which may complicate the task of achieving even the historical rate in the future.

POLICY ISSUES AFFECTING SAVINGS

In the next few years government policies regarding interest rates, taxation, public expenditures, and subsidies will crucially impinge on the level of domestic savings. Public savings, as already indicated, averaged 6 percent of GNP during 1968–73 but were quite modest during 1974 as a result of a combination of circumstances, principally the stagnation of the budgetary current account surplus and the rapid rise in the extrabudgetary deficit. The former reflects a long-standing weakness in Korea's public finances. During 1970–73 the general budget revenue rose in real terms at an average annual rate of only about 3.6 percent. As a result even though the annual increase in current expenditure was held to 5 percent the real current account surplus in the general budget declined by about 10 percent. Revenues turned up sharply during 1974, rising by some 18 percent in real terms as tax collections reflected the 1973 boom, but the improvement in the current account surplus was limited by an equally large rise in current expenditures, owing mainly to substantial salary increases to government employees during the year. The ratio of central government taxes to GNP peaked at 15.4 percent in 1971 but declined sharply in the ensuing two years and recovered only to 15.1 percent in 1974. Notwithstanding additional taxation measures introduced recently and related to the need for increased defense spending,[19] the ratio of central government taxes will rise at best only modestly during 1975 and 1976.

The recent sluggish tax performance reflects such special factors as the impact of the recession on incomes and the tax reductions provided under the 1974 reforms for low-income taxpayers. As the relative inelasticity of tax receipts during 1970–74 clearly indicated, however, the revenue problem basically reflects underlying weaknesses in the tax structure. One major weakness is clearly the sizable loss in revenues resulting from the extensive exemptions granted to exporters from internal taxes and duties on imported raw material and equipment. Another debilitating element in the revenue structure appears to be the time lag in tax collections, indicated by the fact that the 1973 boom was not strongly reflected in government receipts until the following year. Failure to collect taxes on a fully current basis can of course seriously undermine real revenues in the sort of highly inflationary environment to which Korea has been subject. Revision of the exemption system and other basic changes in tax structure need to be considered to ensure a major improvement in revenue performance over the longer run, but the potential for

19. These measures include a defense tax of 10 percent on worker incomes in excess of W70,000 per month ($145), a tax equal to 0.1 percent of land value on paddy farmers, increased sales taxes on luxury items such as jewelery (to 20 percent) and private cars (to 30 percent). A surtax of 2.5 percent on all imports (except those brought in by authorized foreign investors and raw materials for exports) has also been levied. The new tax legislation is estimated to raise nearly W200 billion (US$413 million) a year in additional taxes up to 1980.

boosting revenues significantly in the immediate future appears to lie mainly in indirect taxation.

While real government revenues may grow faster than GNP, considerations of national security will make it difficult to limit the growth in current expenditures in the future. All told, it will not be easy to raise the ratio of current surplus in the general budget to GNP, which had dropped from slightly above 4 percent in 1970 to about 2.5 percent in 1974. It is therefore necessary to reduce as soon as possible the deficits in the extrabudgetary accounts (mainly grain and fertilizer subsidies) which were over 2 percent of GNP during 1975.

The governments' elimination of grain and fertilizer subsidies over the next few years will depend in large part on the expected drop in import costs, estimated at 15 to 20 percent in current dollars between 1974 and 1976. Nevertheless the government decisions on the procurement price of rice and sales prices of fertilizer will also be crucial.[20] Precise information on the breakdown of subsidies for imported and domestically procured rice is not available. It seems, however, that the subsidy on domestic purchases is clearly more important. As mentioned earlier, the domestic purchase price of rice from the 1974 crop was $394 a metric ton, still below the average import price of $485. The international price of rice dropped sharply in 1975, however, and is not expected to show any recovery in real terms during the next few years. The Korean government will therefore have to resist farm pressures to boost the price of rice in order to reduce the burden on the budget, or raise the price of rice to urban consumers above the international price level.

The government policy on interest rates compels as much consideration as that on agricultural prices. During the sixties Korea's heavy reliance on high interest rates successfully mobilized domestic savings and ensured efficient use of investment resources. The continued high rate of inflation, the development of inflationary psychology, and the deteriorating financial position of many enterprises led, however, to mounting concern. In August 1972 nominal interest rates were substantially reduced in

20. Even though fertilizer sale prices to farmers were increased by 65 percent in December 1974, the domestic fertilizer factories were operating at a heavy loss and a further increase of nearly 40 percent was necessary in April 1975. To the extent that the full domestic cost of fertilizer production is not being covered, there is still a subsidy on domestically procured fertilizer. Most of the subsidy, however, relates to imports.

hopes that inflation would be brought to 3 percent a year. International developments reactivated strong inflationary pressures, however, and as a result the real interest rates for loans were substantially negative in 1975, though the rates for savings and time deposits were increased and the spread disappeared. The negative real interest rates have thus been accompanied by interest rate subsidies and increased reliance on direct allocations of credit (see Chapter 5). The government has been reluctant to increase interest rates on the ground that this would push costs further. An additional factor has been the financial difficulties facing many enterprises in the aftermath of the recession. Unless inflationary pressures abate greatly during 1976, a thorough review of the level and structure of interest rates would be desirable to avoid discouragement of savings and unwanted effects on the pattern of investment.

INVESTMENT CHOICES

Because of serious constraints on resources it may therefore be difficult to attain 9 percent growth over the fourth plan period, particularly if the capital intensity of production tends to rise sharply. In the immediate period foreign exchange might be the major constraint, but as the balance of payments deficit is reduced through sustained export expansion, the shortage of domestic savings will become increasingly crucial. Theoretically part of the shortage could be made up by foreign borrowings over and above what is needed for foreign exchange. In Korea's case, however, external requirements are already so large that this option is precluded for any extended period. Even though the external deficit declines as a percentage of GNP, the total requirement of gross inflows will be sizable and its mobilization a major challenge. Furthermore, although the elimination of dependence on foreign savings by 1981 no longer appears practical, the government's desire to rely on external flows as little as possible will tend to limit balance of payments deficits. It is likely that the mobilization of domestic resources on the required scale will prove difficult while the desired structural changes will be capital intensive. Korea will therefore have to lower its goal of 9 percent growth or postpone some long-term investments considered necessary to make the economic structure more self supporting.

Programming the investment for the fourth plan will therefore be a difficult but challenging task for the Korean planners. The multiplication of capital-intensive projects with long gestation periods will place a greater burden on the role of the central authorities in determining the direction of the economy. The excellent macroeconomic planning will have to be even more closely related than in the past to individual development plans for sectors and subsectors and even to the timing of key projects. It would therefore be helpful to provide a ten-year perspective for the fourth five-year plan, covering the period up to 1986, not only to facilitate the planning of subsectors such as energy, food grains, and steel but also to examine the long-term issues of debt management and viability of the balance of payments.

EXTERNAL ASSISTANCE REQUIREMENTS

Table 34 gives the sources and uses of foreign exchange for 1973–81 as estimated in the government's long-term framework. Even before the energy crisis it was our judgment that these medium- and long-term external capital requirements, estimated at $10 billion, represented a substantial underestimate. This conclusion was based mainly on the finding that the saving-investment gap would be substantially larger than projected because of a short fall in savings and that larger external inflows would be needed to supplement domestic savings. The change in

Table 34. Uses and Sources of Foreign Exchange
(million U.S. dollars)

Foreign exchange	1973–76	1977–81
Uses		
Deficit on goods and services	2,922	2,147
Increase in reserves	483	1,491
Loans repayment	1,128	2,080
Interest payment	850	1,920
Export credits	161	748
Total	4,694	6,466
Sources		
Long-term capital, gross	3,995	6,037
Investment	580	1,048
Loans	3,415	4,989
Short-term capital, net of errors and omissions	699	429
Total	4,694	6,466

Source: Economic Planning Board.

the terms of trade in 1974–75, which is by and large likely to be permanent, has, however, dramatically changed the balance of payments outlook. Compounded by the cyclical downturn in exports, Korea's current account balance of payments widened from $300 million in 1973 to $2.0 billion in 1974, bringing the foreign exchange constraint to the forefront and making impractical the original goal of eliminating dependence on net external assistance by 1981. For the next few years the availability of external capital will largely determine Korea's ability to sustain a high growth rate while adjusting to the structural changes in the balance of payments. As the balance of payments improves with the recovery of export expansion, domestic savings will become more of a constraint, particularly if the investment cost of each unit of output rises markedly and there is a bunching of capital-intensive investments. The need for relatively large inflows of external capital may thus continue into the late seventies in part to offset the shortage of domestic savings. In view of the government's policy of increased self-reliance and the possible difficulty of obtaining additional external resources, however, our projections assume that foreign inflows will not be used to overcome a shortfall of domestic resources and that the necessary adjustments will take the form of a reduced growth rate or changes in the pattern of investment.

The other major assumptions underlying the balance of payments estimates for 1976–81 (see Table 35) are that the real growth of merchandise exports will be 14 to 15 percent a year while export prices increase by 6 to 7 percent a year, and that the real growth of imports will be limited to 10 to 11 percent a year, indicating at least moderate import substitution, while import prices increase by 5 to 6 percent. The estimates therefore assume that the terms of trade, which dropped by 25 percent between 1972 and 1975, will improve by about 5 percent over the next five or six years. This assumption is based on the expectation of some decline in real prices of raw materials and food grains from the peak level in 1974–75; the real price of petroleum may also drop somewhat. The export outlook, discussed at length earlier, assumes reasonably high annual growth in the OECD countries of 4 to 4.5 percent. The import growth projected will be consistent with an increase in gross investment at the rate of 10 to 11 percent a year, provided a marginal rate of savings of over 35 percent could be achieved along with considerable progress in import substitution in the capital goods sector. This growth in investment

Table 35. Summary Balance of Payments, 1972–81
(million U.S. dollars)

Item	Actual						Projected			
	1972	1973	1974	1975f	1976	1977	1978	1979	1980	1981
Current account	-371	-309	-2,023	-1,845	-1,717	-1,585	-1,290	-1,090	-915	-850
Trade f.o.b.[a]	-574	-566	-1,937	-1,443	-1,256	-1,105	-815	-690	-515	-300
Exports	1,676	3,271	4,515	5,064	6,414	7,685	9,318	11,175	13,401	16,081
Imports	2,250	3,837	6,452	6,507	7,670	8,790	10,133	11,865	13,916	16,381
Invisibles, net	33	67	-308	-612	-711	-730	-725	-700	-700	-850
Receipts	550	849	838	873	889	1,091	1,246	1,609	1,838	1,839
Payments	517	782	1,146	1,485	1,600	1,821	1,971	2,309	2,538	2,689
Transfers, net	170	190	222	210	250	250	250	300	300	300
Official	51	35	68	65	35	30	15	15	10	10
Private	119	115	154	235	215	220	235	285	290	290
Capital account	478	739	936	2,024	2,077	1,967	1,888	1,603	1,423	1,542
Private direct investment, net	79	143	124	42	175	200	250	300	350	400
Medium- and long-term capital, net	441	552	610	1,093	1,877	1,677	1,513	1,108	838	862
Medium- and long-term capital, gross[b]	698	843	993	1,504	2,515	2,516	2,487	2,176	2,208	2,529
Public loans, gross	324	369	317	528	937	969	940	1,068	1,135	1,230
Amortization of medium- and long-term loans	257	291	383	411	638	839	974	1,167	1,370	1,667
Other items, net[c]	-26	-40	247	216	-50	-35	-50	-70	-90	-100
Short-term trade finance, net	-16	84	-45	673	75	125	175	265	325	380
Errors and omissions	41	19	-8	-229	. . .	. . .	. . .	. . .	. . .	. . .
Overall balance of payments	148	449	-1,079	-50	360	382	598	513	508	692
International Monetary Fund and other items (net)	40	-1	319	130	. . .	. . .	-35	-50	-75	-39
Change in net international reserves[d]	-188	-448	-760	-80	360	382	563	463	433	553
Memo items										
Debt service ratio	18.0	11.3	11.8	12.5	13.9	15.1	14.4	15.3	14.9	14.6
Net international reserves[e]	608	1,056	296	376	656	1,038	1,601	2,064	2,497	3,050

. . . Zero or negligible.
a. Free on board.
b. All loans of maturity one year and above.
c. Includes export credits and other capital transfers.
d. Minus represents increase.
e. Gross net of short-term liabilities.
f. Provisional.

could then make possible a growth of 8 to 9 percent in GNP depending upon the capital-output ratios.

Our estimates of the balance of payments are based on so many assumptions they should be considered as providing only a rough framework for discussion and as indicating essentially the order of magnitude of external capital needs. The estimates in current U.S. dollars are particularly sensitive to assumptions about the rate of international inflation. The pressure of international inflation has been extremely intense during the last couple of years, but we have assumed that it will moderate considerably in the second half of the seventies. If the annual rate of international inflation is higher than the 5 to 6 percent assumed, the need for external capital in current prices will increase correspondingly. Variations in some of the assumptions about real magnitudes would, however, be self-compensating. For instance, if the rate of export expansion and/or import substitution is faster or slower than assumed, the rate of growth of GNP and investment will also vary and thus result to a degree in larger or smaller imports.

With the above caveats, we conclude that the current account deficit will decline steadily from around $1.9 billion in 1975 to $0.9 billion in 1981. This decline will be more than offset, however, by the growing requirements of amortization payments and reasonable additions to foreign exchange reserves. Thus the gross disbursement of medium- and long-term loans will have to rise sharply, averaging $2.4 billion annually during 1976–81.

Mobilization of the required capital would nevertheless be difficult, particularly in the early years, because of the considerable lag between commitments and disbursements. To achieve a high level of foreign loan disbursements during 1976–77 a substantial part of the commitments should be in the form of nonproject assistance that can be disbursed quickly.

CREDITWORTHINESS

The debt service on foreign loans on the scale required is not likely to present a major problem if at least half the loans are on concessionary or semiconcessionary terms and those from private sources have an average term of around ten years. The flow of concessionary assistance to Korea in recent years has not been large and was mainly from the United States and Japan. In response to changing circumstances, the Korean government has modified its earlier goal of not requiring official development assistance beyond 1976. Nevertheless a substantial part of future borrowing from official sources will have to be from multilateral agencies, notably the World Bank, the Asian Development Bank, and the Organization of Petroleum Exporting Countries. Provided the recommended mix of private credit and public assistance can be attained, the debt service ratio would rise only moderately from about 13 percent in 1975 to 16 percent by 1981 and not exceed this level in the first half of the eighties. Total debt service payments would no doubt nearly quadruple from about $700 million in 1975 to $2.5 billion in 1981, but at the same time exports of goods and nonfactor services, in current prices, would rise by over 20 percent a year from $5.7 billion in 1975 to $17.5 billion in 1981. Korea's total debt outstanding would rise from around $6 billion at the end of 1975 to about $16 billion at the end of 1981 but as a percentage of the annual export of goods and services would decline somewhat. The rise in the debt service ratio over the period will thus be entirely due to some hardening of the average terms of the external debt.

In addition to the increased inflow of medium- and long-term loans, our estimates envisage a steady increase in net direct foreign private investment from $124 million in 1974 to around $400 million in 1981. Its share in total net foreign inflows is expected to increase from around 10 percent during 1973–75 to about 20 percent in the early 1980s. In relation to GNP and foreign trade the postulated inflow of foreign investment is relatively modest because of some uncertainty about the growth of Japanese direct investment in Korea. Japan's overall development strategy includes a massive increase in overseas investments during the next decade as a part of its effort to overcome constraints on the expansion of domestic industries caused by shortages of labor and raw materials and environmental concerns. Because Korea lacks basic mineral resources it would not be able to benefit from Japanese investment in resource-based industries, which is the major element in Japan's strategy. Korea could benefit greatly, however, from Japan's drive to develop overseas production in order to overcome the problems of high wage costs and excessive pollution.

The balance of payments projections presented here provide for only modest increases in net international reserves and export credits. Net reserves which during 1970–73 were generally equal to three months' imports had dropped to a level equal to little over half a month's imports at the end of 1974. It is assumed that a recovery equivalent to two months' imports will be made by 1981. This is considered a bare minimum for an economy whose ratio of imports of goods and services to GNP will remain at the high level of 45 percent. Similarly the provision of export credits to finance the sale of ships and other capital goods has been tentatively kept at an average of $200 million a year. This is admittedly inadequate since exports of capital goods may well reach $2 billion annually by the early 1980s. Unless Korea can greatly increase its access to private capital markets and obtain credits at reasonably long-term maturities, say 12 to 15 years, it will be difficult, however, to build up foreign exchange reserves and provide export finance to the extent required.

Social Goals

A major goal of the long-term plans is to disperse the benefits of growth more widely than in the sixties. With rapid economic growth, a continued improvement in the overall employment situation[21] and a sustained rise in real wages will be assured during the seventies. But the past experience of lagging rural income and excessive migration to urban areas has underscored the need to formulate a comprehensive strategy to deal with the economic imbalance of rural and urban areas.

THE SAE MAEUL

The Sae Maeul (New Community) movement initiated in late 1971 by President Park is a concrete expression of this strategy. A nationwide self-help program to improve the rural standard of living, the Sae Maeul movement obviously has economic as well as social and political objectives. It aims to modernize thought and social patterns in the villages, impart to the people a greater sense of participation in the development process, and improve the quality of life in the rural areas. Sae Maeul villages will elect a leader, and after implementation of the program virtually all 35,000 Korean villages should have attained some form of financial viability.

21. For a detailed discussion of long-term employment projections see Appendix A.

The measures to upgrade the living environment in villages include programs to expand or improve roofs, roads, electrification, telecommunications, water supply, and medical facilities.[22] It is planned that 90 percent of the rural households should have access to electricity by 1977 compared with 40 percent in 1972. By 1981 telecommunication facilities will be extended to nearly 20,000 villages (almost 60 percent of the total) compared with less than 5,000 in 1972, and all villages should have a sanitary water supply system as against only 7 percent in 1972.

The total spending in 1974 for Sae Maeul projects at all levels was estimated at $275 million, but less than one-fourth of that amount was from the government budget. Although the financial requirements are likely to double during the next two or three years, they may not prove to be a serious burden on the government budget. The main problems in implementation are likely to be administrative and organizational because successful execution of projects will involve close coordination among many agencies and ministries. On a more fundamental level, the creation of a genuine grass-roots organization like the Sae Maeul constitutes a major departure from the past and will bring about fundamental social changes in the rural areas.

RURAL INCOME TARGETS

The economic goal of the Sae Maeul movement as reflected in the long-term framework was to attain parity of earned income for farm and urban households by 1981. In fact, as discussed in Chapter 2, the ratio of farm to urban household income improved sharply between 1972 and 1974 when full parity was achieved. This was, however, because of the exceptional improvement in agricultural terms of trade and the trend toward better than average agricultural output. Moreover, the official index of household income seriously understates the disparity between average earnings per worker in rural and urban areas. The problem of ensuring a proper balance between the two is therefore likely to continue, and in this context the original projections of desired rural income growth need to be reviewed.

The long-term framework suggests that farm household

---

22. For details see Appendix B on the Sae Maeul movement.

Table 36. Desirable Growth of Urban and Rural Incomes
(*thousand won in current prices*)

Item	1972	Per-cent	1976	Per-cent	1981	Per-cent	Percent a year
A. Urban household income (all cities)	517	100	846	100	1,565	100	13.1
B. Farm household income	429	100	763	100	1,565	100	15.5
Farm income (net)	353	82	566	74	1,082	69	13.3
Off-farm income (net)	76	18	197	26	483	31	22.8
Wage income	31	7	108	14	328	21	29.9
Sideline income	15	4	20	3	39	3	11.2
Other	30	7	69	9	116	7	16.2
Urban-rural household income gap (A/B)	83.0		90.2		100.0		
Urban per capita income (all cities)	98		176		326		
Rural per capita incomes	75		130		285		
Ratio of rural and urban per capita household income (percent)	76.7		73.9		87.4		

Note: The income targets for the average farm household for 1976 and 1981 have recently been revised upward to W788,000 and W1,781,000 respectively from the original targets (W641,000 and W1,400,000) of the Economic Planning Board in June 1973. The revised estimates assume a 5 percent annual price inflation for both farm and off-farm income. The off-farm component would reach 40 percent of total average household income by 1981. This estimate would raise farm household income roughly 15 percent above the expected average income of urban households (all cities) and is therefore unrealistic. Instead, we have estimated a desirable growth of rural incomes which would reach the urban level of W1,565,000 by 1981. This estimate accepted the revised official target for farm income (at current prices) of W1,082,000 in 1981 and accordingly adjusted downward the off-farm component which was thus reduced to a more reasonable 31 percent of the total as against 40 percent in the official estimate. The relative composition of off-farm income by wages, sideline income, and new income is the same as in the official estimates.
Source: World Bank estimates based on official data.

incomes must rise from the 1972 level by an average annual rate of over 15 percent in current prices in order to attain parity of income for farm and urban families by 1981.[23] Korea plans to attain this goal by increasing both net income from farming and off-farm wages, especially from employment in nonagricultural operations. Table 36 shows that the farm income per household will have to

23. This assumes the overall price level will rise 5 percent a year during 1972–81. In fact, the price increases have been much more rapid than anticipated, and therefore the targets expressed in current prices for the 1976–81 period will need substantial upward revision to correspond to real goals. The latter, however, will require some adjustments downward because GNP growth during 1976–81 is now expected to be slower.

increase more than threefold in current prices and the off-farm income will have to rise by more than fivefold if the required growth in overall income is to be ensured. The proportion of income from off-farm sources will thus rise from 18 percent in 1972 to 31 percent in 1981.

The planned increase in net household income from farming operations requires: (a) a 24 percent increase in the cultivated area per household from 0.93 hectares in 1972 to 1.15 in 1981 as the number of farm households decreases 17 percent and the total cultivated area increases about 4 percent; (b) a 51 percent increase in GNP from agriculture, including fisheries and forestry, or 82 percent increase per farm household—to be achieved by the use of new technology, more fertilizer, and other inputs, the acceleration of farm mechanization, and investments to develop land and water resources; and (c) an increase of 22 percent in prices received from farm products relative to prices paid by farmers during 1972–81.

These agricultural targets, which imply an annual growth of 4.7 percent during 1972–81, are discussed at some length in Chapter 6. Although the projected increases in crop production are higher than those realized during 1961–71, they can probably be achieved. The aim of further improving the terms of trade of agriculture by over 2 percent a year is ambitious and will conflict with the goal of reducing sale subsidies on domestic rice. In any case efforts should be made to minimize the regressive effect of some of the policies on the small farmers. The assumption that agricultural productivity can expand 51 percent during 1972–81 while the number of workers in agriculture drops by 8 percent appears even more doubtful. The implied rise in the output for each agricultural worker of 6 percent a year during the next decade compared with 4 percent in the 1960s is certainly an extremely ambitious target. The diversification of output with emphasis on high value crops, reduced underemployment, and increased mechanization will all contribute to a rise in the labor productivity. But the specific targets (for instance, a rise in the number of power tillers from 25,000 in 1972 to 350,000 in 1981) pose difficult problems of land consolidation and pooling equipment. Furthermore a number of operations cannot be mechanized. Labor shortages during planting and harvesting periods therefore threaten to become a serious constraint on expanding food-grain production despite attempts to structure new industries in rural areas in such a way that employees could be released for agricultural work at times of peak need.

Nor will it be easy to raise the share of off-farm incomes in rural incomes from 18 percent in 1972 to 31 percent in 1981. The bulk of the increase will have to come from wage earnings in off-farm work. The World Bank calculations suggest that the number of rural workers engaged in off-farm work will have to increase from 400,000 in 1972 to 1.3 million in 1981 to bring about the required tenfold rise in earnings. The planned regional dispersion of industry will certainly facilitate progress toward this goal, but inasmuch as industrial expansion often takes the form of modernizing and expanding existing facilities, the progress toward decentralization might be slow.

The official projections of farm population and the number of farm households are not consistent with the requirements for labor from farm households. (See Tables 37 and 38.) A decline in the farm population of 24 percent is indicated, which implies that, even if the percentage employed rises from 34.5 percent in 1972 to 40.0 percent in 1981, total farm household employment will come down from 5.0 million in 1972 to 4.5 million in 1981. (The official agricultural employment estimate for 1981 is 4.3 million, which we consider in any case to be low in relation to agricultural output targets.) With the projected decline in farm population the number of farm workers available for off-farm employment will therefore diminish from 0.4 million in 1972 to 0.2 million in 1981. We estimate that even on the basis of optimistic targets for growth of labor productivity in agriculture, the rural population will have to remain more or less unchanged during the next decade if a substantial increase in off-farm employment is to be ensured. But, given the estimates of total income, if the farm population and the number of farm households are revised up-

Table 37. Farm Household Labor Employed Outside Agriculture

Item	1972	1981
1. Number of farm households (thousands)	2,482	2,040
2. Off-farm wages (won)	31,000	328,000
3. Total wage income (1 × 2)(million won)	76,942	669,120
4. Number of workers (thousands)	418	1,312
5. Wages per worker (3 ÷ 4) (thousand won)[a]	184	510

a. This assumes a 12 percent annual increase in nominal wages.

Table 38. Population and Employment by Farm and Nonfarm Households and Sectors
(*thousands*)

Category	1965	1972	1981[a]	Alternative 1981[b]	Percent change 1972–81	Percent change Alternative 1972–81
Population						
Farm	15,811	14,677	11,200	13,965	−23.7	−4.9
Nonfarm	12,763	17,681	25,509	22,744	44.3	28.6
Total	28,574	32,359	36,709	36,709	13.4	13.4
Farm/total (percent)	55.3	45.3	30.5	38.0	—	—
Employment by sectors						
Agriculture, forestry, and fisheries	5,000	5,078	4,674	4,674	−8.0	−8.0
Manufacturing and mining	879	1,423	3,088	3,088	117.0	117.0
Services	2,643	3,525	5,593	5,593	58.8	58.8
Total	8,522	10,026	13,355	13,355	33.2	33.2
Employment: farm households						
Agriculture, forestry, and fisheries	4,586	4,650	4,274	4,274	−8.0	−8.0
Manufacturing and mining	161	418	206	1,312	50.0	213.9
Services	523	5,068	4,480	5,586	−13.6	10.2
Total	5,270					
Employment: nonfarm households						
Agriculture, forestry, and fisheries	414	428	400	400	−6.5	−6.5
Manufacturing and mining	718	4,530	8,475	7,369	87.1	62.7
Services	2,119	4,958	8,875	7,769	79.0	56.7
Total	3,251					
Percent of farm population employed	33.3	34.5	40.0	40.0	—	—
Percent of nonfarm population employed	25.5	28.1	34.8	34.2	—	—

— Not applicable.

a. This assumes a 40 percent employment rate of farm household population and accepts official farm population estimates.

b. This assumes a 40 percent employment rate of farm household population and full parity in rural and urban household incomes by 1981 (W1,565,000 target) but more realistic farm population figures to allow for growth in off-farm employment necessary to generate off-farm wages assumed in Table 36.

ward by about 20 to 25 percent, the difficulties of attaining parity will be increased. Nevertheless the basic thrust of government policies appears to be fully justified. Unless increased job opportunities are provided in rural areas, the drift of the population to urban areas will continue and the task of narrowing rural-urban income differences will become even more difficult.

5

Long-term Industrial Plans

K OREA'S LONG-TERM FRAMEWORK called for an average annual expansion of manufacturing output of about 17 percent during the
1972–81 period, roughly the same rate of growth as in the past
decade. In constant 1970 prices the share of manufacturing in
total output was expected to increase over 40 percent by 1981
compared with about 25 percent in 1972.[1] The shift to heavy and
chemical industries was indicated by the projected rise in their
share in gross manufacturing output from 35.2 percent in 1972 to
51.0 percent in 1981 (see Table 39). Because electronic products
and all machines are classified as heavy industry in the Korean
government reports and documents, the size of the planned shift
in capacity and exports is exaggerated beyond what may
reasonably be described as heavy. We estimate that, in value
added, the contribution of heavy industry (excluding electronics)
to the industrial sector was planned to increase at an annual rate of
20 percent, from a 25 percent share in 1972 to 39.2 percent by 1981.

Korea's emphasis on the development of heavy and chemical
industries is not in any case such a break with the past as it might
at first appear. The second five-year plan (1967–71) initiated feasibility studies for a petrochemical plant based on the naphtha produced by the Ulsan refinery and an integrated steel mill (Pohang
Iron and Steel Company). After Korea's successful implementa-

1. In current prices the rise in the manufacturing share in GNP was to be less
pronounced (34.7 percent in 1981) because manufactured goods were expected to
rise in price less rapidly than agricultural products and services.

Table 39. Composition of Manufacturing Output
(*billion won at 1970 prices*)

Industry	1972	Percent	1981	Percent	Annual growth rate (percent)
Heavy and chemical industry					
Chemical	242	10.2	928	9.7	16.0
Clay, glass, and stone products	83	3.5	344	3.6	17.0
Machinery	208	8.8	1,896	19.8	27.8
Metal and metal products	152	6.4	1,244	13.0	26.3
Petroleum and coal products	149	6.3	469	4.9	13.5
Subtotal	834	35.2	4,881	51.0	21.7
Light industry					
Food, beverages, and tobacco	526	22.2	1,608	16.8	13.3
Textiles and textile products	512	21.6	1,522	15.9	12.9
Wood and furniture	95	4.0	297	3.1	13.5
Other light industries	404	17.0	1,263	13.2	13.5
Subtotal	1,537	64.8	4,690	49.0	13.2
Manufacturing total	2,371	100.0	9,571	100.0	16.7

Source: Economic Planning Board (EPB), June 1973.

tion of these projects it was decided to expand this type of industrial activity, and the third five-year plan stated that as a major priority "heavy and chemical industries would be constructed, thereby improving the nation's industrial structure." But the push toward heavy industries acquired a new urgency in the long-term framework. Whereas the third plan allocated to heavy industry about 50 percent of the planned investment outlays in manufacturing during 1972–76, the long-term framework suggested an allocation of nearly two-thirds during 1973–81 (see Table 40).

The sharp expansion planned in the production of major industrial products under the long-term framework is brought out in Table 41. The figures indicate that steel capacity was expected to rise from less than one million to 15 million metric tons between 1972 and 1981. Shipbuilding capacity was to increase from 190,000 gross tons in 1972 to 6.3 million gross tons in 1981. The production capacity of the electronics industry was to increase from $286 million in 1972 to $6.4 billion in 1981. The capacity of cotton textile yarn was to expand from 108,000 metric tons in 1972 to 629,000 metric tons in 1981 and synthetic fiber ca-

Table 40. Manufacturing Investment, 1973–81

Industry	Million U.S. dollars (1970 prices)
Chemical	
Oil refinery	1,097
Petrochemical	834
Other	422
Subtotal	2,353
Machine	
Electric	353
Electronic	1,197
General	367
Industrial	818
Shipbuilding	768
Transport	233
Other	564
Subtotal	4,300
Metal	
Nonferrous	344
Steel	2,171
Other	425
Subtotal	2,940
Heavy and chemical total	9,593
Manufacturing total	15,006

Source: Data supplied to the World Bank by EPB and Heavy and Chemical Industry Planning Council.

pacity from 320 to 1,900 metric tons a day over the 1973–80 period.

Korea planned this major change in its industrial structure within the framework of an outward-oriented development strategy. As Table 42 shows, a substantial portion of the total output of intermediate and capital goods was expected to be exported in 1981. In order to be competitive in new exports, great emphasis was placed on the optimum size of plants. Thus a capacity of 5.0 million tons for the second steel plant was considered while the capacity of Pohang Steel was to be raised ultimately to 7.0 million tons. Similarly the existing and planned major shipyards in Korea were to be among the largest in the world.

Deepening of Industrial Structure

The deepening of the industrial structure through a relatively greater emphasis on intermediate and heavy manufactures is both

Table 41. The Planned Expansion of Manufacturing Capacity

Industry	Unit	1972	1981	Annual growth rate (percent)
Chemicals				
Cement	Thousand metric tons	7,630	19,260	11
Flat glass	Thousand cases	719	2,900	17
Nitrogen fertilizer	Thousand metric tons	406	789	7.5
Oil refineries	Barrels per stream day	395	1,705	17.5
Petrochemicals (ethylene)	Thousand metric tons	100	600	22
Machinery, electronics, and shipbuilding				
Electronics	Million U.S. dollars	286	6,461	42[a]
Machine tools	Thousand units	4.5	121.3	44
Machinery[b]	Million U.S. dollars	337[c]	4,800	31
Motor vehicles	Thousand units	63	620	29
Shipbuilding	Thousand gross tons	190	6,300	47.5
Metals				
Aluminum	Thousand metric tons	15	200[d]	33
Copper		11	236	40.5
Lead		3.6	62.6	38
Special steel		24	648	44.3
Steel		755	15,000	39.4
Zinc		16.6	184	31
Textiles[e]				
Cotton spinning	Million spindles	1.27	5.12[f]	22
Cotton weaving	Looms	37,000	96,000[f]	15
Cotton yarn	Thousand metric tons	108	629	22
Garments	Sewing machines	6,000	200,000[f]	65
Synthetic fibers	Metric tons a day	320	1,900[f]	29
Wool spinning	Million spindles	0.4	1.5[f]	21
Wool weaving	Looms	3,400	8,900[f]	15

a. 36 percent from 1973–81.
b. Heavy and Chemical Industry Development Plan.
c. 1971.
d. From the Long-term Capital Requirement Program (1973–81).
e. From the Textile Bureau, Ministry of Commerce and Industry.
f. 1973–80 only; equipment investment plans except for synthetics.
Source: EPB, June 1973.

necessary and desirable if the rapid growth of industry is to be maintained. In the domestic market there are fewer opportunities for expanding light industry faster than the increase in domestic incomes, and it is uncertain whether in the long run international markets will be able to sustain rapid industrial growth in Korea that is based on light industry. The international uncertainties

Table 42. Exports as a Percentage of Total Demand

Export	1972	1976	1981
Chemicals			
Cement	17.1	21.5	34.1
Flat glass	38.7	37.5	47.2
Methanol	75.9	91.7	85.8
Nitrogen fertilizer	19.5	26.4	29.5
Petroleum refinery products	18.5	16.9	18.6
Polypropylene	19.4	51.8	65.3
Soda ash	2.5	11.5	20.5
Tires	19.4	38.1	54.1
Machinery, electronics, and shipbuilding			
Bearings	5.7	16.9	37.9
Electronic products	68.6	59.4	55.1
Machine tools	. . .	4.7	44.6
Motor vehicles	. . .	4.0	16.6
Power tillers	. . .	1.4	25.1
Shipbuilding	. . .	70.5	78.5
Textile looms	1.2	1.4	16.7
Transformers	0.2	10.9	37.5
Metals			
Aluminum	31.2	. . .	51.2
Copper (electrolytic)	. . .	. . .	58.2
Lead	6.8	8.8	63.1
Steel	32.1	25.8	35.2
Zinc	. . .	. . .	61.5
Textiles			
Acrylic fiber	71.2	71.4	72.0
Cotton yarn	63.9	76.4	76.5
Nylon yarn	65.5	67.0	72.2
Polypropylene fiber	76.7	86.1	81.8
Viscose rayon	37.0	46.4	49.1

. . . Zero or negligible.
Note: Demand = domestic demand + export demand. It is assumed to be supplied entirely from domestic sources, hence demand = domestic production − change in inventory.
Source: EPB, June 1973.

stem from the protectionist policies in developed countries and the prospect of increasing competition from developing countries as Korean labor costs rise. A relative shift toward heavier industry will also increase net foreign exchange earnings from given exports of light manufactures as the import content of intermediate and capital goods is replaced by domestic production.[2] At present

2. Although Korean domestic production may itself have a fairly high import content.

net foreign exchange earnings of Korea's total manufactured exports amount to only 50 percent of gross foreign earnings, and if indirect import requirements are considered, the ratio of net to gross foreign exchange earnings is probably less than 40 percent.

New Factors Influencing Strategy

In the light of the above, the increased attention being given to planning and development of heavy industries is understandable. The program was drawn up in 1973, however, before the sharp rise in the cost of imported energy and the international repercussions that followed. As a result of these developments, the government is committed to making substantial revisions of its program in the course of preparing the fourth plan (1977–81). Consideration of the main reasons for modifying the long-term industrial plans will indicate the broad direction and form of the likely or desirable adjustments as well as the major issues which will confront the policymakers and influence the course of industrial development in Korea during the coming years.

The original investment program for manufacturing for 1973–81 will have to be revised downward for a number of reasons. First of all, because of the severe overall constraint on resources discussed in the preceding chapter, real investment growth will be considerably below original expectations. Our projections of balance of payments and GNP growth in Chapter 4 are consistent with a total real investment level during 1976–81 which is 20 to 25 percent below the level forecast in the long-term framework. Furthermore, a larger proportion of the smaller total investment is likely to be allocated to social overhead and agricultural investments as greater priority is given to social concerns and the need for food grains and energy. The tentative government target for manufacturing growth during the fourth plan is now 12 to 15 percent a year compared with 16.6 percent for the same period in the long-term economic framework.

With the prospect of a smaller industrial program, the relative priorities of the various manufacturing subsectors demand greater attention. Even initially we had serious reservations about the practicability of many of the export goals set for individual heavy industries. Recent developments—notably the sharp rise in energy cost, increased scarcity of foreign exchange and capital resources, uncertainty about Korean access to the Japanese market, and last but not least the soaring price of imported machinery and equipment—compel a close scrutiny of the original plans for steel, shipbuilding, petrochemicals, and nonferrous metals. As a general principle low priority should be given projects which are extremely capital and energy intensive and heavily dependent on foreign investment, foreign markets, and imported raw material.

As mentioned above, the government fully recognizes the need to prune the plans for heavy and chemical industries. The second steel plant has already been given up, and the program for shipyard construction and expansion of shipbuilding capacity is now being reviewed in the light of the changed pattern and level of international demand for ships. Plans for the petrochemical industry will now focus chiefly on domestic demand and optimum scale. Similarly export plans for aluminum, lead, and copper will be reexamined to take account of financial requirements, comparative cost advantage, and pollution problems. A review along these lines will ensure that the heavy industry program does not preempt a disproportionate share of resources and squeeze the availability of funds for light industry, the potential for which may have been understated. Certainly light industry has done better during 1973–74 than could be expected when the heavy industry plan was drawn up. Furthermore, although the emphasis on intermediate and heavy manufactures is natural, the government should guard against the tendency to regard large and lumpy projects as dominating the process of developing backward linkages. Small and medium firms have a particularly important role to play in the field of industrial machinery and can also contribute significantly to deepening the industrial structure and increasing import substitution.

To illustrate the downward adjustment that will be necessary for the investment plan, we have forecast the growth in manufacturing investment on the assumption that the fixed capital formation will grow by 10 to 11 percent a year[3] between 1975 and 1981 and that its share of the total will gradually rise from 25 to 30 percent over the period.[4] The estimates thus derived are compared

3. This is consistent with our balance of payments estimates in Chapter 4 and implies a GNP growth of 8 to 9 percent a year, depending on the capital-output ratios.

4. The long-term framework provided for a rise in the share of manufacturing investment in total fixed capital formation to well over 40 percent by 1981. As discussed earlier, this will not be feasible because the share of social overhead capital and agricultural investment will fall only gradually.

Table 43. Total Manufacturing Investment
(*billion won at 1970 prices*)

Year	World Bank estimates	Long-term economic framework
1973	238[a]	245
1974	195[a]	294
1975	230	375
1976	260	435
1977	320	487
1978	350	553
1979	400	645
1980	500	752
1981	600	875
1973–81	3,093	4,661

a. Actual

with the manufacturing investment projected in the long-term framework in Table 43. In real terms the manufacturing investment during 1973–75 has fallen short of earlier estimates by over 25 percent while during 1976–81 it might be as much as 35 percent below original targets. It is probably neither feasible nor desirable to reduce to any considerable extent the projected level of investment in light manufactures which accounted for about one-third of the total manufacturing investment in the long-term framework. Thus the major burden of adjustment will fall on the heavy and chemical industry program which might have to be reduced by as much as 50 percent.

Industrial Financing Needs

Even though the industrial investment program is pared down, it will require more than doubling of real outlays between 1975 and 1980. In current prices manufacturing investment will have to rise from an estimated $1.3 billion in 1975 to $4.2 billion in 1981, given only modest rates of international inflation of around 5 to 6 percent a year, and may total $16 billion during 1976–81. The foreign exchange component which at present is over 60 percent will tend to fall only slowly; the increased import substitution in capital goods production will be at least partly offset by the shift toward a more import-intensive pattern of industrial investment. The import requirements of industrial investment alone will be in the range of $8 to $9 billion during

1976–81[5] and will therefore make up a large portion of the requirement for gross foreign exchange loans estimated in Chapter 4 at $14 to $15 billion for 1976–81.

Foreign finance will not be the only problem facing manufacturing enterprises. As discussed in Chapter 2, their weak financial structure has greatly increased their vulnerability in periods of slow growth. As a result of the August 1972 financial measures and the phenomenal expansion of output and profits in 1973, the debt-equity ratio of manufacturing enterprises improved from 4:1 in 1971 to 2.7:1 in 1973. But in 1974 there was again a substantial increase in indebtedness linked with a large increase in inventories.

To supplement earlier attempts to improve the financial position of enterprises, two important steps were announced on May 29 and June 7, 1974. The first focused on three points: dispersion of ownership of large closed business enterprises; tightening controls on bank credit, especially for closed enterprises with outstanding loans in excess of W5.0 billion ($12.5 million); and rationalization of the financial structures of large firms. Enterprises subject to these measures were divided into two categories. Group A includes companies whose financial standing was determined to be unsound by the Ministry of Finance; Group B companies have relatively sound financial standing. Closed enterprises which have foreign investors are exempt from these measures. Group A companies will not be granted payment guarantees of foreign loans for new projects, nor be allowed to establish, purchase, or own new enterprises or invest in shares of stock. They have three years to improve their financial structures. Group B companies are the first firms to be enjoined to go public. Failure to comply with these requirements will lead to suspension of government financial support, foreign exchange privileges, and tax exemptions.

The government also established the National Investment Fund (NIF) as a major component of the master plan to reform the financial system during the 1974–81 period. The main purpose of the fund is to supplement the self-financing and foreign loans of entrepreneurs in heavy and chemical industries, namely shipbuilding, heavy machinery, steel, nonferrous metals, petrochemicals, and electronics. The funds can be used to finance fixed

---

5. In current prices but assuming only modest rates of international inflation of 5 to 6 percent a year.

capital including land, working capital, and export finance requirements. The resources of certain savings institutions and pension and trust funds must be invested in NIF bonds, as must 25 percent of the increase in time and savings deposits in the banks. NIF bonds pay interest at 15 percent (about the same as on time deposits), but funds are reloaned at 9 to 12 percent, with the difference being covered by budgetary subsidy. The bulk of the NIF investments has been in manufacturing and electric power, but it has also made substantial commitments in agriculture and housing.

Although financial intermediation through NIF is a sound attempt to improve the maturity structure of loans, its success will depend largely on the government's ability to stimulate domestic savings. This in turn will depend at least partly on the establishment of realistic interest rates. If real interest rates continue to be negative there will also be a greater danger of the direct credit provided by NIF resulting in a misallocation of resources.

Linked with the issue of overall industrial finance is the need to provide long-term credit to finance the sale of domestically produced capital goods both at home and abroad. The lack of long-term finance may be a key bottleneck in the rapid development of the domestic machinery industry. Similarly the planned export of ships and other capital goods might require substantial export finance. Priority should be given to identifying the needs of the capital goods sector and providing the necessary sales credit either through development of new institutions or the strengthening of existing ones. Insufficient free foreign exchange to meet both these needs may, however, ultimately be a constraint.

Framework for Industrial Planning

Apart from investment allocation and finance, the main determinants of the level and pattern of industrial growth in the future will be trade policies and incentives, research and development, and the industrial planning framework. The trade policies have already been discussed in connection with the prospects for exports which will remain at least in the near future the most dynamic element in manufacturing growth (Chapter 4). While a review of export incentives and trade policies affecting import substitution is necessary in the light of recent changes in the world situation and in Korea's own industrial structure, a fundamental policy reform is unlikely to be needed at this stage. Much more urgent is the strengthening of the industrial planning framework. In the past, although the government's direct support and guidance have been important to industry, responses to new opportunities and market incentives have come mainly from the private sector. With the change in the structure of industry, however, centralized programming of investment is becoming more important. Even though the 1977–81 program for heavy and chemical industries will be substantially reduced, the role and responsibility of the central authorities in determining the direction of industrial growth will inevitably expand with the number of capital-intensive projects requiring long gestation. As suggested earlier, the excellent macroeconomic planning will have to be related even more closely than in the past to development plans for individual sector and subsectors and even to the timing of key projects.

A more systematic exploration of projects within industry is needed to weigh the costs and benefits of the alternatives. The analysis that the Korea Institute of Science and Technology (KIST) undertook in 1969–70 of the steel and associated industries illustrates what can be done, and the Ministry of Commerce and Industry, with help from other organizations both within and outside government, should be able to do this. Obviously private industry should be an integral part of the team that undertakes the work. Korea has arranged with the United Nations Development Programme for technical assistance in planning in six industries (steel, shipbuilding, mechanical engineering, electronics, petrochemicals, and textiles). It is important, however, that this planning should not be a one-shot affair but should be established on a continuing basis.

There are several other areas in which industrial planning and investment could be strengthened. First and most important, little attention has been paid to developing backward and forward linkages in industry, particularly the mechanical engineering of parts, components, and specialized items. Because assembly of imported materials has been common practice, the mechanical engineering industry has been underdeveloped or lacking in Korea. Shipbuilding and automotive programs should stimulate development of the engineering industries. The Hyundai Shipyard, for example, encourages potential suppliers to visit the yard and see what parts and components are needed, and there have been recent attempts to get automobile companies to develop specific suppliers. But the laws seeking to obtain 100 percent domestic content in a few years are going too far. The last 10 percent or so of inputs may be very expensive to obtain domestically, and greater flexibility in the requirements seems genuinely desirable.

At any rate, since planning is always an imperfect exercise, it should be decentralized to a certain extent so that Korean entrepreneurs can take advantage of domestic and overseas business opportunities that might not be apparent to the economic planners. After all, Korea was started along its present lines of development when entrepreneurs perceived an overseas market for light manufactured goods during the first plan period, at a time when reconstruction was, quite correctly, the overriding concern of the planners. As a result of the export-oriented development strategy, overseas markets became increasingly important. A reasonable degree of decentralization is therefore needed for flexibility so that Korea can react rapidly to changes in these markets.

Research and Development

Recognizing that research and development activities (R and D) can contribute significantly to the economy, most developing countries provide some support to such programs, but they are also aware that the resources are in fact often insufficient. It is somewhat rare to find programs that are focused directly on key industrial needs. Korea cannot be faulted on these grounds. A decade ago it took steps to create institutions for research and development and allocated the necessary funds. During the late 1960s key organizations such as the Korea Institute of Science and Technology were created and flourished. The programs now planned for the 1970s and 1980s, however, are far more ambitious than anything previously undertaken. Total expenditures on R and D in all fields was about $30 million or 0.3 percent of GNP in 1972. By 1981 it is projected that the percentage will rise to about 1.0 percent. Taking into account the projected growth in GNP, the 1.0 percent figure implies expenditures on the order of $220 million (in constant 1972 dollars). The private sector now accounts for about one-third of these expenditures, and its share is expected to increase to 50 percent, clearly a great acceleration, if the targets are to be met.

It is agreed that an increased R and D effort is essential to successful industrial development in the next decade and should be more than a simple extension of activities that have already been undertaken. Certain key industries have reached a plateau and require new directions in product development and industrial investment in the future. Nevertheless the programs proposed for the next decade are ambitious and costly, and it is clearly desirable to review their relative priorities, their implications for policy decisions, and the adjustment of commitments of funds and manpower that may follow.

The major innovation in R and D involves the construction and operation of five research institutes in the completely new "science town" of Daeduk. The institutes cover shipbuilding, mechanical engineering, ocean research, petrochemical technology, and electronics and communications. Those for mechanical engineering and electronics and communications are presently scheduled to be completed in 1978 and 1979 respectively, among the last. The greatest pay-off from R and D may come in these two industries, however, and we recommend a higher priority for them.

Problems and Prospects of Major Industries

The three major export industries—textiles, electronics, and shipbuilding—are discussed in greater detail in Appendixes C, D, and E. Their current problems and future prospects are presented briefly here, together with a short discussion of iron and steel and engineering industries.

THE TEXTILE INDUSTRY

The textile industry is one of Korea's most important in terms of output, value added, employment, and exports. In 1973 textiles and apparel accounted for 18 percent of manufacturing employment, 15 percent of value added, and 43 percent of exports. During 1972–74 the value of output increased over 30 percent a year, and exports reached $1.45 billion in 1974.

This rapid growth in the textile and garment industry has been accompanied by several important structural changes. The composition of the product has been shifting from pure cotton toward cotton blends and synthetics which now account for over 60 percent of the total fabric output. This shift has been beneficial for the import substitution of raw materials. Raw cotton is wholly imported, and its share in total fiber consumption dropped from 75 percent in 1960 to 45 percent in 1973. At the same time domestic production of synthetic fibers grew to supply nearly 60 percent of the industry requirement. Another important structural change has been a shift toward more labor-intensive products such as garments and knit goods which account for nearly 60 percent of value added and exports of the industry.

The changing composition of textile products is comparable to the projected changes in the international textile trade during the 1970s. Although world exports of fabrics are expected to grow at the annual rate of only 5 to 6 percent, synthetics and cotton blends will be entirely responsible for this growth, and garment exports from developing countries will grow 15 percent annually during the decade.

In the light of the above considerations, Korea's original export goal of $2.4 billion[6] in textiles and garments by 1981 can probably be exceeded. The attainment of the goal will require only 7.5 percent annual real growth from the 1974 base of $1.45 billion. Korea has only to hold on to its present share of textile exports from developing countries to substantially exceed the 1981 goal. This does not imply, however, that there will be no problems.

The major constraint facing textile exports is the quota limitations of developed countries, particularly since the long-term agreement for cotton has been replaced by multifiber trade agreements which cover the whole gamut of textile products. A new agreement between Korea and the United States covering the period from October 1, 1974, to September 30, 1977, has been signed which calls for an increase in exports to the United States by 7 percent in 1976 and 6.5 percent in 1977. These quotas are stated in terms of volume and thus permit some scope for product upgrading. There are no official quota limitations on Korean textile exports to Japan, though from time to time there has been some restriction on selected products such as silk in 1974. If Japan does impose quota limitations, Korea will have serious difficulty in significantly expanding exports. For this reason Korea should try to diversify its export markets despite some initial cost in doing so. Whenever there is as much uncertainty as there is today, concentration on a few markets has to be replaced by a

---

6. Reinterpreted as the target in 1974 prices.

somewhat more expensive mixed strategy to limit the risk of a larger loss.

The basic thrust of the long-term plan for expanding the textile industry (see Table 41) is sound, but a number of elements need to be carefully reconsidered in the light of recent experience. During 1970–74 the industry had two very good years and two marginal ones, which affected the various segments of the industry in different ways. As could be expected, the production of labor-intensive goods such as knitting and apparel was able to expand quite rapidly to meet demand and contract at small cost in times of difficulty by reducing shifts and overtime. The hardest hit during the recession were the capital-intensive integrated spinning and weaving units and particularly the synthetic fiber industry because idle capacity had a marked effect on cost and profitability. The synthetic fiber industry managed to weather the difficulties in 1970–71 without significant losses because its output was mainly directed toward the protected domestic market. But when the industry expanded in 1974, most output was either directly or indirectly exported. It therefore became more vulnerable to fluctuations in demand, particularly as it had to compete with imports produced on a much larger scale and at lower cost.

To provide more resiliency during the next three or four years the industry should be structured so that the capital-intensive segment is of economic size and can operate at full capacity. Inasmuch as the export market for synthetic fibers is expected to be relatively sluggish, this industry should be designed to supply 80 to 90 percent of the total requirement of the labor-intensive segment. Accordingly, it might be necessary to prune some of the capital-intensive elements of the investment program provided it does not adversely affect the labor-intensive segment. The most obvious place for selective pruning is in synthetic fibers, which could be cut from about 1,900 to 1,600 metric tons a day with most of the reduction in acrylics and nylon, followed by a reduction of the cotton spinning and weaving sectors by about 15 to 20 percent.

In addition to expanding productive capacity, attention should be given to institutional development in marketing. More intense market research is needed to identify new products and quickly feed back information on design trends in the world, as well as actively promote Korean products in diversified markets. The Korean Traders' Association (KOTRA) could possibly expand its function and assume some of these responsibilities, but as the industry grows it might be preferable to develop, with government assistance, an industry-supported technical institution. In addition to its marketing functions, such an institute might also provide consultancy services and technical assistance to upgrade quality and improve productivity, particularly for small and medium firms. This is done to a limited extent by the Korean Productivity Center, but the activities need to be expanded and integrated with other services.

ELECTRONICS

The electronics industry has been and will remain one of the leading growth industries in Korea. Electronics production increased nearly fourteenfold between 1965 and 1973, from a mere $33 million to $462 million. The trend in exports has been even more dramatic; electronics exports rose from $6 million in 1967 to $142 million in 1972 and $370 million in 1973. Exports in 1973 accounted for 80 percent of production compared with less than 20 percent in 1967. In 1973, 49 percent of the exports came from wholly owned foreign subsidiaries with a further 20 percent from joint ventures. In terms of the type of goods produced, in 1973 consumer goods accounted for 29 percent of both production and exports, capital products had 9 percent of production and 4 percent of exports, and components took the lion's share with 61 percent of production and 66 percent of exports. Reflecting in part the fact that much of production consists of assembling components, total imports of electronics are substantial and indeed exceed exports; the domestic value added in sales probably does not exceed 30 percent. Nevertheless the capital-labor and capital-output ratios are quite low.

The plans for 1981 aim at domestic production of about $6 billion of which about half will be exported. This export target represents a quarter of the country's total export goal. The investment requirements will, however, be relatively small; electronics has been allocated less than 10 percent of total industrial investment. Similarly, the capital cost of job creation in electronic industries will probably be in the range of $4,000 to $5,000 compared with about $15,000 for the manufacturing sector as a whole.

The rapid expansion of electronics no doubt appears extremely attractive, but the high growth targets set for the industry will pose a considerable challenge. The obvious weaknesses in the present structure of the industry will have to be overcome. Without adequate domestic technological capabilities and design skills, the present heavy reliance on component production places the industry in the precarious position of being made obsolete. To overcome this problem, consumer goods are being stressed because changes in the technology for TV sets, radios, and tape recorders are relatively small. In addition the rapid growth in domestic demand for consumer durables will give strong support to the industry. At the same time, component production should be geared toward supplying parts for consumer products, thereby increasing the domestic value added. The present low value added exposes electronics firms to the possibility of being squeezed out when margins start declining. In order to penetrate overseas markets for consumer goods, strong marketing arms will have to be built. Consideration should be given to channeling goods toward a few trading companies that deal with the standardized output of several manufacturing plants under brand names belonging to the trading company.

In considering the acquisition and diffusion of technology Korea will have to decide whether to acquire semiconductor technology, which is becoming the most important foundation of electronics, or else risk a substantial erosion of its electronics industry over the next five to ten years.

The experience of European and Japanese firms suggests a number of guidelines for the acquisition and diffusion of the semiconductor technology. First, Korea should concentrate on a few relatively stable technologies that can upgrade the design and reliability of products where the semiconductor input is small enough and the remaining labor content high enough to discourage developed countries from producing it, but still large enough to provide a reasonable manufacturing volume for Korea. Second, since the financial and human resources required are beyond the individual capabilities of Korean firms, the cooperation of industry, research institutions, and government in formulating and financing this program is absolutely essential. Third, the structure of the industry will have to be improved by inducing firms to rationalize production by, among other things, standardizing some of their output and exporting it through trading companies under joint brand names. Finally, the government should also encourage licensing arrangements and technological assistance contracts to fill in whatever gaps might exist in the short and medium run.

SHIPBUILDING

Shipbuilding in Korea has developed since 1973 into a major industry, with export orders on hand totaling over 1.5 million gross tons (over 90 percent in tanker tonnage). The completion of the new Korean Shipbuilding and Engineering Company yard at Okpo would give the country an annual shipbuilding capacity of 2 to 2.5 million gross tons and could place Korea among the major shipbuilding countries of the world. Further doubling of shipbuilding capacity to around 5 million gross tons a year was originally planned by the government, but such a step would require careful justification on the basis of the new world market conditions that followed the oil crisis and the financial resources required.

New tanker tonnage under construction or on order in the world shipyards would just about double the existing world tanker fleet; the bulk of the orders originated during the unprecedented shipping boom that lasted from the last quarter of 1972 to October 1973. The continuing oil crisis, the reopening of the Suez Canal, the anticipated expansion of oil-refining capacity in the oil-producing countries, and rising public concern over oil spillage can be expected to change the future pattern of demand, reversing or at least slowing the recent trend to very large tankers. World demand could shift to smaller tankers (200,000 deadweight tons and below), "clean" vessels carrying refined products, and new types such as liquified gas carriers.

Ship construction for the domestic market deserves better planning. As of August 1974 domestic orders comprised less than 2 percent of the total tonnage under construction in Korean shipyards. Korea's neglect of its domestic fleet is also apparent from the fact that its bottom share in foreign trade declined in recent years from the already low level of around 25 percent in 1969–70. An active domestic ship construction program will not only complement the ship export program and provide stable growth of the industry in the face of a changing world market, but it will also provide an opportunity for supplier industries to develop.

Shipbuilding has emerged as one of the strategic industries of Korea—not surprisingly, since it effectively utilizes the country's comparative advantage in low-cost skilled labor. It should add to Korea's advantage if the marine supplier capability can keep pace with the progress in shipbuilding. This would require some form of integrated planning to link shipbuilding with the planned expansion of the steel industry and the developmental programs in the auto supplier and heavy machinery sectors. The integrated machinery complex in Chang Won was conceived by the government, in part, for the backward integration of the manufacture of machinery and parts with the shipbuilding industry. There is some doubt, however, as to whether the program can develop in time to contribute effectively to the shipbuilding industry over the critical growth period of the latter half of the seventies.

Japan established her dominance in world shipbuilding by offering fast delivery, low prices, and easy credit terms. Now that material and labor costs have soared in Japan, it should be possible for countries such as Korea to exploit the same selling points. The timely entry of Korea into the ship export market in 1973 has given it a head start over other countries with comparable labor advantages, but in the future competition will be against the established shipbuilding powers. Korea will have to be competitive not only in price and delivery time but also in the provision of credit to shipowners. The institutional mechanism and the availability of financial resources for extending such credit will, in the final analysis, determine the extent to which Korea will be successful in penetrating the world market.

IRON AND STEEL

The production of iron and steel and a wide range of iron and steel products is a well-established industry in Korea. Plants producing pig iron, steel, and rolled-steel products date back in some cases to the 1940s. Unfortunately much of the industry's equipment is obsolete, and a serious lack of balance in production facilities has made it necessary for Korea to import substantial quantities of intermediate products. Nevertheless Korea's investment in iron and steel producing and fabricating facilities can make an important contribution to the nation's future economic development.

The industry's deficiency in pig iron, billet, plate, and hot-strip capacity has recently been reduced by the opening in 1973 of the Pohang Iron and Steel Company (POSCO) about 40 kilometers from Ulsan. This new plant, with an annual crude steel capacity of 1.03 million tons,[7] is now being expanded to produce 2.6 million tons of crude steel with attendant increases in product out-

7. All tons are metric.

put. Planning for a third phase, expansion to at least 5 million tons on an accelerated timetable, has begun, and a subsequent phase will lead to the ultimate goal of 7 million tons.

The output of the expanded POSCO plant will provide an important raw material for Korea's machinery industry which the government is planning to expand at a rapid rate for both export and domestic markets. A special steel plant is also under construction by an American steel company as a joint venture that would provide valuable support for Korea's machinery industry.

The government originally intended to construct a second integrated steel plant with an initial capacity of 5 million tons of crude steel beginning in 1976 and starting production in 1980 at an estimated investment cost (at 1970 prices) of $1,094 million. Ultimate expansion to more than 10 million tons was envisaged. The plans for this plant were dropped after a major U.S. steel company's consulting subsidiary conducted a feasibility study.

Korea is at a relative disadvantage in projects such as steelmaking which makes lavish use of its most limited resource, capital, and rather little use of its plentiful supplies of labor. Total investment in the government-owned POSCO works will exceed a billion dollars by 1979 when it will reach an annual output capacity of 7 million tons. The project's capital-output ratio will exceed 3.0. Despite its extremely high capital-labor ratio (4,200 workers in phase one at about $70,000 per job, $210,000 per job for phase two, and an average of $120,000 for both phases), POSCO appropriately meets Korea's economic needs at the present time: It bolsters the effort toward import-substitution, it consumes a certain amount of domestically available raw materials, and most important of all the basic units already exist. Present domestic demand for iron and steel and their products remains substantially greater than present supply, and the further development of industry in Korea (particularly shipbuilding) will lead to significant annual increases in this demand. Provided the Korean economy remains buoyant and a major proportion of the output targets set for industry are met, POSCO will play an important role as a supplier of domestically made products.

The economic case for the construction of additional steel capacity in Korea will need much more scrutiny. It is true that elsewhere many major steel plants have been built to operate on imported raw materials and fuel, but these are usually in countries with a large and growing domestic market for steel, industries that can produce steelmaking equipment, and a relatively plentiful supply of capital for investment. The situation in Korea is fundamentally different. Moreover the domestic demand, estimated on the basis of the KIST study at 9 million tons of crude steel by 1981, needs to be revised downward. Not only will industrial growth be somewhat slower than anticipated but also shipbuilding demand could be substantially less than the 1.8 million tons originally forecast for 1981.

INDUSTRIAL MACHINERY

Even though it expanded at an annual rate of over 20 percent during 1970–74, the industrial machinery industry in Korea is relatively backward. It suffers from the limited size of the domestic market, submarginal scale of operations, poor technology, and unspecialized production. The demand for industrial machinery will, however, rise sharply in the coming years with the rapid growth in manufacturing investment. Since government plans imply net import substitution in this field, domestic output will have to grow eight- to tenfold to meet the targets. Fortunately, the simultaneous development of steel, shipbuilding, and automobile industries will greatly increase the possibilities of backward and forward linkages. Furthermore, the expansion of the textile industry could spur the development of the budding textile machinery industry.

Domestic production of textile machinery has increased substantially since 1972 and accounts for a substantial portion of the total industrial machinery output in Korea. Silk looms are a major product—11,500 sets in 1973 compared with 500 in 1968. The looms are purchased by small firms at about one-third to one-half the price of imported equipment to produce low and medium quality products. The major potential for growth lies, however, in sewing machines, particularly if produced in collaboration with a foreign firm that would be willing to keep Korea abreast of technological developments and export a significant share of the output. The same applies, though to a lesser extent, to high quality looms. These are currently imported from Europe and Japan but could be manufactured domestically if Korea would specialize in a few products and produce them on a large scale in one or two large firms for both domestic and export markets. In the analogous case of machine tools, even technologically advanced countries with excellent design and manufacturing capabilities such as Germany and Switzerland specialize in a few products for domestic and export markets and import about half their requirements. The prospects for spinning machinery are less favorable as technology is rapidly changing from ring-spinning to the more labor-saving open-end machines.

Substantial allocations for industrial machinery and machine tool industries have been made, and the large new industrial complex being developed at Chang Won will itself absorb about 50 percent of the total investment. In view of the high priority given this industry, however, more attention to planning and policy direction seems necessary. Progress will be slow unless the government restricts the import of foreign machine tools by tightening credit terms to suppliers, improves quality control, achieves a reasonable degree of standardization, and provides export financing assistance to encourage exports to developing countries in Asia and elsewhere. It may also be desirable to reexamine the decision to invest more than one billion dollars in the Chang Won complex. Centralized operations and facilities such as the proposed special steel plant will undoubtedly offer valuable operating economies, but these should not be bought at too high a cost in scarce resources.

In general Korea should avoid emphasizing heavy, capital-intensive industry where it may not have any comparative advantage. Instead more emphasis needs to be given to the development of light industries such as instruments and optical goods that can offer employment to a large number of skilled laborers at lower foreign exchange costs as well as provide a breeding ground for the development of suppliers. At present the plans for the machinery industry consist of a large shopping list of seemingly unrelated projects and do not focus on ways to improve the existing structure of the industry or develop a balanced and integrated sector.

The machine tools now being made in Korea are apparently not well received on the local market, and they have at this time no foreign market at all. To build up a machine tools industry that offers an internationally acceptable product would certainly be a long and difficult process, with technical as well as economic problems of considerable complexity. In a field which is widely considered of limited profitability it is questionable whether the eventual results would justify the effort, and it might be noted that some highly developed countries (the Netherlands, for example) do very well without an indigenous machine tools industry.

Although prospects for complex machine tools are dim, simpler specialty items are in demand. There is an opportunity for metal-working, including standardized tool and machine components, to develop into an export industry without too much difficulty, provided quality and price are at competitive levels.

OTHER HEAVY INDUSTRIES

Also planned for expansion are cement, motor vehicles, and nonferrous metals. Copper, aluminum, and zinc smelters are proposed with the expectation of producing initially mainly for the home market, but by 1981 substantial exports are planned. All these projects, like steel, are capital intensive. Further drawbacks are that ore for copper and bauxite for aluminum refining will have to be imported, and in the case of aluminum Korea does not have the basic prerequisite for economic success—low-cost electric power. The program for 1975–78 should therefore be particularly closely scrutinized and investment commitments made only if foreign investment and loans are available on good terms and some assurance of export offtake is provided. The 50 percent electric power subsidy promised recently to Taehan Aluminum Refinery Company for expansion does not appear to be justified.

Plans for the cement industry call for a threefold increase in production between 1972 and 1981 and an increase in cement exports from 1.2 million to 7.4 million tons over the period. If this target is achieved Korea will be one of the world's largest exporters of cement. The large limestone deposits and port facilities at Mukho, which will be substantially expanded, give Korea a strong comparative advantage over Japan, which has not hitherto imported Korean cement but is expected to become a major market. It is, however, important to note that since 1964 world production in cement has tended to increase at a somewhat lower rate than total industrial production; Japan recently expanded its own cement capacity; and cement is sensitive to ocean transport costs, and Korea is not well located in relation to any large cement-using countries except Japan.

A tenfold increase in capacity is projected for the motor vehicle industry during 1972–81, but in the light of the oil crisis these plans need drastic revision. Even without the steep rise in the price of crude oil, it seems unrealistic to expect passenger car sales to rise from less than 20,000 in 1972 to half a million annually by 1981. There is a growing recognition that private automobiles are wasteful, and their social costs greatly exceed private costs. In any case, with its urban population concentrated in two centers, Korea should focus on improving mass transit; a good beginning has already been made by the construction of a subway system in Seoul.

6

Agricultural Development: Past Performance and Future Plans

THE AGRICULTURAL SECTOR has been greatly affected by Korea's rapid industrial growth. In other sectors employment more than doubled and GNP rose more than three times from 1962 to 1974. Approximately 3.5 million rural people (more than one-fifth the urban population in 1971) moved to urban areas during 1961–71 to take advantage of better employment and income opportunities. Agricultural employment did not change during the early 1960s, but it decreased about one percent annually between 1966 and 1971. More recently the agricultural labor force has tended to increase, reflecting in part the government's deliberate efforts to discourage rural-urban migration and in part the sharp improvement in rural incomes during 1971–74. Nevertheless the share of agricultural employment in the total dropped from 67 percent in 1961 to 49 percent in 1974. The agricultural sector's real growth rate of 4.6 percent a year during 1962–74 was much lower than that of the rest of the economy, and consequently agriculture's share of GNP in current prices dropped from 42.2 to 26.3 percent over the period.

Within the agricultural sector the value added in livestock, forestry, and fisheries has grown much more rapidly than the total. The growth in value added in crop production was in turn attributable mainly to higher value crops, especially fruits and vegetables and raw silk. Total food-grain production, which was an esti-

Table 44. Food-Grain Production
(thousand metric tons)

Year	Rice	Barley	Potatoes	Wheat	Pulses	Total
1965	3,501	2,136	1,045	300	203	7,185
1966	3,919	2,374	972	315	195	7,776
1967	3,603	2,253	631	310	235	7,032
1968	3,195	2,453	759	345	288	7,039
1969	4,090	2,459	778	366	273	8,066
1970	3,939	2,352	783	357	277	7,709
1971	3,997	2,197	707	322	263	7,486
1972	3,957	2,222	674	241	261	7,351
1973	4,211	1,953	611	162	283	7,221
1974	4,445	1,851	543	136	368	7,343

mated 7.3 million tons[1] in 1974, has grown little during the last decade, the steady rise in rice production being counterbalanced by declines in other major food crops (see Table 44). Thus total grain imports have increased from 700,000 tons annually in 1962–74 to over 3 million tons in 1972–74, increasing the dependence on imports from 10 to 30 percent of supply. The cost of imported grain in 1974 was $613 million.

While agricultural growth has inevitably lagged behind the rest of the economy, the overall performance has been satisfactory considering Korea's limited land resources and adverse natural circumstances. There is only 0.07 hectare of cultivated land per capita, about the same as Japan and Taiwan. Because of low natural fertility and high acidity, the soil requires large applications of fertilizer and lime to be productive; highly variable rainfall often causes water shortages during rice planting in the spring and flood damage in the summer and fall; and inadequate irrigation and drainage systems together with low temperatures prevent double cropping of much of the cultivated land. Despite these problems land and labor productivity in agriculture has expanded by 3.5 to 4 percent a year during 1965–74. The entire increase in crop production during this period was attributable to larger yields and double cropping inasmuch as the cultivated area changed little. Similarly, the output per worker rose at the same rate as the value added in agriculture because the labor force remained more or less unchanged. Still the growth in agricultural productivity lagged

1. All tons are metric.

considerably behind the increase in labor productivity in the non-agricultural sectors and was a major factor in the relative worsening of rural incomes till 1970 when corrective action was taken in the form of a major and sustained shift in the terms of trade in favor of the agricultural sector.

Contributing to increased land and labor productivity were the diversification of production to include more fruits, vegetables, tobacco, sericulture, livestock, and other labor-intensive activities to utilize available labor more fully throughout the year; wider use of fertilizer, pesticides, and other intermediate inputs to increase yields; and additional double cropping made possible by improved drainage and irrigation.

Korean farmers have achieved high crop yields. That of rice, for example, is twice as high as in Thailand, Indonesia, India, and the Philippines and only about 20 percent lower than in Japan. The use of fertilizer more than doubled during the last decade and now averages about 190 kilograms per hectare of rice and about 170 kilograms per hectare of other crops. These rates are much higher than in most developing countries, although lower than in Japan and Taiwan. Well-developed research and extension programs helped improve techniques.

The development of irrigation has played, and will continue to play, a major role in the expansion of rice production and the achievement of self-sufficiency. In 1962 the total irrigated area was 660,000 hectares or 53 percent of the total paddy area. At present 1,100,000 hectares (86 percent of all paddy area) are irrigated, though not all areas have fully adequate supplies. In recent years emphasis has shifted from small-scale to large-scale irrigation projects, but future planning will stress both kinds of projects.

Despite this rather impressive level of agricultural development, however, the government is concerned with growing grain deficits and lagging rural incomes and attaches a very high priority to sustaining relatively high growth of agriculture during the second half of the seventies (see Table 45). Though the specific targets for 1981 are likely to be revised under the fourth plan, the major elements in the long-term program (1972–81) listed below give the essence of the government's agricultural development strategy:

1. The contribution to GNP from agriculture, forestry, and fisheries in constant prices will increase by 4.7 percent

Table 45. Annual Growth Rates of Principal Subsectors in Agriculture
(*percent*)

Subsector	Actual 1962-72	Targets 1972–81
Crops and livestock	3.7	4.0
Forestry	6.7	5.0
Fisheries	13.8	7.8
Total	4.4	4.7

Source: World Bank projections (except for the total) based on data reported by the Ministry of Agriculture and Fisheries, "An Outline of Long Range Projections," September 1973.

annually. Output per worker will rise about 6 percent annually (compared with about 4 percent during 1961–71), almost as much as in other sectors. The agricultural labor force is expected to decline 8 percent during 1972–81.

2. Farm mechanization will proceed rapidly and the use of fertilizer, pesticides, and other inputs will increase substantially. By 1981 enough power tillers will be available to prepare almost all land under cultivation. The use of fertilizer and pesticides will increase by about 50 percent and almost 200 percent respectively.

3. A larger agricultural output is expected from the expansion of special crops (vegetables, tobacco, fruits, mulberries), large increases in sericulture and livestock production based on improved pasture and imported feeds, and some increases in the total area cultivated as well as in cropping intensity.

4. The total irrigated area (paddy and upland) will be increased 19 percent from 1,045,000 hectares in 1972 to 1,246,000 hectares in 1981.

5. Construction or improvement of drainage systems on about 140,000 hectares of low-lying paddy lands will correct drainage problems.

6. Land rearrangement and land consolidation on about 290,000 hectares will improve productivity and facilitate mechanization.

7. Reclamation of unpland and tidal flats will develop about 120,000 hectares of new land.

8. Fishery production is expected to double and exports to rise from $153 million in 1972 to $577 million in 1981.

9. Nearly one million hectares are to be reforested, and all rural villages would have adequate supplies of firewood by 1981.

10. In line with recent policies (see Chapter 2), the government plans to increase prices of farm products relative to those paid for farm supplies by 22 percent (2.2 percent a year) during 1972–81.

The long-term plan proposes important and far-reaching changes in the structure and organization of the rural sector by the early eighties. In fact Korea reached a turning point in its economic development in the late 1960s when farm population and agricultural employment began to decline in absolute numbers. A continuation of this trend will leave fewer people dependent upon Korea's limited land resources for a livelihood, while the potential for raising output and incomes per farm worker will increase as the land-labor ratio rises. Farm mechanization and further capital-labor substitution will become more profitable as farm wage rates increase. Farming will become more commercialized as a larger share of production is marketed and farmers increase purchases of production inputs.

Production Prospects

The agricultural sector is expected to increase by 4.7 percent annually during 1972–81 compared with 4.4 percent during 1962–72. The growth rate of forestry and fisheries is expected to come down during 1972–81, and therefore crop and livestock output will need to grow at a slightly higher rate than in 1962–72 to achieve the projected targets (see Table 45). The growth rate of rice, projected at 3 percent annually during 1972–81 compared with 1.5 percent during 1961–71, seems too optimistic. A World Bank survey of the agricultural sector concluded that rice production could be expected to rise 1.5 percent annually, provided irrigation and drainage are improved and advanced technology is adopted. Prospects are good for large increases in vegetables, fruits, tobacco, and mulberries as land is available to expand the area of these crops. But it will be possible to increase the total cultivated area by 2.3 percent and total crop area by 5.8 percent from 1972 to 1981 as projected only if plans to improve irrigation and drainage and cultivate additional upland are realized.

Livestock production (meat, eggs, and milk) is projected to increase about 10 percent annually during 1972–81, about twice as rapidly as during 1962–72. Breeding herds will need to increase greatly to achieve the projected number of cattle. There is considerable potential for expanding the yield of forage and pasture to increase dairy and beef production, but much larger feed-grain imports will also be required to achieve the targets for livestock output. Sericulture targets seem reasonable as land is available for growing more mulberry trees. More labor and capital investment in buildings and other facilities will be required, however, to expand cocoon and silk production.

Forest production during the next decade will depend mainly on harvesting present timber resources. The government plans to plant new forests on 2.6 million hectares and expand firewood production to meet the fuel requirements of rural families by 1981. The Forest Development Law enacted in 1973 should contribute greatly to a more effective use of about two-thirds of Korea's land area classified as forest.

Fishery production is to rise from 1.3 million tons in 1972 to 2.6 million in 1981. Fishery production in the last decade rose from 477,000 tons in 1961 to 2.0 million tons in 1974, mainly owing to the greatly expanded catch from off-shore and deep-sea fishing. Prospects for substantially exceeding these targets are thus good.

Grain Self-Sufficiency

The government places high priority on achieving self-sufficiency in rice, barley, and soybeans. Korean officials believe that rice production can be increased almost 3 percent a year by a wider use of high-yielding varieties such as IR-667, earlier planting in the northern part of the country to allow earlier harvesting and reduce frost damage, and the application of more fertilizer and pesticides. It is also believed that yields and hectarages of barley and soybeans can be increased.

It is not unrealistic to expect Korea to become self-sufficient in rice and barley if imports of wheat and feed grains increase. The survey of the agricultural sector pointed out that self-sufficiency in rice could be achieved by 1976 if production increased 1.5 percent a year and imports of other food grains continued between 2.5 and 3.0 million tons a year. Government projections indicate that wheat imports will rise from 1.9 million tons in 1972 to 2.5 million in 1976 and 2.8 million in 1981. Imports of maize for feed are expected to grow from 380,000 tons in 1972 to almost 900,000 in 1976 and over 1.1 million in 1981. Between 1968 and 1972 imports of high-protein feeds (soybean cake and fish meal) for livestock increased from 16,000 to over 60,000 tons. Imports of soybean and other vegetable oils for human consumption have also gone up greatly.

It seems more meaningful, however, to look at self-sufficiency with respect to the total grain supply. Korea imported 36 percent of its food grains in 1971 compared with 22 percent in 1963 (Table 46). Japan imported 62 percent and Taiwan 41 percent of their total grain supplies in 1971. All three countries have about the same area of cultivated land per capita and are becoming increasingly dependent upon imports for both food and feed grain. Japan and Taiwan consume much larger quantities of feed grain per capita than Korea, but Korea will depend more and more on imports to support the projected livestock production.

Table 46. Grains: Per Capita Disappearance and Share of Total Supply Imported

	Korea		Japan		Taiwan	
Category	*1963*	*1971*	*1963*	*1971*	*1963*	*1971*
Per capita disappearance (kilograms a year)						
Food grains	196	240	156	139	190	210
Feed grains	8	14	45	90	4	46
Soybeans and other pulses	10	12	31	39	20	48
Total	214	266	232	268	214	304
Share of total supply imported[a] *(percent)*						
Food grains	23	35	23	34	6	20
Feed grains	8	68	79	94	13	90
Soybeans and other pulses	—	10	79	92	73	87
Total	22	36	41	62	13	41
Share of wheat in total food-grain supply	21	26	26	36	12	20

— Not applicable.

a. Total supply is production plus net imports.

Source: Computed from Food and Agriculture Organization Yearbooks on *Agricultural Production* and *Agricultural Trade.*

Foreign Trade

Exports of crop and livestock products are projected to rise from $77 million in 1972 to about $250 million in 1981 with large increases for silk, canned food, pork, and other meats (see Table 47). These targets appear feasible in view of the potential for expanding livestock production and sericulture. Imports of agricultural products are also expected to rise. Food- and feed-grain imports totaled about $325 million in 1971 and could reach over $500 million by 1981 as more feed imports are needed to support a larger livestock industry. Imports of raw sugar, cotton, and other products not produced in Korea will also rise with the growth of incomes and population. Consequently Korea's trade deficit in agricultural products is likely to increase.

The gross value of fishery exports increased from $44 million in 1965 to $187 million in 1972 and is projected to go over $1 billion in 1981. The prospect of greatly increasing the fishery output is good, but it may be difficult to achieve the export target.

Development of Land and Water Resources

The official long-range projections propose a 2.3 percent increase in total cultivated area during 1972–81. Paddy area is to expand 2.5 percent and cultivated upland 2 percent. In the last dec-

Table 47. Exports of Agricultural Products
(*million U.S. dollars*)

Product	1965	1972	1976	1981
Canned food	—	9	26	55
Fruits	—	2	2	4
Grain products	5	3	8	23
Pork	—	6	25	53
Other meat	—	2	6	14
Silk	8	52	63	87
Swine hair	1	1	1	1
Vegetables, processed	—	—	1	2
Other	1	3	5	9
Total agriculture	15	78	137	248
Fishery products[a]	42	187	633	1,020

—Not applicable.
a. Gross value of exports before deducting the cost of servicing fishing fleets abroad.

ade, however, there has been little change in total cultivated area because new land brought under cultivation was offset by the appropriation of agricultural land for urban-industrial use. Land will continue to be taken from crop production as industry is decentralized; it will therefore be difficult to increase the total cultivated area as projected.

Irrigated paddies are projected to increase by 170,000 hectares and cultivated upland by 31,000 hectares, but investment costs for irrigation systems and the development of upland are high. Feasibility studies of large-scale irrigation projects and watershed development in upland areas are being carried out to decide what investments will be economic in the future. The adjusted 1972–76 plan called for large investments for land and water resource development, but these were reduced and spread over the 1972–81 period in the new long-range projections. It is planned to consolidate 588,000 hectares, about half the total paddy area, to provide better irrigation, drainage, and flood control and facilitate access to fields and farm mechanization. Almost 200,000 hectares were consolidated by the end of 1972, but in view of the high cost there is need to review investment plans for land consolidation. Ways must be found to reduce the cost of irrigation and drainage structures and the most economic kinds of improvements determined.

Korea's increased emphasis on comprehensive planning for land and water use is commendable, including its plans for the development of forestry in highly elevated areas and pasture on the slopes. The projected decrease in the total farm labor force makes it especially important to avoid investment for land and water development in upland areas that may later become submarginal with a labor shift to nonfarm activities.

Farm Mechanization and Labor Productivity

The government targets for farm mechanization have been revised upward. During peak periods in the spring and autumn the usual labor shortages become more acute, and demand for power machinery and equipment is expected to increase greatly. Cash wages of hired farm workers have increased at the rate of 20 percent a year since 1965 and are likely to rise further.

The plan provides for the number of power tillers to jump from 25,000 in 1972 to 167,000 in 1976 and 350,000 in 1981, that is one

tiller for every 15 farm households and 15 hectares under cultivation in 1976 and one for every 8 farm households and 8 hectares
under cultivation by 1981. The use of power sprayers, threshers,
grain driers, and irrigation pumps will also be increased considerably. Seed-bed preparation is to be mechanized for 1.1 million
hectares (over half the total cultivated area) by 1976 and for almost all cultivated land by 1981. Total investment costs of mechanization programs during 1973–76 are estimated at $200
million with an import component of $160 million. The pro-
jected growth of farm mechanization will be much more rapid
than in Taiwan but not as fast as in Japan during the late 1940s
and early 1950s—Japan had one power tiller for every two farm
households and two hectares of arable land in 1967.

Although farm mechanization should move ahead rapidly,
more economic analysis is required to support the projected large
increase in the number of farm machines. Planting and harvesting
operations for grain production are difficult to mechanize, and
much hand labor will still be necessary. Land consolidation will
help make the use of power machinery profitable on Korea's
many small fields, but it is estimated that less than half the total
paddy area is suitable for consolidation.

With increased mechanization agricultural output per worker
is expected to increase 65 percent or almost 6 percent a year
during 1972–81. This growth will depend heavily upon diversification of crops and the expansion of livestock production to utilize
farm labor during slack periods of the year. It might be difficult to
achieve the projected increases in crop production, however, if the
agricultural labor force declines by 8 percent as projected for
1972–81.

Investment Projections and Priorities

The government has revised its investment projections in agriculture only marginally to W836 billion from W807 billion in its
original five-year plan for 1972–76 (see Table 48), but a substantial increase of nearly one-third is projected for the next plan
period. Investment outlays for agriculture, forestry, and fishery
projected for 1973–81 account for 10.5 percent of total investments.

Agriculture's parity price ratio was increased from 94 percent
in 1968 to 104 percent in 1971 (1965 = 100) as prices of farm
products were increased while those of fertilizer and other inputs
were kept almost stable under government programs. There is

Table 48. Investment Projections for Agriculture, Forestry, and Fisheries
(*billion won at 1970 prices*)

Item	Original five-year plan 1972-76	Long-term framework		
		1972-76	*1977-81*	*1972-81*
Agriculture	553.4	548.9	741.2	1,290.1
Forestry	54.0	42.3	48.5	90.8
Fisheries	130.9	134.0	261.5	395.5
Rural electrification	52.9	58.7	16.9	75.6
Rural hospitals	16.1	52.2	30.6	82.8
Total	807.3	836.1	1,098.7	1,934.8

Source: Economic Planning Board, September 1973.

economic justification for maintaining prices of import-substitution commodities (rice, barley, wheat, soybeans, corn) at levels above the nominal exchange rate of imports. Since manufactured exports receive government assistance in various forms, including interest subsidies, tariff concessions on imported materials, and internal tax exemptions, reasonable protection for agricultural imports appears desirable. Furthermore the international prices of thinly traded commodities such as rice do not necessarily represent equilibrium levels.[2]

A rise in the price ratio has different effects on net farm income, depending on how the ratio is increased. Because only a small share of total farm receipts goes for production expenses, an increase in the ratio achieved by reducing the price of inputs would not increase net farm income as much as would raising the price of farm products.

Prices paid by farmers for fertilizer and pesticides are lower relative to those received for rice and other crops in Korea than in most other countries. For example, farmers could purchase a kilogram of fertilizer with only 0.7 kilogram of rice in Korea in 1971 compared with 1.2 to 1.4 kilograms in Taiwan, the Philippines, and Pakistan. This ratio was lower in Japan than in Korea, however.

Questions arise as to the economic merit of even lower crop-fertilizer price ratios. Farmers use about as much fertilizer for a hectare of cultivated land in Korea as in Taiwan and much more than in the Philippines and Pakistan but not as much as in Japan.

2. Only a small proportion of the world production of thinly traded commodities appears on the international market.

Projections call for the amount of fertilizer used to increase by 43 percent during 1972–81. Low prices may encourage the increased use of fertilizer, but it is doubtful whether Korean farmers will find it profitable to apply as much fertilizer per hectare as in Japan where irrigation, drainage, and flood-control facilities are highly developed and additional applications of fertilizer are likely to produce a higher yield. Moreover, it may be more beneficial to the national economy to reduce damage from diseases and insects by a greater use of pesticides than to increase sharply the use of fertilizer.

In view of the changing economic conditions affecting agriculture and rural development, high priority should be given to investments in the following areas:

Marketing. There is need to upgrade and modernize facilities for marketing farm products and distributing production inputs as farming becomes more commercialized, as farms decrease in number and increase in size, and as the nonfarm population rises from 55 percent of the total in 1972 to the 70 percent projected for 1981.

Farm mechanization. Current credit programs provide only inadequate help for financing the purchase of a relatively small number of farm machines. Although, as mentioned above, it remains to be determined whether the projected large increase in power machinery is justified, farmers would undoubtedly be able to utilize effectively more machines than those supplied under existing programs.

Livestock and sericulture. Korea has the land and labor resources to achieve the large output targets set for livestock and sericulture, but more credit facilities will be necessary.

Fisheries. Korea has exceeded output targets set in the past and can continue to do so in the future if the necessary capital is made available.

Forestry. Prospects are good for a substantial expansion of firewood production within the next five or six years and a large increase of timber supplies over the long term.

Land and water development. Investments for these purposes may yield high returns, especially if combined with comprehensive regional projects for expanding forestry, pasture, and forage production for livestock in upland areas in addition to a more intensive use of lowland areas for crop production. Studies of irrigation and regional development projects currently under way should help determine the pattern of future investments.

Long-term Employment Projections

THE KOREAN GOVERNMENT'S long-term macroeconomic projections assume that the population growth will decline from the current rate of around 1.7 to 1.8 percent a year to an average of 1.5 percent in the 1972–76 period and further down to around 1.3 percent during 1977–81. This target seems to be overoptimistic; the government's earlier target for 1981 had been a growth rate of 1.5 percent. Korea's current age structure would indicate a further increase in the number of females of reproductive age (15–49) during the seventies, reflecting the baby boom of the years following the Korean War. Officials in the Ministry of Health and Social Affairs predict a temporary rise in the growth rate of the population during the late seventies up to around 1.8 percent or even higher unless measures to limit the size of families are considerably intensified. The population growth rate during the 1970s will not affect estimates of the labor force for the time span of Korea's current long-term framework or indeed up to 1985.

An important aspect of Korea's demographic trends has been a significant change in the age structure of the population (see Table A1). The proportion of the population below 14 years of age has begun to decline in recent years as a result of a drop in the birth rate. The crude birth rate fell from 4 percent in 1962 to 3.49 percent in 1966 and further down to 2.8 percent in 1970. Consequently in 1972 only 37 percent of the total population was below 14 years as compared with 41 percent in 1966. The reduction of the growth rate to 1.3 percent envisaged by 1981 implies a more rapid decline of the age group below 14 years to only 28.5 percent

Table A1. Population and Age Distribution, 1966–81

Year	Total	Below 14	Percent	14 and over	Percent
1966	29,193	12,025	41.2	17,168	58.8
1970	31,435	12,512	39.8	18,923	60.2
1972	32,359	11,958	37.0	20,401	63.0
1976	34,345	11,156	32.5	23,189	67.5
1981	36,709	10,480	28.5	26,229	71.5
Annual rate of growth					
1966–72	1.80		−0.10		2.90
1972–76	1.50		−1.75		3.25
1976–81	1.30		−1.25		2.49
1972–81	1.41		−1.48		2.86

Source: Census figures for 1966 and 1970; for 1972, 1976, and 1981 new Economic Planning Board estimates based on the last census figures (1.3 percent population growth variant for 1976–81).

of the total. In contrast the population 14 years and over would grow at a more rapid rate of 3.25 percent during 1972–76 and then at around 2.5 percent a year during 1977–81. There would thus be 5.8 million more people in 1981 who are 14 years and over than in 1972.

Employment estimates in the 1972–81 long-range plan which are based on the quarterly Employment Sample Survey show sizable discrepancies from the forecasts of the working-age population based on past census figures. The discrepancies, summarized in Table A2, indicate that the population aged 14 years and over was underestimated in the survey data for 1972. Furthermore the annual growth rate of this population group for 1972–76 was projected at 3.0 percent on the basis of survey data, which is below the 3.25 percent rate indicated by the census figures. After 1976 the projections based on survey data show a much larger growth than do the forecasts based on the census figures and their age pyramids, and therefore the difference in the two series is reduced. Still the projections based on census data show nearly a million more persons 14 years and over in 1981 than was assumed in the long-term framework.

If the survey data estimate the economically active population by and large correctly, they indicate a level and trend in participation rates which are difficult to reconcile with the rapid growth in school enrollments (Table A2). During 1967–72 school attendance of those 14 years and over rose by 12.3 percent a year owing to the government promotion of vocational schools as well as growing incomes, especially among the urban middle classes.

Table A2. Availability of Labor Force, 1966–81
(thousands)

Item	1966	1972	1976	1981	Rate of growth (percent)		
					1966–72	1972–76	1976–81
Population 14 years and over							
Employment Survey data excluding armed forces and prisoners	16,840	18,764	21,126	24,402	1.82	3.00	2.85
Census figures adjusted for armed forces and prisoners[a]	16,391	19,586	22,345	25,353	2.90	3.25	2.49
Difference	−459	+822	+1,229	+951			
Economically active population	9,325	10,507	11,761	13,763	2.00	2.90	3.20
Participation rate							
Survey data	55.4	56.0	55.7	56.4			
Census figures	56.9	53.6	52.6	54.3			
Unemployment rate (official)	7.4	4.5	4.0	3.0			

a. Based on the 600,000-man strength of the armed forces in 1970. Prison population at the level of 1970 is assumed to grow at the same rate as overall adult population.

153

More recently the increase in rural incomes also added to the number of young people continuing education after 14 years of age. Korean parents have always been particularly eager to provide the best possible education for their children, and this desire has been further encouraged by rising incomes and increasing job opportunities for women with greater educational background. Female school attendance increased by 14 percent a year during 1967–72. Official estimates of school attendance during the long-term plan are not available, but our estimates (see Table A3) assume a continuing rapid increase during 1972–76 in line with the government's stepped-up technical and vocational training program. The growth rates should decline during 1976–81 but will still be higher (4.2 percent a year) than the estimated overall growth rate of population 14 years and over (2.5 percent). School attendance in 1981 will on this basis be 41 percent of the inactive population compared with only 24 percent in 1970.

The above suggests that the relatively stable participation rates of 55.5 to 56.0 implied by survey data during 1966–76 are probably overstated. In contrast, the generally higher census population figures indicate a relatively sharp drop in participation rates from 56.9 percent in 1966 to 52.6 percent in 1976, which appears more reasonable. An increase in the participation rate to 54.3 percent[1] by 1981 is, however, projected in the census figures, which seems consistent with the expected slowdown in growth in school attendance. On the basis of higher population estimates and a small net increase in the participation rate between 1972 and 1981, we estimate that over 3.5 million additional jobs would have to be created during 1973–81 in order to reduce the unemployment rate to 3 percent by 1981. This compares with the official estimate of over 3.3 million jobs.

By 1981 the Korean plan foresees a drastic change in sectoral employment (see Table A4). Agricultural employment will decline from 51 percent in 1972 to 35 percent in 1981; the shares of the secondary and tertiary sectors will increase from 14 and 35 percent to 23 and 42 percent respectively. In absolute terms 1.6 million more jobs will be created in industry and mining and

1. Japan's overall participation rate was around 70 percent during the fifties and early sixties and then declined to 65 percent by 1970. Taiwan's current overall participation rate is around 60 percent. Male participation rates in Japan and Taiwan are considerably above Korea's, and Japan's female participation rates have traditionally been high.

Table A3. Economically Active Population and School Attendance

Item	Average annual growth rate		
	1967–72	1972–76[a]	1976–81[a]
Economically active population	2.0	2.9	3.2
Economically inactive population	1.5	3.2	2.6
School attendance	12.3	8.2	4.2
Male	11.0	7.1	4.2
Female	14.1	9.7	4.2
School attendance (thousand persons)	1970	1972	1976[a]	1981[a]
14 years and over	1,888	2,593	3,559	4,362
Male	1,116	1,485	1,957	2,399
Female	772	1,108	1,602	1,963
Percent of economically inactive population	23.8	31.4	38.0	41.0

a. Estimates.

over 2 million jobs in the services sector, while agriculture is forecast to release around 400,000 workers to the other sectors.

Table A5 shows that the official forecasts assume hardly any change in the overall employment-income elasticities. The expected decline in agricultural employment makes the coefficients for the primary sector negative. Despite an 8 percent decline in the labor force during 1973–81 the gross value added in agriculture is projected to grow at around 4.7 percent a year as compared

Table A4. Trends in Employment
(thousand persons)

Sector	1972		Change		1981	
	Status	Percent	1972–76	1976–81	Status	Percent
Agriculture, forestry, and fisheries	5,078	50.6	−186	−218	4,674	35.0
Mining and manufacturing	1,423	14.2	+696	+899	3,088	23.1
Services	3,525	35.2	+768	+1,300	5,593	41.9
Total employment	10,026	100.0	+1,278	+2,051	13,355	100.0

Table A5. Employment, Gross Value Added, and Employment-Income Elasticities

	Annual percent growth			
Item	1963–67	1967–72	1972–76	1976–81
Employment				
All industries	2.9	2.4	3.1	3.3
Agriculture	−0.5	−0.6	−0.08	−0.1
Mining and manufacturing	13.4	4.6	9.1	7.9
Services	6.3	4.3	3.5	5.5
Gross value added[a]				
All industries	8.7	10.3	9.5	11.0
Agriculture	4.5	3.7	4.8	4.7
Mining and manufacturing	15.6	18.9	16.6	16.4
Services	9.8	10.7	7.5	9.1
Employment-income elasticities				
All industries	0.330	0.300	0.326	0.300
Agriculture	−0.111	−0.170	−0.017	−0.021
Mining and manufacturing	0.860	0.240	0.548	0.482
Services	0.643	0.404	0.467	0.604
Labor productivity				
All industries		7.8	6.4	7.7
Agriculture		3.1	4.9	4.8
Mining and manufacturing		14.3	7.5	8.5
Services		6.4	4.0	3.6

a. GNP at 1970 prices by employed persons.
Source: Economic Planning Board.

with 3.5 percent during 1961–71. As discussed in Chapter 6, this is an ambitious goal since it will require labor productivity to increase by over 65 percent during the period of the long-term plan. For secondary industries the employment and GNP share targets seem more realistic. A fairly rapid annual growth in employment during 1972–76 (9.1 percent), slightly lower during 1976–81 (7.9 percent), would generate growth of around 16.5 percent a year in the gross value added during the long-term plan. This appears to be in line with the planned rapid expansion and diversification of Korean industry and the deepening of its structure. The strong emphasis on heavy industries is not inconsistent with this since the program also provides for the substantial expansion of labor-intensive subsectors such as shipbuilding and machinery as well as further expansion of light industries such as textiles, garments, and electronics. A factor adversely affecting the employment target, however, may be that, with wages rising more quickly than in the past, employers may tend to increase investment in labor-saving capital equipment.

In the services sector the official long-term projections imply a substantial increase in employment during 1976–81. The reduction in agricultural employment is apparently to be absorbed here. The employment-income elasticity shows a sharp increase over the preceding period (1967–72 and 1972–76) almost approaching the 1963–67 level. This would indicate a much higher increase in labor-intensive low-productivity services during 1976–81 than in the preceding periods, which seems unlikely in view of the expected sustained rise in real wages. As explained elsewhere, however, the expected decline in agricultural employment may have been overstated.

In summary, the government's overall employment targets are acceptable, although the 3 percent unemployment rate by 1981 is considered optimistic since it is based on population statistics that are understated.

The Sae Maeul Movement

THE SAE MAEUL (NEW COMMUNITY) movement was initiated in late 1971 by President Park as a nationwide, comprehensive self-help program to improve the standard of living in the rural areas. The program is in line with the government's determination to arrest the growth rate of Korea's metropolitan centers by discouraging the rate of migration to the cities. Coordinated by the Ministry of Home Affairs, the Sae Maeul movement has three main objectives: "spiritual enlightenment," the modernization of thinking and social patterns in the villages; physical and environmental improvement; and increased productivity and incomes, principally by the creation of more nonagricultural jobs in the rural areas. The latter objective conforms with the government's plan to disperse industrial locations in Korea, which includes tax incentives to induce new enterprises to locate in rural areas, and tax penalties on new plants in metropolitan centers.

Due to the evolving nature of the Sae Maeul movement and its emphasis on decentralized decisionmaking, small-scale projects, and self-help, it is difficult to determine exactly the total investment in and the physical achievements of the movement. Available data are summarized in Tables B1 and B2. According to official figures, a total of W275 billion (approximately $567 million) was invested in Sae Maeul projects during 1971–74 with W133 million in 1974 alone. Only 22 percent of the total investment was provided from government budgets, with the remaining 78 percent contributed by the villagers, mainly in volunteer labor which totaled 215 million man-days.

Table B1. Physical Achievements of the Sae Maeul Movement, 1971–74

Sector	Up to 1971	1972	1973	1974	Total
Rural roads (kilometers)					
Village roads	6,046	12,000	10,842	5,361	34,249
Farm feeder roads	27,200	7,351	5,367	39,918	79,836
Rural housing					
Roof improvements (thousand buildings)	. . .	413	477	400	1,290
Housing units (number)	. . .	. . .	4,407	3,043	7,450
Water supply systems (number of villages)	235	2,640	2,556	4,556	9,988
Public facilities (number of villages)					
Village halls	13,494	4,452	5,135	1,545	24,626
Public bathhouses	2,111	2,063	1,390	351	5,915
Public laundries	24,129	9,035	14,049	4,984	52,197
Agricultural infrastructure (number of projects)					
Irrigation facilities	. . .	4,102	5,393	9,416	18,911
Public warehouses	. . .	1,699	1,601	5,946	9,246
Public compost pits	51,793	3,097	1,522	3,590	60,002
Common-use barns	. . .	757	162	405	1,324
Other					
Reforestation (hectares)	231,159	. . .	12,385	39,855	283,399
Nursery stocks (million trees)	. . .	. . .	86	203	289
Rural electrification (thousand households)	849	164	308	177	1,497

. . . Zero or negligible.

The Sae Maeul villages go through three stages. After the movement is initiated with the government's moral and financial support, the village is officially designated a Basic Village. In the second stage the village undertakes Sae Maeul projects with government support. Villages in stage three are called "self-reliant" or "independent," that is, most or all of the improvements are implemented, incomes have been significantly raised, and some degree of financial viability has been reached. The government's

Table B2. Gross Investment under the Sae Maeul Movement, 1971–74
(*billion won*)

Source	1971	1972	1973	1974	Total
Government support					
All programs	4.1	4.4	21.5	30.8	59.7
Environmental improvement	4.1	3.3	4.8	4.8	17.0
Contribution by villages[a]					
Total	8.1	28.0	76.9	102.0	215.0
Environmental improvement	8.1	28.0	36.3	25.6	98.0
Total	12.2	31.3	98.4	132.8	274.7
Environmental improvement	12.2	31.3	41.1	30.4	115.0

a. Includes loans and voluntary labor contributions.

target is to have all of Korea's 35,000 villages in the third stage by 1981. The actual and projected numbers of Sae Maeul villages are shown below:

	Actual		Projected	
Stage	1973	1974	1976	1981
Basic	18,415	10,665	. . .	. . .
Self-help	13,943	20,000	20,165	. . .
Independent	2,307	4,000	14,500	34,665
Total	34,665	34,665	34,665	34,665

The Sae Maeul village elects a leader, as well as a woman to handle affairs relevant to females. The administrative village headman is appointed by the provincial government, but his responsibilities regarding the Sae Maeul movement have not yet been spelled out. The role of women in village life has been enlarged by their activities within Sae Maeul proper and indirectly affected by the availability of cash-earning jobs in Sae Maeul industries and related services, which has brought women, especially among the younger generation, greater financial independence from their families. All these factors are bound to bring about fundamental changes in traditional village society.

Each Sae Maeul village will draw up, under the guidance of the provincial and/or county (*gun*) government, a five-year plan which will at a later stage be coordinated with the plans of other villages. Because the planning as well as the implementation of large projects such as water supply, sewerage, and feeder roads are beyond the scope of an individual village, the government encourages cooperation among Sae Maeul villages on the *gun* or sub-*gun* level.

Another important change will be the greater financial independence of the villages themselves. Income derived from revenue-yielding Sae Maeul projects such as reforestation will be distributed in equal shares to the villagers who participated in the projects and to a village fund for reinvestment in other modernization and improvements. Self-reliant villages in stage three are planned to have their own banks (in effect credit unions), established in accordance with the 1972 Credit Union Law. These banks will be entrusted with the village funds so that the villagers will learn to manage their own financial affairs. This may also contribute to the grass-roots acceptance of cooperatives by the farmers. The cooperative movement has no tradition in Korea and has to a certain degree been superimposed on the local level under the guidance of the National Agricultural Cooperative Federation (NACF) and following U.S. and Western European patterns.

NACF has in the past dominated institutional credit at the village level, and its future relationship with the village banks has apparently not yet been defined. It is noteworthy, in this context, that the recently announced campaign to mobilize rural savings of about W1,000 billion by 1980 does not, at least in the preliminary blueprint, provide for the involvement of village banks. The program is to be administered by NACF, although the drive for rural savings has all the features of a genuine grass-roots campaign.

The Sae Maeul movement includes the following major programs:

Roof improvement program. By 1976 virtually all 2,075,000 farm houses should have replaced their traditional straw-thatched roofs with tile or tin. The government provides the materials free for this self-help program.

General village improvement. This includes improving and widening village lanes, clearing and rearranging village streams, constructing public laundry and bathing facilities, and village compost piling stations. Methane tank heating systems that use compost as fuel are to be installed in the southern provinces.

Construction and improvement of rural roads. The road network in rural areas is to be expanded from 32,400 kilometers in

1972 to 58,200 kilometers in 1981. This program is to improve connections between villages and the national network of main roads.

Sanitary water supply. By 1981 all villages should have a sanitary water supply system in comparison with only 7 percent in 1972. The water systems are to be managed by village cooperatives.

Reclamation of idle land. Sae Maeul projects will play an important role in implementing the upland development program to expand forests, pastures, and the production of forage for livestock. Responsibility for reforestation and forest management has therefore been transferred to the Ministry of Home Affairs. The target is to reforest almost one million hectares of farm area by 1981. This would provide virtually all rural villages with adequate supplies of firewood. Cooperative efforts to plant and harvest firewood and timber should increase the incomes of farmers and villages. Saplings for reforestation are provided free by the government.

Rural electrification. In 1972 only 40 percent of rural households had access to electricity. With the crash program planned by the Korea Electric Company of 300,000 hookups a year, 2.53 million households will be connected by 1977. This will leave only 300,000 households which for geographical reasons will not be connected with electric power.

Communications. Telecommunication facilities will be extended to almost 20,000 villages (almost 60 percent by 1981, compared with less than 5,000 in 1972).

Medical facilities. Medical facilities in rural areas are poor. At present there are no public hospitals outside the cities and towns, and only 12 percent of the country's medical doctors work in rural areas. The target is to have small clinics in each of the 140 *guns* by 1976, in addition to 46 provincial hospitals and 9 large provincial medical centers headed by the National Medical Center in Seoul. On the village level, infirmaries are to be established. The rural clinics will also coordinate family-planning programs. Moreover, the 1973 National Service Law provides that young doctors must spend at least two years in a rural area before getting a license to practice in a city.

Sae Maeul industries. The aims of this important program are to raise off-farm cash incomes of rural households, utilize seasonally idle rural labor, facilitate specialization of rural industries, and encourage linkages between rural and urban production lines.

The Sae Maeul factories will also make a sizable contribution to exports as shown below:

Targets	1973	1974	1975	1976	Total 1973–76
Number of plants to be established	170	200	200	200	770
Employment creation (thousands)	34	62	74	86	256
Exports (million U.S. dollars)	23	185	342	550	1,100

By mid-1973, 85 factories employing a total of 12,000 workers had been established. Employment ranged from 50 to 700 employees a plant, wages were between W12,000 and W27,000 a month, and most of the jobs provided were for female labor.

Emphasis is on labor-intensive industries that can take advantage of seasonal underemployment in the rural areas. Sae Maeul industries will produce textiles, garments, footwear, handicrafts, and toys; electrical and electronics factories are also planned. Some Sae Maeul plants will be located in towns outside the large metropolitan centers and will provide employment for the adjacent rural areas. The government supports the program by providing eight-year investment loans and three-year operational loans (both at interest of 8 percent a year) to enterprises establishing Sae Maeul factories. They are also exempt from local property tax until 1976 and eligible for a 50 percent deduction for four years thereafter. Land as well as power and water facilities are being provided; the *gun* governments will recommend workers for the factories, but vocational training is to be provided by the enterprises themselves.

The Textile Industry

KOREA'S MOST IMPORTANT INDUSTRY, textiles in 1973 contributed 15.2 percent of manufacturing value added, 18 percent of employment, and 43.2 percent of exports. The extent of the growth may be gauged from the following: value added increased nearly six-fold from W25.9 billion in 1962 to W152.6 billion in 1973; employment tripled from 100,000 to over 300,000; and exports increased from $8 million in 1962 to $1.3 billion in 1973. The increase in output was accompanied by a substantial improvement in the structure of the industry, particularly through strong forward linkages with the production of garments and knit goods and backward linkages with synthetic fibers.

The first major change took place in the composition and source of the raw materials. Because of their cheapness and durability, synthetic fibers and fabrics have expanded far more rapidly than cotton, and the proportion of cotton in total fiber consumption dropped from 75 percent in 1960 to about 45 percent in 1973. Concurrently the production capacity of synthetic fibers increased remarkably from 37 tons a day in 1967 to 314 tons in 1973 and 510 tons a day in August 1974.[1] An additional 200 tons a day was expected to come on stream in 1975. Production of synthetics in 1973 totaled about 122,000 tons or 60 percent of the total industry requirement of 204,000 tons. This development goes a long way toward assuring the industry a stable supply of raw materials. (See Tables C1 and C2.)

1. All tons are metric.

Table C1. Production of Yarns
(*metric tons*)

Year	Cotton	Woolen and worsted	Raw silk	Spun rayon	Synthetic
1969	89,926	5,201	2,075	2,709	10,957
1970	98,804	5,108	2,027	2,983	34,875
1971	108,671	3,476	2,319	2,657	76,051
1972	108,274	4,088	3,012	3,148	93,398
1973	140,000	6,114	3,531	2,411	121,640

Source: Ministry of Commerce and Industry.

Table C2. Production of Fabrics
(*million meters*)

Fabric	1970	Percent	1971	Percent	1972	Percent	1973	Percent
Cotton	78.8	26	93.7	26	153.5	32	225.0	31
Embroidered	6.8	2	8.9	3	13.6	3	23.2	3
Rayon	95.9	31	75.3	21	94.5	20	124.8	18
Silk	12.6	4	14.3	4	20.4	4	26.2	4
Synthetic	109.9	36	153.4	43	185.5	39	306.6	43
Woolen	2.8	1	8.2	2	9.5	2	16.4	2
Total	306.8	100	353.8	100	477.0	100	709.4	100

Table C3. Structure of the Textile Industry, 1972
(*percent*)

Section of industry	Gross output	Value added	Number of workers
Cotton textiles	17.0	17.8	13.3
Knitting	15.2	13.9	19.2
Man-made fiber textiles	19.7	19.0	17.0
Woolen and worsted textiles	5.0	4.9	4.6
Other	43.7	44.4	45.9
Total	100.0	100.0	100.0

Source: Report on Mining and Manufacturing Survey, 1972.

The second major structural change was a shift toward more labor-intensive activities such as garments and knitting. The output of wearing apparel increased fourfold from 1970 to 1973 (while that of textile fabrics and yarn only doubled) and now accounts for half the value added and 65 percent of employment in the industry. Similarly, exports of apparel and knit goods more than tripled from $214 million in 1970 to about $750 million in 1973, equivalent to 60 percent of total textile exports and 26 percent of total manufactured exports. (See Tables C3 and C4.)

The share of small and medium firms declined markedly to only 28 percent of the industry's output compared with 56 percent in 1965. The fact that this has happened with only a negligible decline in the number of firms tends to indicate that a large part of the overall expansion is attributable to the organic growth of firms. Despite this growth, however, over 75 percent of the firms have less than 50 employees. Most of the larger firms are concentrated in the primary section of the industry such as spinning and fiber production, where economies of scale are important, and to a lesser extent in weaving. They are equipped with up-to-date machinery, have access to technical know-how from their foreign collaborators, and have developed their own export marketing organizations. An increasing number of these firms are developing into large integrated operations that range from spinning to manufacturing apparel. As might be expected, the small and medium firms concentrate either in garments and knitting, where economies of scale are not important, or in weaving.

Cotton Textiles

Production of cotton yarn increased by 50 percent from 95,000 tons in 1969 to 140,000 in 1973, but cotton fabrics increased by only 30 percent from 203 million meters to 265 million over the same period because a larger portion of the cotton yarn is used in blends. Domestic demand for cotton yarn and cloth has continued to decline in both absolute and relative terms as a result of the increased attractiveness of synthetic fibers. But the slack was more than taken up by a substantial increase in exports from 57.8 million meters in 1969 to 228 million meters in 1973; exports now account for 66 percent of the total output of yarn and 92 percent of cotton cloth. Among the many reasons for this development are the rising international demand for cotton fabric, contraction of the Japanese industry, improved competitiveness of

Table C4. Textile Exports
(metric tons and thousand U.S. dollars)

STTC[a]	Commodity	1969 Quantity	1969 Amount	1970 Quantity	1970 Amount	1971 Quantity	1971 Amount	1972 Quantity	1972 Amount	1973 Quantity	1973 Amount
26	Textile fibers	3,966	27,090	7,415	42,575	5,804	44,575	9,221	62,452	11,298	93,255
261.3	Raw silk	1,721	23,951	2,020	35,061	2,246	38,700	2,543	52,956	2,170	72,844
651.3–4	Cotton yarn	1,595	1,569	4,955	4,855	16,229	5,513	12,970	16,794	11,166	24,580
651.6	Yarn and thread of synthetic fibers	358	996	1,569	3,248	10,685	19,197	6,314	11,413	14,530	30,746
652	Cotton fabrics	18,050	18,646	22,247	26,355	24,771	31,004	22,789	34,859	33,267	56,987
653.1	Silk fabrics	65	841	122	1,091	118	1,891	220	7,576	837	83,341
653.2	Woolen fabrics	491	3,343	499	3,382	417	2,509	1,116	7,193	1,367	12,466
653.3	Linen, ramie, and true hemp fabrics	48	68	4	24	5	19	128	169	256	593
653.5	Woven fabrics of synthetic fibers	3,779	12,642	2,762	9,962	4,925	14,402	15,464	38,511	34,903	108,841
653.6	Woven fabrics of regenerated fibers	1,091	2,283	1,054	2,482	824	2,026	958	2,730	2,532	9,317
84	Clothing	29,819	160,771	34,839	213,566	50,471	304,265	50,870	430,129	122,529	749,863
26 + 65 + 84	Total	70,949	253,562	90,398	341,084	135,656	486,655	155,953	669,194	272,901	1,278,345

a. Standard International Trade Classification.
Source: Statistics of Spinners and Weavers Association of Korea.

the Korean industry following the devaluation of the won, and improved quality and productivity. (See Table C5.)

The average count of yarn increased from 23 in 1968 to 25 in 1972; indeed, most of the additional capacity is used to produce fine yarn of 40 counts and above. This improved quality was also reflected in weaving where shirting accounted for the bulk of the increase in production at the expense of jeans and sheeting. Upgrading the product has not only helped supply the expanding demand for these goods but also—and more importantly—enabled Korea to overcome the trade barriers imposed by the Long Term Agreement (LTA) on cotton textiles where quotas are expressed in quantity rather than in value.

Besides improving quality, the Korean textile industry has expanded productivity. The output of yarn per worker increased by 48 percent from 22.46 kilograms in 1968 to 33.28 kilograms in 1972. Compared with Japan's 41.52 kilograms and 48.60 kilograms in 1968 and 1972 respectively, these figures represent a 26 percent improvement in productivity in relation to Japan. The increase in productivity was offset by an 80 percent increase in wages from 1968–72. This trend was significantly reversed in 1973, however, and wage rates are now rising only maginally more rapidly—if at all—than productivity. On the whole, Korean wages are still, competitive—one-sixth of Japanese wages and 10 to 25 percent lower than Taiwan, Korea's major competitor. The combination of high productivity and low wages has enabled the industry to compete effectively in the export market, and Korea's output of cotton yarn and fabrics has expanded at the expense of most other countries.

Table C5. Supply and Demand for Cotton Yarn and Cloth
(yarn in metric tons, cloth in kilometers)

	Supply		Domestic		Export	
Year	Yarn	Cloth	Yarn	Cloth	Yarn	Cloth
1968	87,396	183,527	71,320	93,573	16,076	89,547
1969	94,723	203,725	72,778	76,690	21,944	127,034
1970	103,408	212,804	73,628	69,996	29,779	142,808
1971	114,149	223,408	59,403	52,987	54,745	170,421
1972	114,563	237,199	44,505	24,780	70,057	212,418
1973	139,944	265,328	58,632	19,120	81,312	246,207

Source: Spinners and Weavers Association of Korea.

The prospects for further growth of the cotton textile industry depend on the development of the export market. Exports were not expected to recover before the end of 1975, and although growth in 1976–81 is not expected to continue at the spectacular rate of 1972–73, prospects are still encouraging for a number of reasons. First, only a third of the total exports is fabric or yarn for which world demand is expected to grow only marginally; the balance is made up of apparel and garments for which demand is expected to grow by about 15 percent during the rest of the decade. Second, the proportion of synthetic raw material used in textiles is expected to increase from 20 percent in 1973 to 40 percent in 1981. Third, there is increasing emphasis on improving productivity and quality; the latter is particularly important if Korea is to overcome the quota restrictions imposed by the United States, the European Economic Community (EEC), and Canada, which together account for over 50 percent of textile exports. Fourth, substantial investment has recently improved the industry's structure. In 1973, 45 percent of spinning and 34 percent of weaving capacity was over 11 years old. The investment program undertaken in 1973–74 and the one envisaged for 1975 at a total cost of about $350 million should reduce both ratios to about 25 percent.

Knitting Industry

The knitting industry continues to make good progress. From 1969 to 1973 the production of jerseys increased twentyfold, gloves twofold, hosiery threefold. Total production facilities consisted of 59,100 looms in 1973, up about 90 percent from 1969. Most of the increase took place in flat knitting machines which comprise 58 percent of the total, circular knitting machines (28 percent), and hosiery knitting machines (10 percent).

Before 1965 cotton yarn constituted over 65 percent of the weight of raw material used by the knitting industry, but in subsequent years there has been a rapid shift to synthetics. In 1973 cotton yarn constituted only 25 percent of the total weight of raw materials while synthetic yarn, particularly acrylic for sweaters, gained the bulk of the difference. Most of the raw material for the export market is currently available locally at international prices.

Since 1965 exports of knit goods have increased at a rate of 70 to 90 percent annually, except for 1969–70 when the rate of increase was only 25 percent. Total exports in 1973 were valued at $417 million compared with $10 million in 1965 and $100 million in 1969. The major growth was accounted for by sweaters ($171 million) and wearing apparel ($182 million).

The prospects of the knitting industry will depend to a large extent on the growth of export demand, which has not been as fast as first expected, mostly because knit goods have not made the expected strong inroads in menswear. Prospects for the further expansion of medium- and high-quality items would be better, provided designers are trained to keep up with the fast-changing world of fashion. Korea has developed a strong manufacturing base and diversified export market, and it still has an abundant supply of skilled labor at fairly low wages (currently about $50 a month). Furthermore, new capacity can be quickly added in response to market demand.

Garment Industry

The Korean garment industry has been one of the fastest and consistently growing segments of the industry with an annual growth rate that averaged 45 percent in the past few years. Most of the output is exported, and by 1971 Korea was the largest producer and exporter of shirts in the world. The industry employs 293,000 employees in 2,275 establishments, an average of about 130 employees per establishment compared with 55 in Hong Kong and 155 in Taiwan. Although the average size of Korean firms is relatively small (300 employees a firm is usually required to support strong product design and marketing capabilities), their productivity is roughly 75 percent of European counterparts. For example, the time required to produce a long-sleeved shirt is 27 minutes in Korea compared with 20 minutes in Germany, and for short-sleeved shirts 18 minutes compared with 14 minutes. But salaries in Korea are one-sixth to one-tenth of those in Japan and Europe.

Most of the growth in export demand originated from Japan, which has replaced the United States as Korea's major trade partner in garments. There has also been a successful diversification of exports to EEC which currently imports about 30 percent of total output. The bulk of the exports is low- to medium-quality apparel purchased by large department stores and designed to their specifications. Only a small number of large firms develop and actively market their own designs.

The prospects for the further growth of exports are promising; developed countries are expected to import about 15 percent more garments each year till 1980. Korea is in an excellent position to take advantage of this growth, provided locally produced raw materials are quality and price competitive and wage rates, which account for 50 to 60 percent of value added, do not increase faster than productivity. The industry has a sound financial structure, and the investment undertaken in the last few years has increased production capacity by 70 percent. By all the indicators the garment industry should be the main center of growth in textiles. Its influence could be considerable if it improves the quality of its products and enlarges its scope to include suits and other apparel with large value added. The major weakness is in marketing, which requires much more sophisticated market research, fast feedback of fashion changes, and a more dynamic marketing strategy. The assistance of the Korean Traders' Association (KOTRA) in this respect could be particularly valuable to small and medium firms.

Synthetic Fibers

The synthetic fiber industry has developed through sequential backward integration, first by substituting fibers and filaments made from imported resins and other intermediate raw materials, followed in 1972 by domestic production of intermediates for principal synthetic fibers such as nylon acrylics and polypropylene. Production of synthetic fibers increased over sevenfold from 16,700 tons in 1968 to 122,000 tons in 1973. Until 1969 most of the output was consumed locally; in 1973 only 36 percent was used domestically and the rest (77,400 tons) was exported either directly as fibers (16,400 tons) or indirectly in fabrics and knit goods (61,000 tons). Despite this increase, local production did not keep up with the large growth of demand stimulated by exports, and during 1969–73 imports grew at a rate of 10 percent to reach 82,000 tons, of which 76,700 tons were re-exported in fabrics and goods. (See Tables C6 and C7.)

Until recently most raw materials such as caprolactam, acrylonitrate monomer (AN), dimethyl terephthalate (DMT), ethylene chloride (EC), polyvinyl acetate (PVA), powder and chemical pulp had been imported from the United States and Japan because Korea did not possess a petrochemical industry. Capro-

Synthetic Fibers

Table C6. Consumption of Synthetic Fibers
(*metric tons*)

Use	1969	1970	1971	1972	1973
"Cotton" fabrics	8,500	10,000	12,400	20,500	24,300
Mixed fabrics	19,800	21,900	22,300	24,900	34,800
Knit goods	37,100	52,100	58,500	58,400	63,700
Worsteds	14,100	18,300	23,300	35,900	52,600
Woolens	1,000	1,500	1,400	1,800	2,900
Export	400	2,000	8,300	10,000	16,400
Other	1,100	2,000	2,000	700	8,500
Total consumption	82,000	103,900	128,700	149,700	204,300
Production	33,400	53,100	74,800	97,300	121,900
Import	48,500	50,800	53,900	53,400	82,400

lactam has been mainly imported from foreign countries providing technical assistance to Korean counterparts. Imports of raw materials increased 250 percent from 39,700 tons in 1969 to 138,000 tons in 1973. The fastest growth was registered by DMT which increased more than ten times to 47,000 tons after the polyester processing facilities were enlarged. Domestic production of two important raw materials—AN in 1972 and caprolactam in 1974—began when two plants were completed at the Ulsan petrochemical complex. But total capacity for AN

Table C7. Domestic Production of Synthetic Fibers
(*metric tons*)

Type	1969	1970	1971	1972	1973
Acetate filament	1,602	1,599	1,598	1,615	1,706
Acetate tow	. . .	23	700	975	1,103
Acrylic fiber	10,476	15,813	17,801	24,255	28,349
Nylon filament	11,756	17,428	23,963	28,523	35,803
Nylon fiber	. . .	. . .	. . .	. . .	553
Polyester filament	2,633	6,329	5,914	21,019	30,951
Polyester fiber	899	3,109	3,884	7,853	9,351
Polypropylene filament	303	508	616	754	1,463
Polypropylene fiber	1,005	2,804	4,522	5,876	6,021
Polyvinyl acetate fiber	143	157	. . .	. . .	608
Viscose filament	4,624	5,315	5,809	6,479	6,035
Total	33,441	53,085	64,807	97,349	121,944

. . . Zero or negligible.
Source: Korea Chemical Fibers Association.

(27,000 tons a year) and caprolactam (33,000 tons a year) cover only about 80 percent of current demand.

The industry could not take full advantage of its large aggregate growth to develop in an efficient way because a number of firms started production simultaneously on a relatively small scale. They were probably encouraged by the large investment incentives (eight-year loans at 10 percent interest) domestic protection in the form of 50 percent tariff and quantitative restrictions, and the normal export incentives. The industry is now composed of 16 plants of which 14 produce synthetic fibers and the remaining two produce regenerated and semisynthetic fibers. Only two firms, together accounting for about 40 percent of production capacity, were of economically viable size in 1972 (about 60 tons a day for staple fiber and 40 tons a day for filament yarn). Since then the structure of the industry has somewhat improved because the rapid expansion has been concentrated in a few firms. As of July 1974 four firms were of minimum international size and accounted for about 55 percent of the total output.

The current world recession and the accompanying decline in world demand for textiles has, however, exposed some structural weaknesses in the synthetic fiber industry. First, the industry depends on a few suppliers for a substantial part of its raw materials. Some of these suppliers also control the marketing outlet for textiles and have taken advantage of their position to squeeze manufacturers between the rising cost of raw materials and the falling price of fibers and fabrics by stipulating in the export letter of credit the source of raw materials used in the fibers. Second, during the early days of import substitution when the entire output was destined for domestic consumption, the price of synthetic fibers on the domestic market was sometimes more than twice that of equivalent imports. Prices have since declined but a dual pricing system has evolved: one price for exports and another for the domestic market. Domestic prices which are subject to tax were still roughly 25 to 45 percent higher than equivalent imports. On the whole, production costs of synthetic fibers are 25 percent higher in Korea than in Japan. A comparison of the cost structure of major synthetic fibers prior to the December 1974 devaluation indicates that these high production costs can be attributed to the high cost of raw materials and other inputs, the penalty of small-scale production, and the 20 percent import duty on equipment.

The original government program calls for expansion of the industry's capacity to 1,900 tons a day by 1981 (660,000 a year) to meet domestic demand and export about 100,000 tons a year. Of the planned capacity 45 percent will be for polyester, 15 percent nylon, 15 percent acrylics, and the balance for polypropylene, viscose, acetate, and PVA. These targets would bring the capacity of the Korean industry to that of Japan in 1969 and Germany in 1972 and would require capital investment of $1.1 billion at 1974 prices. This plan, formulated prior to the recent world developments, now seems to aim somewhat high. It is estimated that from March 1974 to December 1975 world production capacity increased about 23 percent for acrylics, 36 percent for polyester, and 2 percent for nylon and rayon. This expansion comes at a time when demand has slackened not only because of the general recessionary trend but also because the rising cost of oil and construction has increased the price of synthetic fibers. Recent studies suggest that the price of acrylics and polyester staple fiber will increase by about 8 to 10 percent for every 100 percent increase in the price of crude oil from a base price of $2.50 a barrel. Accordingly an oil price of $10 a barrel will increase the cost of producing fiber by 32 to 40 percent. In addition, prices of equipment and construction increased by 50 percent in 1974 and will increase the price of synthetic fiber by roughly 15 to 20 percent because capital costs account for 30 to 40 percent of the price of synthetic fiber produced in medium-size plants. These two factors will tend to reduce the growth rate of consumption from the 20 to 30 percent experienced in the early 1970s to about 7 percent by 1980. The excess developed in world capacity in 1974–75 will thus be maintained for a few years, making it difficult for Korea to achieve plans to export synthetic fibers directly on a profitable basis.

It would therefore be advisable for Korea to postpone some of the investment planned for 1976 to allow capacity utilization to increase from its current low level of 65 percent and enable firms to digest the large investments already undertaken. The Korean government, through its investment incentives, can regulate the activities of individual firms by ensuring that rationalization of production goes hand in hand with expansion and by coordinating investments so as to synchronize supply and demand.

The Electronics Industry

T HE ELECTRONICS INDUSTRY was originally established in the late fifties to manufacture radios and other consumer goods for import substitution. The product mix was expanded in the early sixties to include communication equipment to meet local needs. Because of the limited domestic market for consumer electronics and the budgetary constraints of the telecommunication field, the industry was only moderately successful in its early stages of development, and total production in 1965 was only $10 million. In the following years electronics began to grow rapidly, however, and production increased to $462 million in 1973, an average growth rate of 60 percent a year. (See Table D1.) Over 80 percent of the production is exported. The industry has attracted over $150 million in investment and provides employment opportunities for over 80,000 Koreans.

The major factors responsible for this remarkable growth are: (a) an abundant, highly skilled, and literate labor force that works for wages about one-tenth and one-sixth of those in the United States and Japan and has attracted large foreign investments in assembly operations; (b) the government's effort in developing sound infrastructure (transportation, communication, and electric power); and (c) an aggressive and balanced government development strategy.

Structure and Performance

The response of foreign and local investors has been quite favorable. At the end of 1973 foreign investment in electronics

Table D1. Growth of Electronics Industry Production
(million U.S. dollars)

Category	1965	1966	1967	1968	1969	1970	1971	1972	1973	Average annual growth rate (percent)	
										1965–73	1970–73
Consumer goods	5.0	9.9	16.2	16.8	24.4	30.3	33.4	55.2	135.0	51	65
Industrial equipment	2.1	8.4	10.8	15.5	16.4	17.4	18.4	25.3	43.0	46	36
Components	3.5	4.5	9.8	23.8	40.0	58.4	86.2	127.0	284.0	74	70
Total	10.6	21.8	36.8	56.1	79.8	106.3	138.0	207.6	462.0	60	63

Source: Ministry of Commerce and Industry.

Table D2. Exports by Investor
(thousand U.S. dollars)

Type of firm	1969		1970		1971		1972		1973	
	Amount	Percent	Amount	Percent	Amount	Percent	Amount	Percent	Amount	Percent
Local	9,586	23	13,757	25	24,531	27	39,387	28	113,664	31
Joint venture	559	1	8,342	15	11,320	13	25,164	18	74,424	20
Foreign	31,766	76	32,865	60	52,752	60	77,582	54	181,204	49
Total	41,911	100	54,964	100	88,603	100	142,133	100	369,292	100

Source: Korea Electronic Products Exports Association.

amounted to $104 million, 60 percent in 12 fully owned foreign subsidiaries and 40 percent in 42 joint ventures. Japan accounted for over two-thirds of the total investment and the United States for 31 percent. The inflow of foreign capital and technology further stimulated the development of local suppliers of components, and the number of such firms increased from 41 in 1965 to 202 in 1973.

There is a substantial difference in size, production activities, and marketing outlets among foreign firms, joint ventures, and local operations (Table D2). Local firms are usually small-scale operations with less than 200 employees, which produce components and consumer goods—the latter under either a subcontract or U.S. and Japanese brand names—for both domestic and export markets. They account for 48 percent of the industry's output and 31 percent of exports. Foreign firms operate on a much larger scale with the number of employees ranging from several hundred to several thousand and are principally engaged in assembling electronic components. They include subsidiaries of foreign giants such as Motorola, Signetics, American Micro Systems Inc., Fairchild, Control Data, Applied Magnetics, and Toshiba. Although their share in output and export has substantially declined from the late sixties when they were the prime movers of the industry (50 percent of output and 80 percent of exports), their contribution is still substantial with 25 percent of output, 50 percent of exports, and about 22 percent of employment. Joint ventures are intermediate in size (500 employees). They were established in the early seventies in response to the special incentives provided by the Electronics Industry Promotion Law and now account for 27 percent of output, 21 percent of exports, and 26 percent of employment.

The large growth in output was accompanied by a decided shift in the share of the three major categories of electronic goods—consumer electronics, industrial equipment, and components. Because of the large foreign-owned assembly operations, the production of electronic components grew at an average annual rate of 71 percent from 1965 to 1973 compared with only 51 percent for consumer goods and 46 percent for industrial equipment. Accordingly the share of components in total output increased from 44 percent in 1965 to 62 percent in 1973 while that of consumer goods declined from 47 percent to 29 percent over the same period. (See Table D3.)

The production of electronic components amounted to $284

Table D3. Composition of the Electronics Industry
(percent)

Category	1965	1966	1967	1968	1969	1970	1971	1972	1973
Production									
Consumer goods	47.2	45.4	44.0	29.9	30.5	28.5	24.1	26.6	29.2
Industrial equipment	19.8	33.9	29.3	27.6	20.6	16.5	13.3	12.2	9.3
Components	33.0	20.7	26.7	42.5	50.1	55.0	62.6	61.2	61.5
Export									
Consumer goods	72.2	76.4	30.0	18.0	16.9	16.2	17.9	24.4	29.4
Industrial equipment	. . .	0.5	1.4	0.6	0.6	0.8	0.8	3.0	4.3
Components	22.8	23.0	68.6	81.4	82.5	83.0	81.3	72.6	66.0

. . . Zero or negligible.
Source: Ministry of Commerce and Industry.

million in 1973 of which 86 percent was exported to the United States and Japan. The assembly of semiconductor products by off-shore U.S. and Japanese firms accounted for 85 percent of the output and 85 percent of exports. The balance consisted of passive and electromagnetic devices produced by local and joint-venture firms. Despite its growth this sector contributed only $45 million to GNP because value added is extremely low (15 percent). Korea's major advantage in this field is essentially the lower wage rates of its labor force, the productivity of which is at least as high as and probably higher than Japanese and U.S. counterparts.

Production of consumer electronics, which increased from $4.5 million in 1965 to $135 million in 1973, is somewhat more integrated than assembly operations, and value added is estimated at 27 percent of output. Monochrome televisions contributed about 53 percent of total output followed by radio receivers (20 percent) and tape recorders, the fastest growing segment of consumer electronics (19 percent). With the exception of televisions, of which only 36 percent were exported, over 90 percent of consumer goods are exported to Japan and the United States. Most of the exports, however, are sold under American or Japanese brand names with very little marketing effort by Korean producers. This field is dominated by joint ventures and local firms with technological collaboration from U.S. and Japanese counterparts. The major firms include Gold Star, the largest local electronics company, with 4,500 employees and $54 million in revenues, producing a diversified product line (radios, televisions, speakers, and components); Sam Sung with 1,200 employees and $20 million in revenue (televisions and desk calculators); and Tai-

Han Electric employing 2,400 employees with a sales volume of $17 million (televisions and radios). The scale of operation of these firms is reasonable for assembly operations but too small to support a major design and marketing effort to compete effectively on an individual basis with large- or medium-size international firms.

The production of industrial equipment concentrates in the fields of telecommunication—telephone sets, telephone exchange equipment, and PABX systems ($30 million in 1973)—and assembly of electronic calculators ($14 million), although internationally calculators are classified as consumer goods, not industrial equipment as in Korea. Telecommunication equipment is produced by two local firms: Gold Star Company produces PABX and telephone exchange systems under license from Siemens AG of Germany, and Oriental Precision Company produces telephone sets and center office equipment in collaboration with Nippon Electric Company and Tamura Electric Works of Japan. The value added in this industry is in the order of 30 percent and products are of high quality. But the telephone exchange systems produced are electromechanical, a design at least 15 to 20 years old. Although still competitive for the Korean market and other developing countries, the systems cannot compete with the newer electronic type produced by major U.S. and Japanese companies such as Ericson, Siemens AG of Germany, and Nippon Electric. Switching to the new type would require sophisticated computer and electronic technologies which are far beyond Korea's financial capability and resources. Production of pocket electronic calculators, mainly an assembly operation with little value added, faces considerable difficulties because the rapid change in large-scale integrated (LSI) technology has reduced the labor content to less than 50 cents an item.

The changing pattern of output and exports in the last few years suggests some deepening in the industry's structure. The range of products has significantly expanded from integrated circuits and transistors to oscilloscopes and television sets. There is also increasing evidence that government encouragement of local firms and joint ventures is starting to bear the fruits of transferring technical and managerial know-how. The share of local firms in exports has increased from 23 percent in 1969 when the program was initiated to 31 percent in 1973, while that of joint venture firms increased from 1 to 21 percent, both at the expense of fully owned subsidiaries.

To sum up, the industry has developed considerable manufacturing capability which compares favorably with that in developed countries. But as it now stands the industry does not have a good base for sustained expansion of output and exports in a rapidly changing technological and marketing environment. By and large it is still an assembly operation with value added of only 20 percent and an import content of more than 70 percent. Its marketing capability is undeveloped because consumer goods are sold abroad under foreign brand names, and its design capability is almost nonexistent. Korea is expected to have a comparative advantage in consumer goods because of somewhat slower technological change. But the small firms in this sector will find it difficult to sustain long-range efforts in design and marketing to compete effectively with the increasingly structured and vertically integrated operations of international giants.

Furthermore, because the Korean electronics industry is labor intensive it is vulnerable to both short-term economic decline and long-term technological change. During 1974 there were dramatic reductions in personnel within the electronics assembly sector. Fairchild Semiconductor, for example, reduced its worldwide labor force from 25,500 in 1973 to 18,000 in 1974. Signetics, another major participant in semiconductor assembly in Korea, is estimated to have furloughed over half its work force. The recent progress in automated equipment for assembling integrated circuits probably signals a lesser demand for manual assemblers in the future. In contrast to conventional wire bounders that produce 100 integrated circuits an hour, the new gang-bounding equipment can assemble 5,000 an hour. A single technological change such as this would be likely to reduce personnel requirements 50 to 1.

Development Plans and Issues

The long-term plan for the electronics industry calls for $4.76 billion in production and $2.47 billion in exports by 1981 (see Table D4), which is one quarter of the country's total export target. This implies an average growth rate of 36 percent for output and 32 percent for exports for the 1973–81 period compared with 60 percent achieved in the last decade. The government estimates the total investment requirement at $1.2 billion, of which 50 percent is expected to be in foreign investment. Government and industry plan to achieve these ambitious targets through vig-

Table D4. Korean Electronics Industry Supply and Demand Projection
(*million U.S. dollars*)

Category	1975	1976	1977	1978	1979	1980	1981
Total industry							
Local consumption	844.7	1,133.3	1,500.4	1,949.8	2,492.1	3,056.1	3,553.1
Export	567.0	765.0	1,009.0	1,311.0	1,665.0	2,081.0	2,471.0
Production	914.5	1,275.0	1,739.6	2,341.0	3,083.3	3,926.4	4,760.0
Import	497.2	623.3	769.8	919.8	1,073.8	1,210.7	1,264.1
Consumer goods							
Local consumption	118.52	175.95	268.23	402.63	559.3	730.70	939.54
Export	238.14	359.55	514.59	721.05	982.35	1,311.03	1,630.86
Production	356.66	535.50	782.82	1,123.68	1,541.65	2,041.73	2,570.40
Import	. . .	. . .	. . .	. . .	. . .	. . .	. . .
Industrial equipment							
Local consumption	217.93	276.24	316.76	441.68	544.75	628.63	752.75
Export	22.68	38.25	60.54	91.77	116.55	166.48	197.68
Production	91.45	127.50	191.36	257.51	339.16	431.90	571.20
Import	149.16	186.99	230.94	275.94	322.14	363.21	379.23
Components							
Local consumption	365.67	474.29	608.38	781.90	996.29	1,237.64	1,354.39
Export	306.18	367.20	433.87	498.18	556.10	603.49	642.46
Production	448.11	561.00	695.84	866.17	1,079.16	1,295.71	1,428.00
Import	223.74	280.49	346.41	413.91	483.21	544.82	568.85

. . . Zero or negligible.

orous development programs that will restructure the Korean electronics industry by 1981 to resemble that of the Japanese as shown in the table below (the figures given are percentages):

		Components	Industrial electronics	Consumer
United States	(1973)	13	65	22
Japan	(1973)	30	33	37
Korea	(1973)	62	12	29
Korea	(1981)	34	12	54

Efforts will be concentrated on developing electronic consumer goods as a major export-oriented segment (see Table D5), backward integration into raw materials and components, and a broad technological base.

The desire to deemphasize component production, which now accounts for over two-thirds of total output, is presumably prompted by the evolving LSI technology. As evidenced by recent developments in pocket calculators, the labor-intensive assembly of components is fast being replaced by capital-intensive LSI circuits produced in vertically integrated facilities in the United States. By contrast, in the case of some consumer electronics where technology is fairly stable, manufacturing operations appear to be shifting from the United States to developing countries. The total consumption of monochrome television receivers in the United States increased by only 3.5 percent a year from 6 million sets in 1969 to 7.3 million sets in 1973, while imports showed a marked gain from 1.3 million to 5 million sets. Similar patterns

Table D5. Projected Exports of Consumer Electronics
(*thousand sets*)

Product	1975	1976	1977	1978	1979	1980	1981
Phonographs	101	180	365	690	1,132	1,800	2,250
Radios, auto	159	282	570	1,075	1,761	2,800	3,200
Radios, home	4,047	5,603	7,637	10,895	13,133	15,091	18,937
Tape recorders	1,420	1,903	2,728	4,444	6,424	9,100	11,429
Television, color	213	421	665	869	1,111	1,323	1,653
Television, monochrome	1,135	1,527	1,818	2,202	3,127	4,531	5,802

can also be observed for traditional consumer products such as radios, recorders, and phonographs. (See Table D6.)

This shift from developed to developing countries, together with the technological trends toward vertically integrated operations, confirms the soundness of the new direction and emphasis of Korea's development plan for consumer electronics. With a fairly stable technology for a large segment of consumer goods such as monochrome television and radios, Korea has only to develop a moderate capability to be able to incorporate minor improvements in these products. Domestic manufacture of components could then be geared to the needs of consumer goods manufacturers, thus increasing Korean value added in electronics output.

It must be pointed out, however, that business opportunities, promotional efforts, and resource requirements for an assembly operation would differ dramatically from those for an industry integrating product design with planning, manufacturing, and marketing. For aggressive penetration of the consumer electronics market, the growth target and plans formulated by the government and industry must be supplemented as soon as possible by a comprehensive master plan for the development of the industry. This plan should integrate market research, product strategy, diffusion of technology, marketing strategy, and resource requirements.

Although the growth forecast for Korean exports has been scaled down considerably from the spectacular rate enjoyed in the past, projections for electronics exports appear to be ambi-

Table D6. U.S. Imports and Consumption of Electronic Consumer Goods
(*thousand sets*)

Year	Monochrome television receivers		Auto radios		Phonographs	
	Imports	Consumption	Imports	Consumption	Imports	Consumption
1967	1,290	6,001	621	9,527	1,964	6,626
1968	2,043	6,996	1,814	12,510	2,129	6,495
1969	3,121	7,117	1,791	11,939	2,063	6,320
1970	3,596	6,900	2,232	10,378	2,040	5,620
1971	4,166	7,647	3,150	13,505	1,926	6,034
1972	5,056	8,239	2,924	13,162	2,451	7,207
1973	4,989	7,296	4,459	12,546	2,423	6,135

tious. The following tabulates the seven-year forecast for Korean electronics exports from 1975 to 1981 and the progress of Japanese electronics exports from 1964 through 1970 (in millions of U.S. dollars):

	1975	1976	1977	1978	1979	1980	1981
Korea	567	765	1,009	1,311	1,665	2,081	2,471

	1964	1965	1966	1967	1968	1969	1970
Japan	513	623	894	1,053	1,425	1,986	2,403

The two patterns are similar, but Japan's electronics industry had a much larger technological, production, and marketing base in 1964 than Korea's in 1975. Production in 1964 registered $2.3 billion with a high added value, highly integrated large-scale operations, substantial design capabilities, and a developed marketing network with first-class after-sales service. The Korean electronics production, in contrast, is estimated to be about $914 million with an import figure approaching $500 million in 1975, and as mentioned earlier Korean firms are still small with limited capability in design and marketing.

Marketing Development

The export targets for the electronics industry imply that Korea will have to capture from 50 to 70 percent of the increase in U.S. imports or about 30 to 50 percent of the total increment in world trade in some consumer items. The industry will obviously continue to do subcontracting work and sell its output under foreign brand names, but the large increase in exports constitutes a significant departure from previous practice. A major effort will be required to solve the serious marketing problem. It will have to include market research and product planning, as already discussed, and the development of effective distribution channels and after-sales service. One possibility mentioned earlier is to establish a trading company to market a standardized product. This would pool the resources of Korean firms and develop the critical mass required to develop strong overseas market channels and brand recognition. But such a strategy would be expensive, and the consumer electronics industry will have to weigh the cost carefully in analyzing the profitability of its marketing activities.

The Shipbuilding Industry

IN 1974 KOREA BECAME the sixteenth nation in the world with the capacity to build supertankers;[1] yet about 10 years previously the country was building only wooden fishing boats and a few small cargo vessels. Government strategy calls for several more supertanker-class shipyards, aimed at giving the country an annual shipbuilding capacity of around 5 million gross tons[2] by 1980. Projects under way include the Hyundai Shipyard at Ulsan and the Korean Shipbuilding and Engineering Company (KSEC). Hyundai, the first yard of supertanker class built in the country, has an annual shipbuilding capacity of one million gross tons. Expansion already begun will lengthen the existing dock and add a second. Investment to date is $68.7 million, and the project should cost an additional $60 million. Before Hyundai the KSEC yard in Pusan was the largest in Korea with a shipbuilding capacity of 66,000 gt a year. The company is building a new yard at Okpo on Koje Island which will have two docks for supertankers and will cost an estimated $128 million. The government was originally planning at least three additional supertanker yards

1. For some other shipbuilding countries, see Table E1.
2. There are several measures used in reporting ship tonnage. The two most commonly used in connection with merchant ships are the gross ton (gt), which gives the size of the vessel or more precisely the closed cubic space (one gross ton equals 100 cubic feet), and the deadweight ton (dwt) which gives the carrying capacity of the vessel (difference between ship displacement when fully loaded and when empty). Since ship registration and insurance are based on the gross ton, the term gross registered ton (grt) is often used in reporting gross tonnage.

**Table E1. Launchings by Major Shipbuilding Countries
of Ships 100 Gross Tons and Over**
(million gross tons)

Country	1955	1960	1965	1970	1971	1972	1973 Total	1973 Tankers
A. Japan	0.83	1.73	5.36	10.48	11.99	12.87	15.67	9.25
Sweden	0.53	0.71	1.17	1.71	1.84	1.81	2.52	1.38
Germany (Federal Republic)	0.93	1.09	1.02	1.69	1.65	1.61	1.98	0.82
Spain	0.07	0.16	0.30	0.93	0.92	1.14	1.57	1.01
France	0.33	0.59	0.48	0.96	1.11	1.13	1.13	0.65
United Kingdom	1.47	1.33	1.07	1.24	1.24	1.23	1.02	0.35
B. Norway	0.14	0.20	0.41	0.64	0.83	0.98	1.07	0.57
Denmark	0.15	0.22	0.26	0.51	0.81	0.91	0.92	0.73
Netherlands	0.40	0.57	0.23	0.46	0.82	0.76	0.90	0.74
United States	0.07	0.48	0.27	0.34	0.48	0.61	0.89	0.36
Italy	0.17	0.43	0.44	0.60	0.81	0.95	0.75	0.38
World total[a]	5.32	8.36	12.22	21.69	24.86	26.71	31.52	16.64

Note: Countries in group A neared or surpassed 1 million gross tons annual launchings in 1970. Countries in group B neared or surpassed 1 million gross tons annual launchings in 1972–73.

a. World totals do not include vessels built in the Soviet Union and the People's Republic of China.

Source: OECD, *Maritime Transport*, p. 150.

plus several medium-scale yards for cargo ships and large fishing vessels.

Recent Developments

In 1973 the first order for two supertankers was received by the Hyundai yard while it was still in the early stages of construction. The KSEC yard in Pusan received orders for six tankers of 20,000 to 30,000 dwt each. The order book of Korean shipyards increased from 360,000 gt in December 1972 to 1,300,000 gt in December 1973. As of August 1974 the Korean yards had contracted to export 1,650,000 gt valued at $709 million. Table E2 lists the export orders on hand by type and size of ship and country of registration. It is noteworthy that the list includes several orders from Japan.[3]

3. Until 1973 Italy, Japan, and Spain built no ships abroad. In 1973 Italy procured 15 percent of its newly registered 786,000 gt from Sweden. The Japanese and

Table E2. Ship Export Contracts on Hand, August 1974

Type	Size[a]	Number	Country of registration
Tankers	260,000 dwt	2	Greece
	258,000 dwt	2	United States
	258,000 dwt	4	Liberia
	229,000 dwt	2	Liberia
	227,000 dwt	2	Japan
	30,000 dwt	5	Liberia
	20,000 dwt	4	United States
Bulk carriers	18,000 dwt	5	Liberia
Cargo ships	6,130 gt	3	England
	4,000 gt	2	Liberia
	4,000 gt	2	Japan
Log carriers	4,000 gt	2	Panama
Container ships	1,600 gt	1	United States
Fishing vessels	420 gt	4	Japan
	420 gt	9	United States
	230 gt	3	Japan

a. In deadweight tons (dwt) and gross tons (gt).
Source: Ministry of Commerce and Industry, 1974.

The almost totally export-oriented character of the emerging modern shipbuilding industry in Korea may be seen from the following table, which describes the ship construction activities as of August 1974:[4]

Ship size	Domestic orders Number	Domestic orders Thousand gt	Export orders Number	Export orders Thousand gt	Total construction Number	Total construction Thousand gt
Below 1,000 gt	32	12	6	2	38	14
1,000–10,000 gt	4	4	5	18	9	22
10–30,000 gt	—	—	5	71	5	71
Above 30,000 gt	—	—	6	786	6	786
Total	36	16	22	877	58	893

the Spanish fleets acquired 4,760,000 and 516,000 gt respectively in 1973, but all were built at home (OECD, *Maritime Transport,* 1973). The supertanker order received by Korea from Japan in 1974 is possibly the first time ever that such orders were placed overseas by Japanese shipowners.

4. Ministry of Commerce and Industry, *Shipbuilding Industry in Korea,* 1974.

Thus at the end of 1974 Korea had export contracts for 1.65 million gt, 90 percent of it for tankers; 0.89 million gt were under construction, over 98 percent of it for export.

Export Market

The world merchant fleet in mid-1973 totaled 287 million gt (448 million dwt). Tankers totaled 115 million gt, 40 percent of the fleet, or 210 million dwt, 47 percent of the fleet. The tonnage under construction or on order in world shipyards as of October 1973 stood at 165 million gt, of which 110 million gt was tankers. During the twelve-month period preceding October 1973 orders for tankers increased by almost 50 million gt. In fact, the tanker tonnage then on order in world shipyards would have just about doubled the existing tanker fleet.

All long-term shipping forecasts made prior to October 1973 must be revised in the light of the upheavals in the oil trade, which in 1972 accounted for over 65 percent of the ton-miles of world seaborne trade. Prior to October 1973 projections of world tonnage by 1980 ranged from 380 million gt (the Association of West European Shipbuilders—other sources projected even lower figures) to 440 million gt (the Japan Shipbuilders' Association).[5] The shipbuilding capacity needed to meet these forecasts varies from over 30 million gt to reach the Japanese figure to under 20 million gt to reach the lower figure. Because shipbuilding capacity in 1973 was about 25 million gt and increasing each year, indications even before the oil crisis were that the world shipbuilding industry could have an overcapacity by as early as 1975 to 1976, particularly with regard to tankers. The events subsequent to October 1973 will undoubtedly change the shipping pattern and the ship demand. Not all effects are predictable, but certain developments can be expected as a result of the increase in oil prices.

Only a short time ago a strong growth of oil imports to the United States was expected to be one of the mainstays of shipping demand for the next 10 to 15 years. U.S. oil imports were projected to make up about 20 percent of world shipping demand by

5. *The Motor Ship*, vol. 54, no. 636 (London), July 1973, as reported in UNCTAD, *Review of Maritime Transport*, 1973, p. 59. The Japanese forecast would roughly obtain if the world tanker requirement grows at an average of 10 percent a year during the seventies (during 1970–73 growth averaged about 15 percent a year with the U.S. oil shipping demand more than doubling in three years), and if in 1980 the tanker tonnage comprises half the world gross tonnage.

1980 compared with only 7 percent in 1972 and 9 percent in 1973. It is now the declared intention of the U.S. government to reduce the country's dependence on imported oil through the development of indigenous oil resources (in Alaska and offshore wells), the substitution of other forms of energy (coal, nuclear, solar), and energy conservation measures. These programs will take some years to bear fruit, but their success could substantially decrease future overall growth in tanker demand.

The closing of the Suez Canal in 1966 changed the pattern of world oil movements and led to dramatic increases in tanker sizes up to 483,000 dwt. The reopening of the canal will likely have the greatest impact on transport between the Persian Gulf and Europe and, depending on the canal dues and bunker prices, could lead to the greater use of small ships. Because the canal can accommodate laden vessels of only 60,000 dwt and vessels in ballast up to 200,000 dwt, there could be a significant decline in future orders for giant tankers exceeding 200,000 dwt, and some orders already placed could be canceled. In fact one leading Japanese shipyard recently announced that for the time being it will not accept future-delivery orders for tankers exceeding 200,000 dwt.

Because Korea's shipbuilding strategy was aimed at capturing a substantial share of the world's future market for supertankers and other large vessels, these developments will require a major revision of its plans.

Domestic Market

Planning for ship export was given such high priority that building ships for the home fleet does not appear to have received much attention. During recent years the domestic demand for ships was largely satisfied by secondhand vessels procured from abroad (especially ships above 1,000 gt), as is typical of most developing countries. (See Table E3.) Prices of secondhand vessels tend to follow closely the fluctuations in the freight markets, and the strong demand conditions in 1972 and 1973 resulted in sharp increases in prices of all types of secondhand tonnages as shown below (average values in millions of U.S. dollars).[6]

---

6. Fearnley and Egers Chartering Co., Ltd., *Review*, 1973. The prices are market value estimates at existing exchange rates for a charter-free tanker in good condition, with fairly prompt delivery, and payment in cash.

Dwt	Built	1971	1972	1973
18,000	1952–53	0.8	0.7	1.9
50,000	1963–64	7.0	6.0	13.0
100,000	1967–68	16.0	13.5	30.0

Financing the purchase of secondhand vessels has become increasingly difficult not only because they are more expensive than ever before but also because the terms are more stringent than on new ships. Nevertheless the issue of whether to build or buy is a complicated one for domestic shipowners to resolve. From the national perspective of industrialization, the case for building ships at home can be reinforced by the argument that it provides opportunities for developing domestic suppliers. Ship components must satisfy higher standards of quality and reliability than their land counterparts, and shipowners usually reserve the right to designate the source of major components. Consequently, until Korean suppliers of marine parts establish their reputation it should be difficult for them to participate significantly in ship export activities. It would be possible, however, for these makers to supply machinery and parts for domestic ships because the technical demands as well as the specifications of the shipowners will presumably be less exacting.

The total tonnage registered under the Korean flag as of July 1973 was 1,104,000 gt or 1,620,000 dwt, counting only ships larger than 100 gt. The dwt/gt ratio of the fleet is 1.47.[7]

The growth of the domestic fleet appears not to have kept pace with the increased shipping demands, particularly on international runs. Available statistics suggest that Korean-flag vessels carried only about 20 percent of the international freight in 1973, down from the 25 percent level in the late sixties. This trend runs counter to the goverment's aim to build up an oceangoing fleet large enough to carry half Korea's import and export trade. In order for the Korean fleet to have carried 30 percent of the international freight in 1973, it would have required additional ton-

---

7. The dwt/gt ratio for the world fleet increased from 1.40 in 1965 to 1.56 in 1973. Tankers and bulk carriers give higher ratios. The ratio indicates cargo-carrying capacity, and its increase reflects technological advances as well as an increase in the size of ships. Larger ships require less horsepower per dwt to supply a given speed; thus the engine and bunker space and weight are reduced, and less crew space is required. These savings in space and weight lead to an increased dwt/gt ratio.

Table E3. Ship Construction, Import, and Export, 1965–72
(thousand gross tons)

Item	1965	1967	1969	1970	1971	1972
Capacity	63	88	156	187	189	190
Vessels launched	14	20	38	39	43	50
Merchant ships above 100 gt only	3	8	12	12	16	38
Ship import	61	266	233	132	195	115
Merchant ships	46	234	220	115	160	72
Fishing vessels	15	32	13	17	35	43
Ship export (million U.S. dollars)	—	0.90	4.73	3.34	4.73	8.86

— Not applicable.

Source: Ministry of Commerce and Industry; Korea Development Bank, *Industry in Korea,* 1973.

nage on the order of 0.5 million gt. To look at the question another way, if the seaborne trade were to increase to 50 million tons by 1976 (probably a conservative figure; trade volume increased from 22 million tons in 1970 to 40 million in 1973) and if the domestic fleet were to carry 30 percent of this trade, the present fleet would have to almost double in tonnage. As an emerging shipbuilding power, Korea probably has good reason to expand its merchant fleet and build more of it at home. For international runs, a doubling of the existing fleet could be an early goal. If about half this expansion is built at home, the shipbuilding program of 4–500,000 gt, say, over three years should keep the dozen or so medium-scale yards operating near full capacity, provide the opportunity for these yards to become more competitive through mergers and modernization of facilities, and enable the marine supplier sector to develop.

Statistical Appendix

Table SA1. Total Population Trends and Projections, 1960–81

Year	Population[a] (millions)	Annual growth (percent)	Crude birth rate (percent)	Crude death rate (percent)	Density (per square kilometer)
1960	24.95	2.96	n.a.	n.a.	253.5
1961	25.50	2.96	n.a.	n.a.	259.0
1962	26.23	2.88	4.00	1.05	266.5
1963	26.99	2.72	3.93	1.02	274.2
1964	27.68	2.45	3.85	0.99	281.2
1965	28.33	2.28	3.74	0.96	287.8
1966[b]	29.16	2.12	3.49	0.93	296.1
1967	29.54	2.08	3.36	0.89	300.0
1968	30.17	2.01	3.16	0.87	306.4
1969	30.74	1.85	2.93	0.83	312.1
1970[b]	31.44	1.77	2.80	0.80	319.2
1971	31.83	1.69	n.a.	n.a.	323.2
1972	32.36	1.67	n.a.	n.a.	328.6
1973	32.91	1.68	n.a.	n.a.	333.2
1974	33.46	1.67	n.a.	n.a.	339.8

Projected rates of population growth

1975	1976	1977	1978	1979	1980	1981
1.5	1.5	1.4	1.4	1.3	1.3	1.3

n.a.: Not available.
a. Revised estimates on the basis of the results of the 1970 census. Annual figures are estimates as of July 1. Net emigration is not taken into account in population estimates from 1971 onward; thus the annual increase in 1972 is identical with national growth.
b. Census figures excluding foreigners.
Source: Economic Planning Board (EPB).

Table SA2. Selected Economic Indicators, 1962–74

Item	1962	1963	1964	1965	1966
Population					
1. Midyear population (millions)	26.23	26.99	27.68	28.33	28.96
2. Growth rate (percent)	2.9	2.7	2.5	2.3	2.2
National income					
3. GNP (billion won at 1970 prices)	1,220.98	1,328.31	1,441.99	1,529.70	1,719.18
4. Annual increase (percent)	3.1	8.8	8.6	6.1	12.4
5. Gross fixed capital formation (billion won at 1970 prices)	133.38	167.79	155.12	195.40	294.28
6. Share of GNP (percent)	10.9	12.6	10.7	12.8	17.1
7. Gross national savings (current prices)	5.48	30.49	51.94	60.50	122.45
8. Share of GNP (percent)	1.6	6.2	7.4	7.1	11.1
9. GNP per capita (current U.S. dollars)[b]	87	98	102	106	126
10. Growth rate of per capita GNP (constant 1970 prices)	0.2	5.8	5.6	3.3	9.6
Sector composition of GNP (percent)[a]					
11. Agriculture, forestry, and fisheries	36.6	42.2	45.9	38.4	35.4
12. Annual increase (constant 1970 prices)	−5.8	8.1	15.5	−1.9	10.8
13. Mining and manufacturing	16.5	16.6	17.6	19.8	20.1
14. Annual increase (constant 1970 prices)	14.1	15.7	6.9	18.7	15.6
15. Other sectors' annual increase (constant 1970 prices)	8.9	7.4	3.0	9.9	12.6
Employment (millions)					
16. Population 14 years and over	n.a.	15.1	15.5	15.9	16.4
17. Labor force	n.a.	8.3	8.4	8.9	9.1
18. Persons employed	n.a.	7.7	7.8	8.2	8.4
19. Unemployment rate	n.a.	8.2	7.7	7.4	7.1

n.a.: Not available.

a. Current prices, except as noted.

b. The GNP per capita figures here are derived by converting the GNP in current prices in billion won to U.S. dollars at the official exchange rate. The estimates differ from those in the main text which are derived by the World Bank's uniform system of using several years' average of relative prices and exchange rates as a base.

	1967	1968	1969	1970	1971	1972	1973	1974
1.	29.54	30.17	30.74	31.44	31.83	32.36	32.91	33.46
2.	2.0	2.0	1.9	1.8	1.7	1.7	1.7	1.7
3.	1,853.01	2,087.12	2,400.49	2,589.26	2,826.82	3,026.63	3,522.72	3,825.50
4.	7.8	12.6	15.0	7.9	9.2	7.0	16.5	8.2
5.	358.63	498.30	639.23	650.20	680.63	659.14	851.89	939.07
6.	19.3	23.9	26.6	25.1	24.1	21.8	24.2	24.6
7.	151.81	218.32	365.18	423.20	458.27	577.31	1,089.77	1,302.88
8.	12.0	13.7	17.5	16.3	14.5	15.0	22.1	19.2
9.	143	168	208	242	275	304	376	501
10.	5.3	10.1	13.9	6.0	7.4	5.4	14.4	6.8
11.	31.4	28.5	28.7	28.0	28.9	28.3	26.0	25.3
12.	−5.0	2.4	12.5	−0.9	3.3	1.7	5.5	5.6
13.	20.4	21.8	21.9	22.8	22.8	24.4	27.1	29.0
14.	21.6	24.8	19.9	18.2	16.9	15.0	30.4	17.0
15.	13.8	15.4	14.6	8.9	8.9	5.8	14.7	4.9
16.	16.7	17.2	17.6	18.3	19.0	19.7	20.4	21.2
17.	9.3	9.6	9.9	10.2	10.5	11.1	11.6	12.1
18.	8.7	9.2	9.4	9.7	10.1	10.6	11.1	11.6
19.	6.2	5.1	4.8	4.5	4.5	4.5	4.0	4.1

(Table continued next page.)

Table SA2 *(continued)*

Item	1962	1963	1964	1965	1966
Public finance (billion won)[c]					
20. Current revenue	39.5	45.5	54.7	74.2	113.9
21. Current expenditure	48.7	52.4	59.2	70.4	102.8
22. Capital expenditure	31.0	26.2	28.6	35.7	63.6
23. Net borrowing	0.5	5.1	5.0	−1.5	8.1
24. Tax revenue as percent of GNP	10.8	8.9	7.3	8.6	10.8
Money and Credit (billion won)					
25. Money supply	39.4	41.9	48.9	65.6	85.1
26. Quasi money	12.3	13.5	14.7	31.5	71.9
Domestic credit (outstanding at end of period):					
27. To the public sector				14.9	11.7
28. To the private sector				85.1	118.8
Prices (1970=100)					
29. Wholesale price index	38.4	46.3	62.8	68.5	74.6
30. Rate of increase	9.4	20.6	34.6	10.0	8.9
31. Seoul consumer price index	32.9	39.7	51.4	58.4	65.4
32. Rate of increase	6.5	20.7	29.5	13.6	12.0
33. Terms of trade (1967–69=100)	87.6	82.8	83.4	85.0	95.2
34. Exchange rate (won per U.S. dollar)	130.0	130.0	256.5	272.6	271.5
External account (million U.S. dollars)					
35. Exports of goods and services	163.2	175.5	211.0	289.8	454.7
36. Imports of goods and services	455.2	578.3	432.0	488.4	777.7
37. Deficit on goods and services	−292.0	−402.8	−221.0	−198.6	−323.0

c. General government sector.

	1967	1968	1969	1970	1971	1972	1973	1974
20.	162.8	254.9	327.0	433.5	514.8	618.3	608.8	939.6
21.	136.7	184.8	244.2	315.7	397.4	493.6	474.9	714.4
22.	77.7	123.2	186.3	170.0	203.0	311.9	176.8	258.3
23.	14.4	6.0	21.0	4.1	11.5	81.1	42.8	33.1
24.	12.1	14.4	15.1	15.4	15.6	13.5	13.2	15.1
25.	123.0	177.9	252.0	307.6	358.0	519.4	730.3	945.7
26.	130.9	258.8	452.6	590.2	726.9	932.4	1,243.3	1,489.6
27.	11.5	−2.0	22.3	−52.8	−66.7	16.2	40.6	121.3
28.	221.0	431.7	706.3	919.4	1,201.2	1,463.0	1,899.8	2,862.5
29.	79.4	85.8	91.6	100.0	108.5	123.8	132.4	188.2
30.	6.4	8.1	6.8	9.1	8.6	14.0	6.9	42.1
31.	72.5	80.6	88.7	100.0	112.3	125.6	129.5	160.1
32.	10.9	11.2	10.0	12.7	12.3	11.8	3.1	23.6
33.	98.5	102.7	98.8	100.3	97.5	98.9	93.9	76.4
34.	274.6	281.5	304.5	316.7	373.9	398.9	397.5	404.0
35.	642.9	880.3	1,150.7	1,379.0	1,616.0	2,226.8	4,120.2	5,352.9
36.	1,060.0	1,546.7	1,945.1	2,181.7	2,634.1	2,767.8	4,619.6	7,598.0
37.	−417.1	−666.4	−794.4	−802.7	−1,018.1	−541.0	−499.6	−2,245.1

Table SA3. Expenditure on Gross National Product, 1965–74, at Current Market Prices

Item	1965	1966	1967	1968	1969	1970	1971	1972	1973	1974
Billion won										
Private consumption	668.80	805.18	985.97	1,204.44	1,493.65	1,884.25	2,337.32	2,844.45	3,359.55	4,734.33
General goverment consumption	76.02	104.82	132.17	175.28	222.69	281.81	355.96	438.24	479.35	741.90
Gross domestic fixed capital formation	119.17	208.69	272.96	411.66	552.94	650.20	729.72	780.23	1,169.43	1,754.95
Increase in stocks	2.81	15.79	8.01	16.21	67.76	54.46	75.63	25.25	122.86	370.93
Exports of goods and nonfactor services	68.61	106.81	144.61	209.30	287.81	381.23	514.21	813.81	1,577.72	2,071.19
Less imports of goods and nonfactor services	127.79	207.82	279.42	416.81	541.86	642.44	865.95	1,013.52	1,739.64	2,923.28
Statistical discrepancy	−9.95	−14.40	−16.30	−25.22	−26.50	−32.15	6.92	−13.14	−3.60	94.72
Expenditure on GDP	797.67	1,019.07	1,248.00	1,574.86	2,056.49	2,577.36	3,153.81	3,875.32	4,965.67	6,844.74
Net factor income from the rest of the world	7.65	13.38	21.95	23.18	25.03	11.90	−2.26	−15.32	−37.00	−65.63
Expenditure on GNP	805.32	1,032.45	1,269.95	1,598.04	2,081.52	2,589.26	3,151.55	3,860.00	4,928.67	6,779.11
Less indirect taxes	47.13	72.31	98.66	147.71	196.90	252.12	297.94	342.83	440.23	689.85
Plus subsidies	0.07	0.02	0.01	0.47	0.06	0.74	1.53	1.41	17.43	184.89
Less provisions for the consumption of fixed capital	45.91	58.50	75.80	101.73	128.37	160.15	192.20	276.71	409.35	600.49
National income at factor cost	712.35	901.66	1,095.50	1,349.07	1,756.31	2,777.73	2,662.94	3,241.87	4,096.52	5,673.66
Composition (percent)										
Private consumption expenditure	83.1	78.0	77.7	75.4	71.8	72.8	74.2	73.7	68.2	69.8
General government consumption	9.4	10.2	10.4	11.0	10.7	10.9	11.3	11.3	9.7	10.9
Gross domestic fixed capital formation	14.8	20.2	21.5	25.8	26.6	25.1	23.2	20.2	23.3	25.9
Increase in stocks	0.3	1.5	0.6	1.0	3.2	2.1	2.4	0.7	2.5	5.5
Exports of goods and nonfactor services	8.5	10.3	11.4	13.1	13.8	14.7	16.3	21.1	32.0	30.6
Less imports of goods and nonfactor services	15.9	20.1	22.0	26.1	26.0	24.8	27.5	26.3	35.3	43.1
Statistical discrepancy	−1.2	−1.4	−1.3	−1.6	−1.3	−1.2	0.2	−0.3	−0.1	1.4
Expenditure on GDP	99.0	98.7	98.3	98.6	98.8	99.6	100.1	100.4	100.7	101.0
Net factor income from the rest of the world	1.0	1.3	1.7	1.4	1.2	0.4	−0.1	−0.4	−0.7	−1.0
Expenditure on GNP	100.0	100.0	100.0	100.0	100.0	100.0	100.0	100.0	100.0	100.0
Less indirect taxes	5.9	7.0	7.7	9.2	9.4	9.7	9.4	8.9	8.9	10.2
Plus subsidies	0.0	0.0	0.0	0.0	0.0	0.0	0.0	0.0	0.0	2.7
Less provisions for the consumption of fixed capital	5.7	5.7	6.0	6.4	6.2	6.2	6.1	7.1	8.3	8.8
National income at factor cost	88.4	87.3	86.3	84.4	84.4	84.1	84.5	84.0	83.1	83.7

Source: Bank of Korea.

Table SA4. Expenditure on Gross National Product, 1965–74, at Constant 1970 Market Prices

Item	1965	1966	1967	1968	1969	1970	1971	1972	1973	1974
Billion won										
Private consumption	1,201.12	1,282.37	1,396.87	1,545.55	1,705.63	1,884.25	2,080.12	2,226.03	2,415.82	2,547.34
General government consumption	181.56	200.30	218.08	240.62	264.17	281.81	311.90	325.55	336.60	387.11
Gross domestic fixed capital formation	195.40	294.28	358.63	498.30	639.23	650.20	680.63	659.14	851.89	939.07
Increase in stocks	1.86	23.21	9.69	10.75	74.84	54.46	68.18	8.79	69.78	162.55
Exports of goods and services	80.29	122.28	165.99	235.03	310.07	381.23	459.35	643.34	1,034.29	1,010.74
Less imports of goods and services	149.55	237.92	320.73	468.04	583.77	642.44	773.55	801.23	1,087.04	1,123.55
Statistical discrepancy	10.08	19.35	−0.71	−1.12	−36.64	−32.15	2.21	−25.88	−71.91	−64.96
Expenditure on GDP	1,520.76	1,703.87	1,827.82	2,061.09	2,373.53	2,577.36	2,828.84	3,035.74	3,549.43	3,858.30
Net factor income from rest of the world	8.94	15.31	25.19	26.03	26.96	11.90	−2.02	−12.11	−26.71	−32.80
Expenditure on GNP	1,529.70	1,719.18	1,853.01	2,087.12	2,400.49	2,589.82	2,826.82	3,023.63	3,522.72	3,825.50
Composition (percent)										
Private consumption	78.5	74.6	75.4	74.1	71.1	72.8	73.6	73.6	68.6	66.6
General government consumption	11.9	11.7	11.8	11.5	11.0	10.9	11.0	10.8	9.6	10.1
Gross domestic fixed capital formation	12.8	17.1	19.4	23.9	26.6	25.1	24.1	21.8	24.2	24.6
Increase in stocks	0.1	1.3	0.5	0.5	3.1	2.1	2.4	0.3	2.0	4.3
Export of goods and services	5.2	7.1	9.0	11.3	12.9	14.7	16.3	21.3	29.4	26.4
Less imports of goods and services	9.8	13.8	17.3	22.4	24.3	24.8	27.4	26.5	30.9	29.4
Statistical discrepancy	0.7	1.1	—	−0.1	−1.5	−1.2	0.1	−0.9	−2.0	−1.7
Expenditure on GDP	99.4	99.1	98.6	98.8	98.9	99.5	100.1	100.4	100.8	100.9
Net factor income from rest of the world	0.6	0.9	1.4	1.2	1.1	0.5	−0.1	−0.4	−0.8	−0.9
Expenditure on GNP	100.0	100.0	100.0	100.0	100.0	100.0	100.0	100.0	100.0	100.0

Source: Based on Table SA3.

Table SA5. Industrial Origin of Gross National Product, 1965–74, at Current Market Prices
(billion won)

Sector	1965	1966	1967	1968	1969	1970	1971	1972	1973	1974
Agriculture, forestry, and fisheries	309.12	365.15	399.26	455.18	597.46	724.59	910.74	1,094.62	1,280.15	1,717.69
Fisheries	13.62	16.66	24.03	29.87	34.68	46.43	61.39	70.35	122.95	126.18
Mining and manufacturing	158.65	207.39	259.82	347.97	454.40	590.74	719.25	940.92	1,338.25	1,962.78
Mining and quarrying	14.77	16.45	20.65	20.49	23.69	30.73	34.18	37.93	48.13	71.19
Manufacturing	143.88	190.94	239.17	327.48	430.71	560.01	685.07	902.99	1,290.12	1,891.59
Other sectors	337.55	459.91	610.87	794.89	1,029.66	1,273.93	1,521.56	1,824.46	2,310.27	3,098.64
Gross national product	805.32	1,032.45	1,269.95	1,598.04	2,081.52	2,589.26	3,151.55	3,860.00	4,928.67	6,779.11
Breakdown of other sectors										
Banking, insurance, and real estate	12.75	16.81	21.47	30.54	41.19	56.93	74.63	86.54	108.34	164.77
Construction	27.64	37.94	49.48	78.79	121.00	150.20	166.85	179.11	237.67	303.37
Electricity, water, and sanitary services	10.26	14.13	17.82	23.49	32.46	45.00	52.48	76.23	85.42	75.68
Electricity and gas	9.18	12.81	15.94	20.53	28.13	39.45	44.84	62.45	70.06	55.81
Ownership of dwellings	27.99	33.42	43.72	49.55	55.17	62.87	73.52	83.52	95.28	125.85
Public administration and defense	39.94	53.84	67.15	85.64	107.28	138.07	168.02	199.46	214.36	289.36
Rest of the world	7.65	13.38	21.95	23.18	25.03	11.90	−2.26	−15.32	−37.00	−65.63
Services	59.04	78.93	106.42	145.04	179.40	230.69	285.19	343.94	401.82	556.90
Education	15.81	23.69	31.81	49.55	56.10	77.93	95.14	120.83	138.51	200.66
Transport, storage, and communication	32.14	50.73	71.92	100.27	124.24	149.66	181.35	223.05	299.18	390.27
Transport and storage	27.00	40.32	59.53	82.89	106.62	123.46	150.11	184.25	252.43	321.46
Wholesale and retail trade	120.14	160.73	210.94	258.39	343.89	428.61	521.78	647.93	905.20	1,258.07

Source: Bank of Korea.

Table SA6. Industrial Origin of Gross National Product, 1965–74, at 1970 Constant Market Prices
(billion won)

Sector	1965	1966	1967	1968	1969	1970	1971	1972	1973	1974
Agriculture, forestry, and fisheries	602.65	667.91	634.78	650.08	731.48	724.59	748.46	760.93	802.95	847.56
Fisheries	27.97	30.87	35.22	39.70	41.72	46.43	55.81	72.91	95.74	115.50
Mining and manufacturing	237.46	274.62	334.02	416.70	499.59	590.74	690.42	794.00	1,035.60	1,212.09
Mining and quarrying	24.11	24.75	27.25	27.03	26.56	30.73	31.21	31.21	36.85	38.97
Manufacturing	213.35	249.87	306.77	389.67	473.03	560.01	659.21	762.79	998.75	1,173.12
Other sectors	689.59	776.65	884.21	1,020.34	1,169.42	1,273.93	1,387.94	1,468.70	1,684.17	1,765.85
Gross national product	1,529.70	1,719.18	1,853.01	2,087.12	2,400.49	2,589.26	2,826.82	3,023.63	3,522.72	3,825.50
Breakdown of other sectors										
Banking, insurance, and real estate	31.72	33.75	37.29	44.01	48.70	56.93	63.98	66.07	70.23	77.43
Construction	50.73	63.71	72.30	102.63	143.61	150.20	150.59	148.47	180.72	182.27
Electricity, water, and sanitary services	15.03	17.66	23.09	28.45	36.98	45.00	52.02	57.91	70.48	79.87
Electricity and gas	12.93	15.63	20.12	24.91	32.56	39.45	45.60	51.59	63.85	72.54
Ownership of dwellings	50.97	52.15	54.24	56.83	59.74	62.87	66.05	69.60	73.89	79.92
Public administration and defense	105.26	112.48	119.56	125.61	131.45	138.07	143.38	141.88	142.83	146.02
Rest of the world	8.94	15.31	25.19	26.03	26.96	11.90	-2.02	-12.11	-26.71	-32.80
Services	153.98	165.92	181.10	196.35	212.42	230.69	250.86	261.60	282.64	289.68
Education	56.36	61.16	64.15	68.39	72.70	77.93	83.00	87.28	91.90	96.38
Transport, storage, and communication	63.93	74.74	90.62	112.57	132.75	149.66	165.21	183.28	232.02	247.27
Transport and storage	52.69	62.02	75.54	93.64	110.46	123.46	135.52	148.13	190.12	197.19
Wholesale and retail trade	209.03	240.93	280.82	327.86	376.81	428.61	497.87	552.00	658.07	696.19

Source: Bank of Korea.

203

Table SA7. Industrial Share of Gross National Product, 1965–74

(percent)

Sector	1965	1966	1967	1968	1969	1970	1971	1972	1973	1974
At current market prices										
Agriculture, forestry, and fisheries	38.4	35.4	31.4	28.5	28.7	28.0	28.9	28.3	26.0	25.3
Fisheries	1.7	1.6	1.9	1.9	1.7	1.8	1.9	1.8	2.5	1.9
Mining and manufacturing	19.7	20.1	20.5	21.8	21.8	22.8	22.8	24.4	27.1	29.0
Mining and quarrying	1.8	1.6	1.6	1.3	1.1	1.2	1.1	1.0	1.0	1.0
Manufacturing	17.9	18.5	18.8	20.5	20.7	21.6	21.7	23.4	26.2	27.9
Other sectors	41.9	44.5	48.1	49.7	49.5	49.2	48.3	47.3	46.9	45.7
Gross national product	100.0	100.0	100.0	100.0	100.0	100.0	100.0	100.0	100.0	100.0
Breakdown of other sectors										
Banking, insurance, and real estate	1.6	1.6	1.7	1.9	2.0	2.2	2.4	2.2	2.2	2.4
Construction	3.4	3.7	3.9	4.9	5.8	5.8	5.3	4.6	4.8	4.5
Electricity, water, and sanitary services	1.3	1.4	1.4	1.5	1.6	1.7	1.7	2.0	1.7	1.1
Electricity and gas	1.1	1.2	1.3	1.3	1.4	1.5	1.4	1.6	1.4	0.8
Ownership of dwellings	3.5	3.2	3.4	3.1	2.7	2.4	2.3	2.2	1.9	1.9
Public administration and defense	5.0	5.2	5.3	5.4	5.2	5.3	5.3	5.2	4.3	4.3
Rest of the world	0.9	1.3	1.7	1.5	1.2	0.5	-0.1	-0.4	-0.7	-1.0
Services	7.3	7.6	8.4	9.1	8.6	8.9	9.0	8.9	8.1	8.2
Education	2.0	2.3	2.5	3.1	2.7	3.0	3.0	3.1	2.8	3.0
Transport, storage, and communication	4.0	4.9	5.7	6.3	6.0	5.8	5.8	5.8	6.1	5.8
Transport and storage	3.4	3.9	4.7	5.2	5.1	4.8	4.8	4.8	5.1	4.7
Wholesale and retail trade	14.9	15.6	16.6	16.2	16.5	16.6	16.6	16.8	18.4	18.6

At 1970 constant market prices

Agriculture, forestry and fisheries	39.4	38.9	34.3	31.1	30.5	28.0	26.5	25.2	22.8	22.2
Fisheries	1.8	1.8	1.9	1.9	1.7	1.8	2.0	2.4	2.7	3.0
Mining and manufacturing	15.5	16.0	18.0	20.0	20.8	22.8	24.4	26.2	29.4	31.7
Mining and quarrying	1.6	1.4	1.5	1.3	1.1	1.2	1.1	1.0	1.0	1.0
Manufacturing	13.9	14.5	16.6	18.7	19.7	21.6	23.3	25.2	28.4	30.7
Other sectors	45.1	45.2	47.7	48.9	48.7	49.2	49.1	48.6	47.8	46.1
Gross national product	100.0	100.0	100.0	100.0	100.0	100.0	100.0	100.0	100.0	100.0
Breakdown of other sectors										
Banking, insurance, and real estate	2.1	2.0	2.0	2.1	2.0	2.2	2.3	2.2	2.0	2.0
Construction	3.3	3.7	3.9	4.9	6.0	5.8	5.3	4.9	5.1	4.8
Electricity, water, and sanitary services	1.0	1.0	1.2	1.4	1.5	1.7	1.8	1.9	2.0	2.1
Electricity and gas	0.8	0.9	1.1	1.2	1.4	1.5	1.6	1.7	1.8	1.9
Ownership of dwellings	3.3	3.0	2.9	2.7	2.5	2.4	2.3	2.3	2.1	2.1
Public administration and defense	6.9	6.5	6.5	6.0	5.5	5.3	5.1	4.7	4.1	3.8
Rest of the world	0.6	0.9	1.4	1.2	1.1	0.5	-0.1	-0.4	-0.8	-0.9
Services	10.1	9.7	9.8	9.4	8.8	8.9	8.9	8.6	8.0	7.6
Education	3.7	3.6	3.5	3.3	3.0	3.0	2.9	2.9	2.6	2.5
Transport, storage, and communication	4.2	4.3	4.9	5.4	5.5	5.8	5.8	6.1	6.6	6.4
Transport and storage	3.4	3.6	4.1	4.5	4.6	4.8	4.8	4.9	5.4	5.2
Wholesale and retail trade	13.7	14.0	15.2	15.7	15.7	16.6	17.6	18.3	18.7	18.2

Source: Based on Tables SA5 and SA6.

Table SA8. Aggregate Distribution of the National Income, 1965–74
(billion won)

Item	1965	1966	1967	1968	1969	1970	1971	1972	1973	1974
National income	712.35	901.66	1,095.50	1,349.07	1,756.31	2,177.73	2,662.94	3,241.87	4,096.52	5,673.66
Compensation of employees	220.18	295.15	401.10	511.35	678.10	850.30	1,037.96	1,258.32	1,523.28	2,090.24
Income from unincorporated enterprises	373.25	448.80	482.39	557.33	748.25	905.35	1,155.71	1,415.87	1,841.30	2,641.92
Agriculture	248.05	291.23	302.36	343.23	457.02	556.88	718.60	869.76	966.47	1,331.19
Income from property	77.17	106.03	142.78	184.09	234.10	292.99	325.92	369.93	483.29	647.72
Rent	39.53	46.78	62.43	72.44	89.00	102.85	121.28	140.31	175.82	220.58
Interest	32.81	50.99	72.53	97.03	126.20	160.40	174.44	194.01	209.55	313.13
Dividends	4.83	8.26	7.82	14.62	18.90	29.74	30.20	35.61	97.92	114.01
Corporate transfer payments	2.66	2.63	4.97	5.61	6.85	9.14	10.16	17.84	23.46	41.74
Saving of corporation	20.71	23.60	29.78	30.31	32.44	35.85	36.28	67.40	136.46	84.80
Direct taxes on corporations	6.26	11.99	16.51	24.81	33.44	42.70	57.06	55.48	52.42	115.42
General government income from property and entrepreneurship	17.19	20.44	25.73	45.16	36.56	58.76	59.87	76.03	53.25	74.15
Less: Interest on public debt	0.73	1.07	1.18	1.81	3.67	4.80	6.74	7.75	4.61	5.17
Less: Interest on consumer's debt	4.34	5.91	6.58	7.78	9.76	12.56	13.28	11.25	12.33	17.16
Gross national product (current market prices)	805.32	1,032.45	1,269.95	1,598.04	2,081.52	2,589.26	3,151.55	3,860.00	4,928.67	6,779.11

Source: Bank of Korea.

Table SA9. Percentage Distribution of the National Income, 1965–74
(percent)

Item	1965	1966	1967	1968	1969	1970	1971	1972	1973	1974
National income	88.5	87.3	86.3	84.4	84.4	84.1	84.5	83.9	83.1	83.7
Compensation of employees	27.3	28.6	31.6	32.0	32.6	32.8	32.9	32.5	30.9	30.8
Income from unincorporated enterprises	46.3	43.5	38.0	34.9	35.9	35.0	36.7	37.4	37.4	39.0
Agriculture	30.8	28.2	23.8	21.5	22.0	21.5	22.8	22.5	19.6	19.6
Income from property	9.6	10.3	11.2	11.5	11.2	11.3	10.3	9.5	9.8	9.6
Rent	4.9	4.5	4.9	4.5	4.3	4.0	3.8	3.6	3.6	3.3
Interest	4.1	4.9	5.7	6.1	6.1	6.2	5.4	4.9	4.3	4.6
Dividends	0.6	0.8	0.6	0.9	0.9	1.1	1.0	0.8	2.0	1.7
Corporate transfer payments	0.3	0.3	0.4	0.4	0.3	0.4	0.3	0.4	0.5	0.6
Saving of corporation	2.6	2.3	2.3	1.9	1.6	1.4	1.2	1.2	2.8	1.3
Direct taxes on corporations	0.8	1.2	1.3	1.6	1.6	1.6	1.8	1.4	1.1	1.7
General government income from property and entrepreneurship	2.1	2.0	2.0	2.8	1.8	2.3	1.9	1.8	1.1	1.1
Less: Interest on the public debt	0.1	0.1	0.1	0.1	0.2	0.2	0.2	0.2	0.1	0.1
Less: Interest on consumers' debt	0.5	0.6	0.5	0.5	0.5	0.5	0.4	0.3	0.3	0.3
Gross national product (current market prices)	100.0	100.0	100.0	100.0	100.0	100.0	100.0	100.0	100.0	100.0

Source: Based on Table SA8.

Table SA10. Gross Domestic Fixed Capital Formation, 1965–74: Amount by Sector
(billion won)

Sector	1965	1966	1967	1968
At current market prices				
1. Agriculture, forestry, and fisheries	13.7	24.8	23.3	30.7
2. Banking, insurance, and real estate	0.5	1.0	0.9	3.7
3. Construction	1.8	2.5	2.6	11.9
4. Electricity, water, and sanitary services	7.1	10.5	22.1	43.6
5. Manufacturing	31.7	66.0	71.0	98.6
6. Mining and quarrying	1.5	2.1	2.5	4.2
7. Ownership of dwellings	13.9	21.2	28.1	48.7
8. Public administration	2.0	2.5	5.3	10.5
9. Services	15.2	18.3	27.1	35.9
10. Transport, storage, and communication	24.1	52.1	78.0	106.5
11. Wholesale and retail trade	7.8	7.8	12.0	17.6
12. Fixed capital formation	119.2	208.7	273.0	411.7
13. Increase in stocks	2.8	15.8	8.0	16.2
14. Total	122.0	224.5	281.0	427.9
At constant 1970 prices				
15. Agriculture, forestry, and fisheries	23.7	35.1	31.5	35.3
16. Banking, insurance, and real estate	0.7	1.3	1.1	4.4
17. Construction	3.0	3.5	3.3	13.5
18. Electricity, water, and sanitary services	11.4	15.7	30.6	55.1
19. Manufacturing	48.8	83.2	82.6	111.0
20. Mining and quarrying	2.3	3.2	3.5	4.9
21. Ownership of dwellings	26.5	35.6	42.1	67.0
22. Public administration	3.3	3.7	7.2	12.7
23. Services	24.8	26.7	36.0	43.0
24. Transport, storage, and communication	37.1	74.6	105.0	131.2
25. Wholesale and retail trade	13.8	11.9	15.9	20.3
26. Fixed capital formation	195.4	294.3	358.6	498.3
27. Increase in stocks	1.9	23.2	9.7	10.8
28. Total	197.3	317.5	368.3	509.1

Source: Bank of Korea, *Economic Statistics Yearbook,* 1973; EPB answers to World Bank questionnaire.

	1969	1970	1971	1972	1973	1974
1.	35.0	52.4	59.6	85.0	100.4	189.8
2.	5.1	6.6	5.3	5.1	7.7	13.0
3.	12.4	7.9	10.3	10.8	21.6	16.9
4.	64.6	73.9	62.8	45.2	53.0	111.2
5.	114.0	128.7	143.4	155.7	338.9	390.0
6.	3.8	3.5	5.5	5.4	8.4	16.6
7.	55.4	87.9	101.1	104.7	157.9	299.3
8.	10.7	13.1	22.7	25.5	23.8	27.8
9.	55.7	70.2	79.3	71.9	110.5	138.6
10.	165.7	167.5	193.3	234.2	299.6	469.0
11.	30.6	38.6	46.5	36.9	47.6	82.8
12.	552.9	650.2	729.7	780.2	1,169.4	1,755.0
13.	67.8	54.5	75.6	25.3	122.9	370.9
14.	620.7	704.7	805.4	805.5	1,292.3	2,125.9
15.	39.9	52.4	55.8	72.0	75.5	98.4
16.	5.7	6.6	4.9	4.3	5.9	7.7
17.	13.5	7.9	9.3	8.6	13.9	8.1
18.	77.3	73.9	60.0	39.7	40.9	63.9
19.	125.9	128.7	132.0	129.2	238.5	194.6
20.	4.2	3.5	5.0	4.3	5.6	7.7
21.	71.5	87.9	96.1	89.5	120.5	171.2
22.	12.9	13.1	21.3	21.9	18.2	15.5
23.	63.5	70.2	74.6	61.8	84.6	74.1
24.	191.3	167.5	177.8	196.6	211.8	250.3
25.	33.7	38.6	44.0	31.5	36.5	47.6
26.	639.2	650.2	680.6	659.1	851.9	939.1
27.	74.8	54.5	68.2	8.8	69.8	162.5
28.	714.1	704.7	748.8	667.9	921.7	1,101.6

Table SA11. Gross Domestic Fixed Capital Formation, 1965–74:
Percentage by Sector
(*percent*)

Sector	1965	1966	1967
At current market prices			
1. Agriculture, forestry, and fisheries	11.2	11.1	8.3
2. Banking, insurance, and real estate	0.4	0.4	0.3
3. Construction	1.5	1.1	0.9
4. Electricity, water, and sanitary services	5.8	4.7	7.8
5. Manufacturing	26.0	29.4	25.3
6. Mining and quarrying	1.2	0.9	0.9
7. Ownership of dwellings	11.4	9.5	10.0
8. Public administration	1.6	1.1	1.9
9. Services	12.5	8.1	9.6
10. Transport, storage, and communication	19.7	23.2	27.8
11. Wholesale and retail trade	6.4	3.5	4.3
12. Fixed capital formation	97.7	93.0	97.1
13. Increase in stocks	2.3	7.0	2.9
14. Total	100.0	100.0	100.0
At constant 1970 prices			
15. Agriculture, forestry, and fisheries	12.0	11.0	8.6
16. Banking, insurance, and real estate	0.3	0.4	0.3
17. Construction	1.5	1.1	0.9
18. Electricity, water, and sanitary services	5.8	4.9	8.3
19. Manufacturing	24.7	26.2	22.4
20. Mining and quarrying	1.2	1.0	1.0
21. Ownership of dwellings	13.5	11.2	11.4
22. Public administration	1.7	1.2	1.9
23. Services	12.6	8.4	9.8
24. Transport, storage, and communication	18.8	23.5	28.5
25. Wholesale and retail trade	7.0	3.8	4.3
26. Fixed capital formation	99.1	92.7	97.4
27. Increase in stocks	0.9	7.3	2.6
28. Total	100.0	100.0	100.0

	1968	1969	1970	1971	1972	1973	1974
1.	7.2	5.6	7.4	7.4	10.6	7.8	8.9
2.	0.8	0.8	0.9	0.7	0.6	0.6	0.6
3.	2.8	2.0	1.1	1.3	1.3	1.7	0.8
4.	10.2	10.4	10.5	7.8	5.6	4.1	5.2
5.	23.0	18.4	18.3	17.8	19.3	26.2	18.4
6.	1.0	0.6	0.5	0.7	0.7	0.6	0.8
7.	11.4	8.9	12.5	12.5	13.0	12.2	14.1
8.	2.4	1.7	1.9	2.8	3.2	1.8	1.3
9.	8.4	9.0	9.9	9.8	8.9	8.6	6.5
10.	24.9	26.7	23.8	24.0	29.1	23.2	22.1
11.	4.1	5.0	5.5	5.8	4.6	3.7	3.9
12.	96.2	89.1	92.3	90.6	96.9	90.5	82.6
13.	3.8	10.9	7.7	9.4	3.1	9.5	17.4
14.	100.0	100.0	100.0	100.0	100.0	100.0	100.0
15.	6.9	5.6	7.4	7.5	10.8	8.2	8.9
16.	0.8	0.8	0.9	0.7	0.6	0.6	0.7
17.	2.7	1.9	1.1	1.2	1.3	1.5	0.7
18.	10.8	10.8	10.5	8.0	6.0	4.4	5.8
19.	21.8	17.6	18.3	17.6	19.3	25.8	17.7
20.	1.0	0.6	0.5	0.7	0.6	0.6	0.7
21.	13.2	10.0	12.5	12.8	13.4	13.1	15.6
22.	2.5	1.8	1.9	2.8	3.3	2.0	1.4
23.	8.4	8.9	9.9	10.0	9.3	9.2	6.7
24.	25.8	26.8	23.8	23.7	29.4	23.0	22.7
25.	4.0	4.7	5.5	5.9	4.7	4.0	4.3
26.	97.9	89.5	92.3	90.9	98.7	92.4	85.2
27.	2.1	10.5	7.7	9.1	1.3	7.6	14.8
28.	100.0	100.0	100.0	100.0	100.0	100.0	100.0

Table SA12. Balance of Payments: Consolidated Account, 1965–74
(million U.S. dollars)

Item	1965	1966	1967	1968	1969	1970	1971	1972	1973	1974
Current account										
Trade f.o.b.	−240.3	−429.5	−574.2	−835.7	−991.7	−922.0	−1,045.9	−573.9	−566.0	−1,936.8
Exports	175.6	250.4	334.7	486.3	658.3	882.2	1,132.3	1,676.5	3,271.3	4,515.1
Imports	415.9	679.9	908.9	1,322.0	1,650.0	1,804.2	2,178.2	2,250.4	3,837.3	6,451.9
Services (net)	46.1	106.5	157.1	169.3	197.3	119.3	27.8	32.9	67.1	−308.3
Receipts	114.2	204.3	308.2	394.0	492.4	496.8	483.7	550.3	849.4	837.8
Payments	68.1	97.8	151.1	224.7	295.1	377.5	455.9	517.4	782.3	1,146.1
Transfers (net)	203.3	219.6	225.2	226.1	245.8	180.2	170.6	169.8	190.1	222.4
Official	134.6	122.0	134.5	120.6	103.9	85.1	64.0	50.6	35.0	68.6
Private	68.7	97.6	90.7	105.5	141.9	95.1	106.6	119.2	155.1	153.8
Total	9.1	−103.4	−191.9	−440.3	−548.6	−622.5	−847.5	−371.2	−308.8	−2,022.7
Capital account										
Direct private investment	5.6	13.4	7.6	19.2	15.9	66.1	42.9	78.8	143.3	124.1
Medium- and long-term, net	33.5	197.0	211.0	390.2	559.6	416.9	466.8	441.0	552.0	610.0
Private short-term trade finance	−23.1	6.4	85.9	13.2	56.5	122.4	134.6	−16.3	84.0	−45.4
Other	−1.8	1.4	−5.5	0.1	0.6	23.2	18.1	−25.5	−39.9	247.0
Total	14.2	218.2	299.0	422.7	631.4	585.2	622.4	477.6	738.7	935.6
Errors and omissions	−7.1	4.4	11.1	4.1	−6.3	−16.2	13.1	41.3	18.8	8.1
Overall balance of payments	16.2	119.2	118.2	−13.5	76.5	−56.5	−172.0	147.7	448.7	−1,079.0
Monetary sector and reserves										
Commercial banks (net)	−1.1	−0.5	−53.9	147.3	45.2	111.6	103.5	−228.9	−116.0	296.8
Central monetary institutions	−8.3	−97.0	−57.0	−134.1	−118.6	−47.9	77.7	81.3	−306.5	601.4
Monetary gold	−0.5	−0.1	. . .	0.1	. . .	. . .	−0.1	−0.6	−0.5	. . .
SDRs (special drawing rights)	. . .	. . .	. . .	. . .	. . .	1.9	1.9	0.4	−0.5	29.8
International Monetary Fund	. . .	−5.2	. . .	6.0	. . .	−12.5	. . .	−1.1	−17.8	155.8
Other	−7.8	−6.4	−7.3	−5.8	−3.1	3.4	−11.0	1.2	−7.5	−5.0
Total	−17.7	−109.2	−118.2	13.5	−76.5	56.5	172.0	−147.7	−448.8	1,079.0

. . . Zero or negligible.   *Source:* Bank of Korea.

212

Table SA13. Balance of Payments: Goods and Services Account, 1965–74
(million U.S. dollars)

Item	1965	1966	1967	1968	1969	1970	1971	1972	1973	1974
Receipts										
Merchandise f.o.b.	175.1	250.3	334.7	486.2	658.3	882.2	1,132.2	1,675.9	3,270.8	4,515.1
Nonmonetary gold	0.5	0.1	...	0.1	...	...	0.1	0.6	0.5	...
Freight and insurance	4.5	9.9	10.7	17.3	31.3	40.6	44.7	53.3	58.4	94.8
Other transport	3.4	3.9	6.4	10.3	13.1	20.7	29.8	55.1	96.4	134.0
Travel	7.7	16.2	16.3	16.9	16.2	18.7	31.2	74.7	264.1	153.3
Investment income	3.7	5.6	10.1	12.4	37.9	38.0	28.8	20.9	40.5	82.9
Government	88.1	136.5	208.9	257.4	299.1	279.9	247.8	244.2	185.3	161.4
Military transactions	74.0	100.9	162.6	216.6	249.4	232.2	219.3	228.1	160.4	155.5
Other	14.1	35.6	66.3	40.8	49.7	47.7	28.5	16.1	24.9	5.9
Other services	6.8	32.2	55.8	79.7	94.8	98.9	101.4	102.1	204.7	211.4
Total	289.8	454.7	642.9	880.3	1,150.7	1,379.0	1,616.0	2,226.8	4,120.2	5,352.9
Payments										
Merchandise f.o.b.	415.9	679.9	908.9	1,322.0	1,650.0	1,804.2	2,178.2	2,250.4	3,837.2	6,451.9
Nonmonetary gold	...	...	...	...	...	...	...	...	...	...
Freight and insurance	32.4	46.8	63.0	90.7	116.5	135.8	166.8	178.6	306.0	428.6
Other transport	10.7	10.6	8.6	13.9	16.8	22.1	32.6	40.6	84.1	140.5
Travel	1.7	3.2	8.4	10.5	11.0	12.4	14.8	12.6	17.1	27.6
Investment income	2.3	5.0	11.9	17.8	42.5	75.0	119.4	161.2	213.0	324.6
Government	12.8	13.7	19.2	24.5	24.8	33.5	36.9	43.8	44.5	43.9
Other services	8.2	18.5	40.0	67.3	83.5	98.7	85.4	80.6	117.6	180.9
Total	484.0	777.7	1,060.0	1,546.7	1,945.1	2,181.7	2,634.1	2,767.8	4,619.6	7,598.0
Goods and services deficit	−194.2	−323.0	−417.1	−666.4	−794.4	−802.7	−1,018.1	−541.0	−499.6	−2,245.1
Goods and nonfactor services	−223.0	−372.3	−498.2	−750.2	−881.2	−842.6	−1,011.6	−501.6	−406.4	n.a.

n.a.: Not available.
... Zero or negligible.

Source: Bank of Korea.

Table SA14. Commodity Composition of Exports, 1965–74
(f.o.b.,ᵃ million U.S. dollars)

SITCᵇ	Commodity	1966	1967	1968	1969	1970	1971	1972	1973	1974
0	*Food*	28.2	37.9	44.5	50.3	65.6	69.7	107.0	245.6	299.7
03	Fish and fish preparations	17.8	26.9	25.8	29.0	40.8	42.4	70.4	143.5	168.4
04	Cereals and cereal preparations	3.6	0.8	0.8	1.5	1.3	2.4	1.5	12.7	6.2
042	Rice	3.2	...	...	...	...	...	...	...	...
05	Fruits and vegetables	5.5	9.0	15.6	16.4	19.5	20.7	19.1	49.3	41.1
054891	Dried laver	3.3	6.5	13.7	12.6	13.0	7.3	2.2	9.0	2.6
1	*Beverages and tobacco*	0.9	7.0	8.6	14.9	14.2	15.3	14.0	22.9	47.5
12	Tobacco	0.9	6.7	7.8	13.6	13.5	14.1	12.6	22.2	46.9
2	*Crude materials, inedible (except fuels)*	37.0	58.0	61.5	73.0	100.0	94.9	119.2	196.1	198.4
26	Textile fibers	7.7	17.0	20.0	27.1	42.6	44.6	62.5	93.3	76.5
2613	Raw silk	6.5	14.9	18.0	23.8	35.1	39.3	53.9	72.8	59.8
27	Crude fertilizers and crude minerals	4.4	5.8	6.3	7.4	9.4	9.7	8.8	18.4	31.6
28	Metalliferous ores and metal scrap	17.7	21.6	25.8	26.4	31.8	23.7	23.6	23.8	31.3
2813	Iron ore	6.7	6.1	7.3	6.1	4.5	4.5	4.6	2.6	1.1
28392	Tungsten ore	6.3	11.0	11.1	12.4	17.2	11.0	10.3	10.3	16.3
29	Crude animal and vegetable material	6.9	10.9	9.3	11.7	15.6	15.9	18.7	31.1	31.0
29241	Ginseng	1.9	2.9	4.4	5.9	9.2	10.5	8.1	13.0	11.3
292911	Agar-agar	2.3	4.7	1.8	1.6	1.2	1.0	1.6	3.6	6.4
3	*Mineral fuels*	1.9	1.8	2.3	4.8	8.7	11.3	18.2	35.4	107.7
4	*Animal and vegetable oils and fats*	0.1	0.1	0.1	0.1	0.1	0.1	0.3	0.6	1.8
5	*Chemicals*	0.4	2.4	3.1	9.8	11.4	14.9	36.1	48.5	91.8

SITC										
6	*Manufactured goods*	66.4	101.4	143.6	172.8	220.9	328.4	514.2	1,102.9	1,475.5
62	Rubber manufactures	1.0	2.0	2.5	2.7	3.7	4.8	11.3	20.9	66.8
63	Wood and cork	18.2	36.6	65.9	80.5	93.5	128.9	170.4	305.2	199.4
631211-16	Veneer sheets and plywoods	18.0	36.4	65.6	79.2	91.7	127.4	153.6	270.8	163.4
65	Textiles	26.3	49.0	61.2	65.7	84.9	137.8	176.6	435.2	492.6
652	Cotton fabrics, woven	10.5	12.6	13.3	18.6	26.4	31.0	34.8	56.5	54.9
66	Nonmetallic mineral manufactures	2.8	1.0	0.9	5.2	6.5	13.6	24.3	46.8	84.8
67	Iron and steel	12.7	1.9	1.2	4.9	13.4	24.4	92.8	188.9	450.3
68	Nonferrous metals	2.9	1.8	1.5	4.8	5.8	3.2	6.0	7.4	11.2
69	Manufactures of metal	2.2	7.0	9.7	9.8	12.2	13.9	22.1	62.8	120.0
7	*Machinery and transport equipment*	5.5	14.2	24.5	53.2	61.5	87.4	171.6	395.9	672.3
71	Machinery (except electrical)	2.5	4.0	4.2	8.9	8.4	12.0	32.2	59.3	77.0
72	Electrical machinery and appliances	1.9	7.4	18.9	36.7	43.9	68.5	223.3	312.5	474.2
73	Transport equipment	1.1	2.8	1.4	7.6	9.2	6.9	14.3	24.0	121.1
8	*Miscellaneous manufactured articles*	34.5	97.2	167.0	242.3	352.5	445.4	642.8	1,169.9	1,547.0
84	Clothing	20.7	59.2	112.2	160.8	213.6	304.3	442.4	749.9	957.0
85	Footwear	4.1	8.1	11.0	10.5	17.3	37.4	55.4	106.4	179.5
89	Miscellaneous manufactures	8.9	27.6	40.9	66.9	114.1	91.8	121.8	243.0	294.9
89995	Human hair and wigs	6.8	23.3	35.5	60.2	101.1	73.1	73.8	81.5	72.9
9	*Unclassified*	0.2	0.2	0.2	0.3	0.4	0.3	0.7	7.1	18.5
	Total Exports[c]	175.1	320.2	455.4	622.5	835.2	1,067.6	1,624.1	3,225.0	4,460.4
	Export to military forces in Vietnam	. . .	14.5	30.8	35.8	47.0	64.7	51.8	45.8	76.2
	Grand Total[d]	175.1	334.7	486.2	658.3	882.2	1,132.3	1,675.9	3,270.8	4,536.6

. . . Zero or negligible.
a. Free on board.
b. Standard International Trade Classification.
c. Customs clearance base.
d. Offshore sales of tuna not included.
Source: Office of Customs Administration.

215

Table SA15. Destination of Exports, 1965–74
(thousand U.S. dollars)

Country	1965	1966	1967	1968	1969	1970	1971	1972	1973	1974
United States	61,695	95,782	137,431	237,021	315,673	395,182	531,814	758,974	1,021,182	1,492,168
Japan	43,974	66,293	84,726	99,744	133,326	234,329	261,988	407,876	1,241,539	1,380,196
Canada	2,542	5,765	7,914	14,165	15,115	19,553	28,935	58,915	124,881	166,764
China (Taiwan)	1,942	2,075	3,104	5,750	13,275	7,210	12,030	16,131	40,942	50,754
France	526	954	2,116	2,590	1,752	1,568	2,560	8,187	23,141	24,491
Germany (Federal Republic)	3,191	6,975	5,286	9,636	16,415	27,330	31,357	51,195	120,338	241,781
Italy	1,180	1,243	1,087	1,600	3,566	7,182	5,570	9,515	16,595	28,711
United Kingdom	3,592	5,066	7,883	7,026	10,560	13,021	14,110	28,680	74,960	106,685
All others	56,440	66,181	70,682	77,869	112,834	129,810	179,234	284,615	561,447	968,821
Total	175,082	250,334	320,229	455,401	622,516	835,185	1,067,607	1,624,088	3,225,025	4,460,371

Source: Bank of Korea, Monthly Economic Statistics, April 1975, pp. 82–83.

Table SA16. Imports by Funding Source, 1962–73
(percent)

Source	1962-66	1967-71	1972	1973[a]
Korean Foreign Exchange	48.2	63.1	65.7	76.6
Loan and investment	11.9	25.2	24.9	17.5
Official aid	30.8	4.9	0.9	0.0
Relief and other	9.1	6.8	8.5	5.9
Total	100.0	100.0	100.0	100.0
Million U.S. dollars (c.i.f.)[b]	2,580.1	8,616.3	2,522.0	4,320.4

a. Provisional.
b. Cost, insurance, and freight.
Source: EPB, Long-term Projection (Balance of Payments), September 1973.

Table SA17. Imports by Country of Origin, 1965–74
(percent in dollar terms)

Country	1965	1966	1967	1968	1969	1970	1971	1972	1973	1974
United States	47.6	41.6	36.2	36.8	35.5	36.0	35.1	25.7	28.4	24.8
Japan	43.5	48.1	52.5	50.8	50.4	49.8	49.4	40.9	40.7	38.3
Canada	0.4	0.4	1.0	1.0	1.5	1.4	2.0	1.4	2.0	1.7
China (Taiwan)	2.7	1.8	3.2	1.3	1.6	2.1	2.0	2.0	1.3	1.6
France	0.7	1.8	2.0	1.1	2.4	3.2	3.7	2.0	1.1	0.5
Germany (Federal Republic)	4.2	3.3	3.7	6.0	5.3	4.1	3.8	2.7	0.8	2.1
Italy	0.5	2.6	0.8	1.8	1.2	1.2	1.0	0.9	0.5	0.4
United Kingdom	0.3	0.4	0.6	1.2	2.1	2.0	2.9	2.9	1.6	1.3
Others	21.1	0.0	0.0	1.0	0.0	0.2	0.1	21.5	23.6	29.3
Total	100.0	100.0	100.0	100.0	100.0	100.0	100.0	100.0	100.0	100.0

217

Table SA18. Commodity Composition of Imports, 1964–74
(*c.i.f.,*[a] *million U.S. dollars*)

SITC[b]	Commodity	1964	1965	1966	1967
0	*Food*	68.2	63.5	72.4	94.1
04	Cereals and cereal preparations	60.8	54.4	61.4	76.6
041	Wheat	36.8	35.9	40.5	46.3
06	Sugar and sugar preparations	3.8	4.0	6.2	9.7
1	*Beverages and tobacco*	0.1	0.2	0.3	0.8
2	*Crude material, inedible (except fuels)*	97.1	110.0	153.9	208.5
23	Crude rubber (except synthetic)	5.8	8.4	9.4	10.2
24	Wood, lumber, and cork	18.5	20.8	43.1	58.5
25	Pulp and paper	9.4	9.4	12.9	16.6
26	Textile fibers (not manufactured)	52.8	59.7	66.6	80.3
2631	Raw cotton	37.3	40.8	42.8	49.3
27	Crude fertilizers and crude minerals	4.3	4.7	5.1	12.6
28	Metalliferous ores and metal scrap	3.9	5.1	13.3	20.6
3	*Mineral fuels and lubricants*	28.5	31.3	42.4	61.6
33	Petroleum and petroleum products	25.9	28.9	40.6	59.4
4	*Animal and vegetable oils and fats*	3.9	3.8	5.5	6.9
5	*Chemicals*	84.3	103.4	134.5	113.0
51	Chemical elements and compounds	13.7	16.1	20.8	33.4
53	Dyeing and tanning materials	3.7	4.8	4.6	7.1
54	Medicinal and pharmaceutical products	3.8	4.9	6.1	7.5
56	Fertilizers, manufactured	55.9	65.8	88.9	43.9
58	Plastic materials	3.3	6.5	7.9	10.9
6	*Manufactured goods*	46.1	71.2	125.2	183.7
65	Textile yarn fabrics	19.6	26.9	45.2	69.6
66	Nonmetallic mineral manufactures	2.1	1.5	6.1	12.7
67	Iron and steel	14.8	24.7	39.5	56.1
68	Nonferrous metals	4.2	9.0	11.2	12.4
684	Aluminum	1.7	4.0	6.1	7.0
69	Manufacture of metal	3.0	7.1	18.8	26.7
7	*Machinery and transport equipment*	69.5	73.1	171.7	310.2
71	Machinery (except electrical)	38.2	35.3	95.6	141.2
72	Electrical machinery	19.7	12.6	26.1	47.6
73	Transport equipment	11.6	25.2	50.0	121.4
8	*Miscellaneous manufactured articles*	5.3	6.8	10.5	17.2
86	Professional, scientific instruments	2.7	3.9	5.4	9.5
9	*Unclassified*	1.3	0.2	. . .	0.1
	Total imports	404.4	463.4	716.4	996.2

. . . Zero or negligible.
a. Cost, insurance, and freight.
b. Standard International Trade Classification.

Statistical Appendix

SITC[b]	1968	1969	1970	1971	1972	1973	1974
0	167.5	301.7	319.4	399.5	357.5	569.6	818.2
04	129.4	250.3	244.8	304.0	282.7	444.1	613.1
041	62.8	90.3	79.5	115.1	128.1	255.4	297.6
06	12.3	21.4	28.9	38.4	43.0	76.5	147.5
1	1.4	1.7	1.6	3.8	7.9	6.3	10.7
2	267.1	332.4	404.5	462.7	454.4	910.5	1,249.9
23	11.9	17.6	17.6	20.2	22.5	46.7	75.5
24	91.5	108.5	125.4	153.7	140.9	311.9	343.8
25	22.5	25.7	33.5	37.3	37.5	76.4	134.5
26	90.3	96.7	119.8	139.2	159.3	259.7	309.0
2631	49.1	52.0	62.7	84.2	85.5	112.4	189.5
27	16.0	22.5	23.3	26.8	25.9	37.3	64.8
28	27.7	48.2	70.3	64.1	45.6	126.2	256.3
3	75.5	110.9	136.0	189.4	218.9	312.5	1,120.0
33	72.8	107.6	132.9	187.1	217.7	296.2	1,120.0[c]
4	8.3	12.3	15.3	21.3	20.3	37.9	57.4
5	128.5	136.7	163.8	201.0	223.5	343.9	630.9
51	47.3	60.8	77.8	101.3	111.2	173.5	349.1
53	7.8	10.3	11.6	13.7	19.2	38.2	56.2
54	11.8	13.1	15.2	13.6	13.0	17.9	24.8
56	30.6	11.9	4.1	7.1	11.1	17.6	52.9
58	18.1	25.2	37.0	44.8	45.2	60.7	92.8
6	242.2	278.7	305.9	363.3	396.1	772.9	1,000.2
65	102.7	109.6	127.8	137.0	129.0	300.7	269.6
66	9.2	9.8	8.9	9.9	18.6	17.9	30.9
67	69.3	84.5	89.6	128.7	167.8	314.4	464.0
68	16.1	18.5	20.4	19.7	19.7	45.0	106.7
684	9.1	10.0	5.2	4.3	4.5	10.1	30.7
69	34.3	45.5	44.0	49.1	40.9	54.2	64.6
7	533.0	593.2	589.5	685.4	761.8	1,156.8	1,848.6
71	282.9	307.0	306.0	350.7	360.2	547.8	723.8
72	95.9	113.7	132.9	167.2	223.3	360.2	513.4
73	154.3	172.5	150.8	167.5	178.2	248.7	611.5
8	38.9	55.2	47.3	66.8	81.3	129.5	167.2
86	14.7	19.9	21.6	28.2	28.9	40.7	69.4
9	0.4	0.9	0.8	1.0	0.2	0.5	6.7
	1,462.9	1,823.6	1,984.0	2,394.3	2,522.0	4,240.3	6,894.3

c. Estimate based on data from the Ministry of Commerce and Industry.
Source: Bank of Korea.

Table SA19. External Public Debt Outstanding as of December 31, 1974, Repayable in Foreign Currency
(*thousand U.S. dollars*)

Creditor	Debt outstanding December 31, 1974[a]		
	Disbursed	*Undisbursed*	*Total*
Suppliers			
Austria	39,313	100,580	139,893
Belgium	20,561	. . .	20,561
France	55,250	29,888	85,138
Germany (Federal Republic)	122,960	27,740	150,700
Hong Kong	81,533	10,813	92,346
India	5,272	14,234	19,506
Israel	188	. . .	188
Italy	30,478	1,379	31,857
Japan	344,167	93,194	437,361
Netherlands	15,154	. . .	15,154
Panama	13,283	22	13,305
Spain	16,946	4,710	21,656
Sweden	5,424	1,378	6,802
Switzerland	7,370	. . .	7,370
United Kingdom	77,362	17,975	95,337
United States	379,092	84,325	463,417
Multiple lenders	34,813	. . .	34,813
Unknown	562	. . .	562
Total	1,249,728	386,238	1,635,966
Private banks			
Bahamas	5,000	2,282	7,282
Canada	21,949	2,926	24,875
France	94,695	136,457	231,152
Germany (Federal Republic)	30,680	. . .	30,680
Japan	2,975	. . .	2,975
Luxembourg	2,000	. . .	2,000
Singapore	10,891	9,719	20,610
United Kingdom	138,197	139,753	277,950
United States	287,957	260,316	548,273
Multiple lenders	10,594	17,050	27,644
Total	604,938	568,503	1,173,441

. . . Zero or negligible.

a. The totals shown here are lower than the total medium- and long-term debt outstanding shown elsewhere, which includes debt not guaranteed by the public sector.

b. Debt with a maturity of over one year.

Source: World Bank data based on Bank of Korea reports.

Creditor	Debt outstanding December 31, 1974[a]		
	Disbursed	Undisbursed	Total
Other private financial institutions			
United Arab Emirates	18,842	. . .	18,842
Germany (Federal Republic)	. . .	17,431	17,431
Hong Kong	3,608	8,092	11,700
Panama	11,236	. . .	11,236
Spain	800	. . .	800
United Kingdom	2,600	. . .	2,600
United States	25,104	55,669	80,773
Total	62,190	81,192	143,382
International organizations			
Asian Development Bank	113,001	212,397	325,398
World Bank	223,837	268,269	492,106
International Development			
Association	78,272	37,112	115,384
Total	415,110	517,778	932,888
Governments			
Austria	. . .	4,201	4,201
Belgium	14,386	. . .	14,386
Canada	15,275	15,139	30,414
Denmark	2,900	640	3,540
France	. . .	953	953
Germany (Federal Republic)	93,477	57,236	150,713
Hong Kong	2,690	191	2,881
India	2,942	5,784	8,726
Japan	570,204	173,224	734,428
Netherlands	2,871	. . .	2,871
Switzerland	. . .	506	504
United Kindgom	7,409	18,755	26,164
United States	984,543	288,258	1,272,801
Total	1,696,697	564,887	2,261,584
Total external public debt[b]	4,028,663	2,118,598	6,147,261

Table SA20. Foreign Trade Quantum and Unit Value Indexes and Terms of Trade, 1965–74
(1970 = 100.0)

Item	1965	1966	1967	1968	1969	1970	1971	1972	1973	1974
Quantum index										
Exports	24.7	32.0	39.2	54.1	77.8	100.0	129.4	194.6	305.2	333.4
Imports	23.1	36.1	50.8	75.6	95.3	100.0	121.2	125.6	158.1	164.2
Unit value index										
Exports	85.7	93.5	97.8	100.8	95.8	100.0	98.8	99.9	126.5	160.2
Imports	100.1	97.9	98.8	97.9	96.4	100.0	99.6	101.3	135.2	210.3
Petroleum	n.a.	n.a.	n.a.	91.1	94.5	100.0	113.2	120.5	147.4	522.1
Cereals	61.4	84.1	78.7	83.3	88.3	100.0	82.7	72.7	96.4	198.5
Other	95.4	95.0	94.2	98.5	97.8	100.0	102.1	105.0	142.0	191.5
Terms of trade	85.6	95.5	99.0	103.0	99.4	100.0	99.2	98.6	93.6	76.2
Excluding petroleum and cereals	89.8	98.4	103.8	102.3	98.0	100.0	96.8	95.1	89.1	84.7

n.a.: Not available.
Source: Bank of Korea and World Bank estimates.

222

**Table SA21. Total Medium- and Long-term Loans
from Official Sources, 1962–74**
(*million U.S. dollars*)

Year	New loans		Debt service			Debt outstanding at end of period	
	Com- mitted	Dis- bursed	Amorti- zation	In- terest	Total	Com- mitted	Dis- bursed
1962	53.0	7.4	1.2	0.4	1.6	71.6	6.2
1963	9.1	42.6	0.5	0.3	0.8	80.1	48.3
1964	35.3	11.6	1.7	0.9	2.6	113.7	58.2
1965	76.1	5.6	0.6	0.6	1.2	189.2	63.2
1966	148.9	73.6	0.9	2.4	3.3	337.2	135.9
1967	71.5	105.6	1.4	3.2	4.6	407.3	240.1
1968	57.1	70.2	2.2	4.7	6.9	462.2	308.1
1969	226.5	138.9	2.9	6.4	9.3	685.9	444.1
1970	148.5	115.3	6.5	9.9	16.4	827.9	552.9
1971	399.2	303.4	15.4	12.9	28.3	1,211.7	840.9
1972	589.6	324.4	24.1	21.7	45.8	1,777.2	1,141.2
1973	473.3	368.5	22.8	30.7	53.5	2,227.7	1,486.9
1974	456.5	316.7	43.2	49.7	92.9	2,641.0	1,760.4

Note: Includes loans with maturities of over three years.
Source: EPB.

**Table SA22. Total Medium- and Long-term Loans
to the Banking System, 1968–74**
(*million U.S. dollars*)

Year	New loans		Debt service			Debt outstanding at end of period	
	Com- mitted	Dis- bursed	Amorti- zation	In- terest	Total	Com- mitted	Dis- bursed
1968	40.0	40.0	. . .	0.7	0.7	40.0	40.0
1969	30.0	30.0	. . .	3.6	3.6	70.0	70.0
1970	25.0	25.0	20.0	6.8	26.8	75.0	75.0
1971	89.5	89.5	4.3	14.0	18.3	160.2	160.2
1972	70.0	20.0	25.7	14.0	39.7	204.5	154.5
1973	83.3	51.3	79.7	11.0	90.7	208.1	126.1
1974	243.9	318.4	26.4	14.0	40.4	425.6	418.1

. . . Zero or negligible.
Source: Ministry of Finance.

**Table SA23. Total Medium- and Long-term Loans
from Commercial Sources, 1962–74**

(*million U.S. dollars*)

Year	New loans		Debt service			Debt outstanding at end of period	
	Com- mitted	Dis- bursed	Amorti- zation	In- terest	Total	Com- mitted	Dis- bursed
1962	1.7	. . .	0.9	. . .	0.9	0.8	−0.9
1963	55.2	23.7	4.1	0.1	4.1	51.9	18.7
1964	63.4	11.9	5.2	0.8	6.0	110.1	25.4
1965	75.1	36.1	5.2	1.1	6.3	180.0	56.3
1966	105.1	111.8	11.3	3.3	14.6	273.8	156.8
1967	154.6	124.1	25.8	8.1	33.9	402.6	255.0
1968	463.6	268.3	42.0	11.6	53.6	824.2	481.3
1969	615.5	408.7	69.2	24.2	93.4	1,449.0	820.9
1970	314.4	366.7	100.3	53.8	154.1	1,663.1	1,087.3
1971	345.9	345.2	119.2	68.2	187.4	1,889.8	1,313.3
1972	297.2	326.4	178.3	91.0	269.3	2,008.7	1,461.4
1973	587.9	338.4	238.6	121.6	360.2	2,358.0	1,561.1
1974	1,086.9	616.0	294.9	160.5	455.4	3,150.0	1,882.3

Note: Includes loans with maturities of over three years.
. . . Zero or negligible.
Source: EPB.

**Table SA24. Medium-term Trade Finance of One- to Three-year
Maturities, 1966–74**

(*million U.S. dollars*)

Year	New loans			Debt outstanding at end of period	
	Committed	Disbursed	Repayments	Committed	Disbursed
1966	25.9	16.7	0.2	25.7	16.5
1967	150.8	58.5	7.7	168.8	67.3
1968	108.3	166.6	13.4	261.2	218.3
1969	30.3	27.1	15.2	258.1	232.8
1970	33.8	31.0	92.1	199.8	171.7
1971	48.2	35.5	94.1	153.9	113.1
1972	32.5	47.5	44.2	142.2	116.4
1973	94.6	84.6	63.1	173.7	137.9
1974	87.4	78.3	65.9	195.2	150.3

Source: Ministry of Finance.

Table SA25. Total Medium- and Long-term External Debt, 1962–74
(million U.S. dollars)

Year	New loans		Debt service			Debt outstanding at end of period[a]	
	Com-mitted	Dis-bursed	Amorti-zation	In-terest	Total	Com-mitted	Dis-bursed
1962	74.5	7.4	2.1	0.4	2.5	72.4	5.3
1963	64.3	66.3	4.6	0.4	5.0	132.1	67.0
1964	98.7	23.5	6.9	1.7	8.6	223.9	83.6
1965	151.3	41.7	5.8	1.7	7.5	369.5	119.5
1966	280.7	202.1	12.4	5.7	18.1	636.9	309.2
1967	376.9	288.1	34.9	11.3	46.2	978.9	562.4
1968	669.0	545.1	58.3	17.0	75.3	1,587.8	1,049.2
1969	902.4	604.7	90.9	34.2	125.1	2,463.0	1,567.8
1970	521.7	538.0	218.9	70.5	289.4	2,765.8	1,886.9
1971	882.8	773.6	233.0	95.1	328.1	3,415.6	2,427.5
1972	989.3	718.3	272.3	126.7	399.0	4,132.5	2,873.5
1973	1,239.1	842.8	404.2	163.3	567.5	4,967.5	3,312.1
1974	1,874.7	1,329.4	430.4	224.2	654.6	6,411.8	4,211.1

a. The estimates of medium- and long-term debt outstanding are somewhat lower than those in Table 22 in the text, which is based on more up-to-date information.
Source: EPB.

Table SA26. External Borrowing and Terms, 1966–72
(January–December 31)

Item	1966	1967	1968	1969	1970	1971	1972
Total							
Interest rate (percent a year)	4.2	5.7	5.5	5.6	5.8	4.6	3.9
Grace period (year)	6.0	3.7	3.9	4.3	5.2	5.7	6.3
Maturity (year)	20.8	11.9	14.5	15.9	18.0	19.8	23.8
Grant element (percent)	41	23	26	27	28	38	46
Amount (millions of U.S. dollars)	372.2[a]	513.1[a]	530.6	672.6[a]	561.7	699.2[a]	790.2[a]
Governments							
Interest rate (percent a year)	2.6	2.8	3.6	2.5	4.7	1.5	1.7
Grace period (year)	8.8	8.6	7.9	6.3	6.6	8.2	8.1
Maturity (year)	31.9	28.3	26.9	26.2	22.7	26.1	30.5
Grant element (percent)	62	60	51	58	39	67	68
Amount (millions of U.S. dollars)	156.3	85.0	156.0	153.6	221.0	309.1	409.2
International organization							
Interest rate (percent a year)	0.0	0.8	5.4	5.8	5.8	7.1	6.2
Grace period (year)	4.0	10.0	3.4	5.8	4.8	4.5	5.7
Maturity (year)	16.0	49.5	14.7	26.5	27.6	21.1	24.8
Grant element (percent)	61	84	27	32	32	20	28
Amount (millions of U.S. dollars)	45.1[a]	11.0	15.3	104.3	75.0	172.9	167.0
Private banks							
Interest rate (percent a year)	6.0	6.7	6.1	6.8	7.7	5.2	6.7
Grace period (year)	2.3	2.1	1.5	3.1	5.6	1.7	3.0
Maturity (year)	7.3	6.0	11.4	11.6	10.0	6.0	7.2
Grant element (percent)	15	11	18	16	12	15	13
Amount (millions of U.S. dollars)	1.9	12.2	57.4	81.1	48.5	10.6	74.3
Suppliers							
Interest rate (percent a year)	5.8	6.3	6.3	6.5	6.8	6.9	6.4
Grace period (year)	3.5	2.5	2.4	3.0	3.1	3.3	2.8
Maturity (year)	10.5	7.8	8.6	9.2	9.6	10.0	11.1
Grant element (percent)	21	14	15	16	15	14	18
Amount (millions of U.S. dollars)	166.6	379.3	301.9	296.5	147.3	204.1	107.9
Other private financial institutions							
Interest rate (percent a year)	0.0	7.3	. . .	8.0	5.9	. . .	5.7
Grace period (year)	4.0	4.2	. . .	4.7	5.1	. . .	4.9
Maturity (year)	16.0	5.0	. . .	5.8	15.8	. . .	14.7
Grant element (percent)	61	10	. . .	8	26	. . .	26
Amount (millions of U.S. dollars)	2.3	25.6	. . .	34.6	69.9	. . .	32.1

. . . Zero or negligible.

a. Total loan commitment includes small "unknown" or unidentified loans which have been excluded from the terms analysis.

Source: World Bank.

Table SA27. Official Loans Classified by Terms, 1959–74
(*thousand U.S. dollars*)

Terms	1959–66	1967	1968	1969	1970	1971	1967–71	1972	1973	1974	1959–74
Interest rate											
0–1 percent	78.0	11.0	...	17.0	15.0	7.0	50.0	26.0	20.0	...	174.0
1–3 percent	194.0	32.0	27.0	111.0	61.0	218.0	450.0	262.0	42.0	25.0	972.0
3–5 percent	64.0	29.0	18.0	11.0	9.0	8.0	75.0	165.0	205.0	203.0	711.0
5–7 percent	5.0	...	7.0	87.0	...	...	94.0	...	...	35.0	134.0
Over 7 percent	...	...	...	...	64.0	166.0	230.0	138.0	206.0	194.0	767.0
Floating rate	1.0	...	5.0	...	...	...	5.0	...	...	...	6.0
Total	342.0	71.0	57.0	227.0	149.0	399.0	903.0	590.0	473.0	457.0	2,765.0
Grace period											
0–3 years	21.0	...	12.0	37.0	22.0	64.0	136.0	33.0	87.0	70.0	347.0
3–5 years	16.0	...	...	8.0	1.0	80.0	89.0	180.0	113.0	38.0	435.0
5–7 years	45.0	30.0	18.0	56.0	61.0	43.0	207.0	83.0	14.0	304.0	661.0
7–9 years	...	...	...	...	...	...	...	...	...	...	...
Over 9 years	260.0	42.0	27.0	126.0	64.0	213.0	472.0	283.0	260.0	45.0	1,321.0
Total	342.0	71.0	57.0	227.0	149.0	399.0	903.0	590.0	473.0	457.0	2,765.0
Repayment period[a]											
3–10 years	6.0	...	...	...	4.0	...	4.0	...	...	...	11.0
10–15 years	15.0	...	12.0	38.0	10.0	70.0	130.0	58.0	30.0	100.0	333.0
15–20 years	67.0	29.0	18.0	60.0	18.0	27.0	153.0	175.0	68.0	142.0	605.0
20–30 years	3.0	1.0	...	3.0	52.0	173.0	229.0	73.0	203.0	190.0	698.0
30–40 years	236.0	31.0	127.0	111.0	49.0	121.0	340.0	258.0	147.0	25.0	1,007.0
Over 40 years	14.0	11.0	...	15.0	15.0	7.0	47.0	26.0	25.0	...	112.0
Total	342.0	71.0	157.0	227.0	149.0	399.0	903.0	590.0	473.0	457.0	2,765.0

... Zero or negligible.   a. Includes grace period.   *Source:* Bureau of Economic Cooperation, EPB.

Table SA28. Commercial Loans Classified by Terms, 1962–74
(million U.S. dollars)

Terms	1962–66	1967	1968	1969	1970	1971	1967–71	1972	1973	1974	1962–74
Interest rate											
0–4 percent	20.0	3.0	...	1.0	...	...	4.0	...	6.0	1.0	32.0
4–5 percent	82.0	2.0	8.0	...	...	...	11.0	4.0	...	...	98.0
5–6 percent	158.0	135.0	369.0	235.0	137.0	87.0	963.0	44.0	156.0	98.0	1,419.0
6–7 percent	36.0	...	59.0	108.0	27.0	88.0	282.0	47.0	47.0	379.0	792.0
7–8 percent	3.0	14.0	18.0	154.0	66.0	17.0	270.0	10.0	45.0	97.0	427.0
8–9 percent	...	...	8.0	18.0	...	75.0	101.0	70.0	22.0	7.0	200.0
Over 9 percent	...	...	...	99.0	42.0	70.0	161.0	...	7.0	15.0	183.0
Floating rate	...	...	...	...	42.0	59.0	101.0	122.0	305.0	490.0	1,018.0
Total	301.0	155.0	464.0	616.0	314.0	346.0	1,894.0	297.0	588.0	1,087.0	4,166.0
Grace period											
0–1 year	59.0	87.0	149.0	127.0	37.0	90.0	491.0	58.0	46.0	139.0	794.0
1–2 years	102.0	29.0	184.0	161.0	43.0	91.0	509.0	49.0	79.0	269.0	1,008.0
2–3 years	84.0	24.0	49.0	185.0	76.0	77.0	410.0	107.0	274.0	316.0	1,190.0
3–4 years	44.0	...	21.0	47.0	7.0	45.0	120.0	74.0	30.0	359.0	628.0
4–5 years	...	14.0	60.0	5.0	40.0	7.0	126.0	9.0	76.0	2.0	212.0
Over 5 years	11.0	...	...	91.0	110.0	37.0	238.0	...	83.0	3.0	334.0
Total	301.0	155.0	464.0	616.0	314.0	346.0	1,894.0	297.0	588.0	1,087.0	4,166.0

Repayment period[a]

3–5 years	6.0	25.0	54.0	161.0	21.0	35.0	296.0	5.0	16.0	14.0	373.0
5–10 years	151.0	95.0	248.0	190.0	85.0	60.0	679.0	93.0	213.0	449.0	1,584.0
Subtotal	157.0	95.0	248.0	190.0	85.0	60.0	679.0	93.0	228.0	463.2	1,958.0
10–11 years	42.0	6.0	4.0	72.0	35.0	24.0	143.0	39.0	228.0	133.0	585.0
11–12 years	60.0	11.0	60.0	22.0	8.0	21.0	101.0	16.0	55.0	3.7	235.0
12–13 years	5.0	4.0	25.0	25.0	49.0	107.0	210.0	38.0	33.0	43.0	329.0
13–14 years	11.0	. . .	15.0	9.0	. . .	. . .	24.0	5.0	. . .	299.0	339.0
14–15 years	25.0	13.0	6.0	105.0	22.0	41.0	186.0	28.0	. . .	145.0	384.0
15–20 years	. . .	. . .	51.0	52.0	95.0	57.0	256.0	37.0	44.0	. . .	337.0
Subtotal	143.0	35.0	161.0	264.0	209.0	251.0	920.0	163.0	360.0	624.0	2,209.0
Total	301.0	155.0	464.0	616.0	314.0	346.0	1,894.0	297.0	588.0	1,087.0	4,166.0

. . . Zero or negligible.
a. Includes grace period.
Source: Bureau of Economic Cooperation, EPB.

229

Table SA29. Public Revenues and Expenditures, 1970–74
(*billion won*)

Item	1970 Central government	1970 Government enterprises	1970 Local government	1970 Consolidated public sector	1971 Central government	1971 Government enterprises
Current revenue						
1. Tax revenue	360.2	. . .	33.5	393.7	439.9	. . .
2. Direct and indirect	330.1	. . .	33.5	363.3	401.9	. . .
3. Monopoly profits[a]	30.1	. . .	. . .	30.1	38.0	. . .
4. Other income	45.5	. . .	21.6	94.9	52.0	. . .
5. Total	405.7	27.8	55.1	488.6	491.9	22.9
Current expenditure						
6. Public consumption	165.9	. . .	102.6	268.5	209.6	. . .
7. Wages and salaries	114.6	. . .	72.3	186.9	137.2	. . .
8. Goods and services	51.3	. . .	30.3	81.6	72.4	. . .
9. Interest payments	4.4	. . .	0.4	4.8	5.1	. . .
10. Extrasystem transfers	37.1	. . .	6.8	43.9	46.4	. . .
11. Total	207.4	. . .	109.8	317.2	261.1	. . .
12. Intrasystem transfers	108.3	. . .	108.3	. . .	136.3	. . .
13. Savings on current account	90.0	27.8	53.6	171.4	94.5	22.9
14. Counterpart funds	28.8	. . .	. . .	28.8	26.3	. . .
Utilization of loans						
15. Domestic	1.3	5.3	2.6	9.2	−3.0	8.4
16. Foreign	−0.3	−2.2	0.6	−1.9	−0.1	6.3
17. Total	1.0	3.1	3.2	7.3	−3.1	14.7
Other capital resources						
18. Loan payment received	27.6	0.1	0.3	28.0	43.5	. . .
19. Depreciation reserves	. . .	6.5	. . .	6.5	. . .	8.4
20. Use of cash balance	−13.7	−11.4	−6.7	−31.8	−9.2	−5.6
21. Other capital transfers	6.7	3.6	16.8	27.1	10.4	0.2
22. Total	20.6	−1.2	10.4	29.8	44.7	3.0
23. Intrasystem capital transfers	33.5	. . .	33.5	. . .	37.8	. . .
24. Extrasystem capital transfers	8.7	. . .	6.3	15.0	9.1	. . .
Investments						
25. Gross capital	48.3	26.0	91.4	169.1	42.6	40.6
26. Fixed capital formation	48.3	. . .	91.4	165.9	42.6	40.3
27. Inventories	. . .	3.2	. . .	3.2	. . .	0.3
28. Subscriptions	20.5	. . .	. . .	20.5	31.0	. . .
29. Loans	29.0	0.3	3.0	32.3	41.9	. . .
30. Subscription and loans abroad	0.4	. . .	. . .	0.4	. . .	. . .
31. Total	98.2	29.7	94.4	222.3	115.5	40.6

. . . Zero or negligible.

a. Monopoly profits include only portions of surplus in monopoly which have been transferred to the general account; the remaining portion is included in enterprise revenues.

Source: Reclassified from government transactions published by Bank of Korea. *Economic Statistical Yearbook,* various issues.

Statistical Appendix

	1971		1972				1973	
	Local govern- ment	Consoli- dated public sector	Central govern- ment	Govern- ment enter- prises	Local govern- ment	Consoli- dated public sector	Central govern- ment	Govern- ment enter- prises
1.	40.3	480.2	472.6	. . .	47.1	519.7	575.1	. . .
2.	40.3	442.2	429.7	. . .	47.1	476.8	518.1	. . .
3.	. . .	38.0	42.9	. . .	. . .	42.9	57.0	. . .
4.	28.7	103.6	48.5	. . .	36.1	129.3	64.3	. . .
5.	69.0	583.8	521.1	44.7	83.2	649.0	639.4	14.9
6.	130.9	340.5	262.3	. . .	163.8	426.1	274.8	. . .
7.	91.8	229.0	164.3	. . .	113.1	277.4	173.7	. . .
8.	39.1	111.5	98.0	. . .	50.7	148.7	101.1	. . .
9.	1.7	6.8	5.8	. . .	2.0	7.8	5.9	. . .
10.	11.2	57.6	62.8	. . .	14.2	77.0	74.4	. . .
11.	143.8	404.9	330.9	. . .	180.0	510.9	355.1	. . .
12.	136.3	. . .	165.8	. . .	165.8	. . .	166.7	. . .
13.	61.5	178.9	24.4	44.7	69.0	138.1	117.6	14.9
14.	. . .	26.3	27.1	. . .	. . .	211.1	16.8	. . .
15.	8.0	13.4	93.3	5.5	4.1	95.7	2.1	52.2
16.	0.4	6.6	59.6	16.2	. . .	75.8	50.6	4.4
17.	8.4	20.0	152.9	21.7	4.1	171.5	52.7	56.6
18.	2.5	46.0	30.5	. . .	1.4	29.5	17.6	. . .
19.	. . .	8.4	. . .	8.2	. . .	8.2	. . .	11.8
20.	−5.7	−20.5	−4.0	−20.2	−11.9	−36.1	−52.9	0.1
21.	17.8	28.4	7.0	10.8	14.0	31.8	13.7	14.0
22.	14.6	62.3	33.5	−1.2	3.5	33.4	−21.6	25.9
23.	37.8	. . .	41.8	. . .	41.8	. . .	37.2	. . .
24.	9.0	18.1	13.9	. . .	14.8	28.7	15.1	. . .
25.	111.2	194.4	63.7	60.8	95.5	220.0	68.5	95.2
26.	111.2	194.1	63.7	56.0	95.5	215.2	68.5	51.5
27.	. . .	0.3	. . .	4.8	. . .	4.8	. . .	43.7
28.	0.1	31.1	84.1	. . .	. . .	84.1	15.1	. . .
29.	2.0	43.9	34.4	4.4	8.1	37.3	29.6	2.2
30.	. . .	. . .	. . .	. . .	. . .	. . .	. . .	. . .
31.	113.3	269.4	182.2	65.2	103.6	341.4	113.2	97.4

(*Table continued next page.*)

Table SA29 (*continued*)

	1973		1974[b]			
Item	Local govern-ment	Consoli-dated public sector	Central govern-ment	Govern-ment enter-prises	Local govern-ment	Consoli-dated public sector
Current revenue						
1. Tax revenue	75.0	650.1	672.7	. . .	79.3	752.0
2. Direct and indirect	75.0	593.1	603.7	. . .	79.3	683.0
3. Monopoly profits[a]	. . .	57.0	69.0	. . .	. . .	69.0
4. Other income	35.5	127.0	82.7	. . .	38.5	88.2
5. Total	110.5	777.1	755.4	−33.0	117.8	840.2
Current expenditure						
6. Public consumption	189.2	464.0	326.8	. . .	205.0	531.8
7. Wages and salaries	126.0	299.7	194.8	. . .	143.6	338.4
8. Goods and services	63.2	164.3	132.0	. . .	61.4	193.4
9. Interest payments	1.4	4.6	8.9	. . .	1.2	7.2
10. Extrasystem transfers	13.0	102.4	90.6	. . .	12.5	154.0
11. Total	203.6	576.0	426.3	. . .	218.7	693.0
12. Intrasystem transfers	166.7	. . .	187.4	. . .	187.4	. . .
13. Savings on current account	73.6	206.1	141.7	. . .	. . .	147.2
14. Counterpart funds	. . .	16.8	13.6	. . .	. . .	13.6
Utilization of loans						
15. Domestic	2.8	56.2	44.5	123.2	−3.9	146.2
16. Foreign	−8.3	46.7	34.8	19.9	0.5	55.2
17. Total	−5.5	102.9	79.3	143.1	−3.4	201.4
Other capital resources						
18. Loan payment received	5.9	16.1	20.5	. . .	6.3	24.3
19. Depreciation reserves	1.9	13.7	. . .	11.7	. . .	11.7
20. Use of cash balance	−13.9	−66.7	−33.0	−10.5	−33.5	−77.0
21. Other capital transfers	27.7	55.4	24.6	15.8	22.9	63.3
22. Total	21.6	18.5	12.1	17.0	−4.3	22.3
23. Intrasystem capital transfers	37.2	. . .	34.3	. . .	34.3	. . .
24. Extrasystem capital transfers	15.9	31.0	60.4	. . .	13.3	73.7
Investments						
25. Gross capital	101.5	265.2	96.5	68.6	94.3	259.4
26. Fixed capital formation	101.5	221.5	96.5	78.7	94.3	269.5
27. Inventories	. . .	43.7	. . .	−10.1	. . .	−10.1
28. Subscriptions	0.2	15.3	26.6	. . .	. . .	26.6
29. Loans	9.3	32.8	28.9	10.5	5.5	44.9
30. Subscription and loans abroad	. . .	. . .	. . .	. . .	. . .	. . .
31. Total	110.0	313.3	152.0	79.1	99.8	330.9

. . . Zero or negligible.

a. Monopoly profits include only portions of surplus in monopoly which have been transferred to the general account; the remaining portion is included in enterprise revenues.

b. Primary budget.

Source: Reclassified from government transactions published by Bank of Korea. *Economic Statistical Yearbook,* various issues.

Table SA30. Central and Local Government Tax Revenues, 1965–74
(billion won)

Type of tax	1965	1966	1967	1968	1969	1970	1971	1972	1973	1974
Central government taxes										
On income and wealth	17.5	31.6	47.4	72.9	103.5	128.4	166.3	161.0	175.3	265.2
Corporate	5.7	10.9	15.9	24.6	33.1	42.4	56.7	54.8	49.8	121.0
Inheritance and gift	0.1	0.4	0.5	0.7	0.8	1.5	2.0	1.5	1.8	2.1
Personal income	11.7	20.3	31.0	47.6	69.6	84.5	107.6	104.7	123.7	142.1
On international trade	15.8	21.3	30.0	49.3	59.5	72.2	84.0	93.9	119.8	249.5
Customs duties	12.6	17.6	25.4	37.9	44.7	50.9	52.5	59.1	82.4	126.7
Petroleum	3.2	3.7	4.6	11.4	14.8	21.3	31.8	34.8	37.4	122.8
On domestic goods and services	21.3	42.2	61.8	88.5	124.1	164.2	202.8	221.4	283.4	398.9
Business activity	4.4	7.3	11.6	17.5	23.0	31.0	37.9	48.7	59.8	89.5
Commodity	7.0	10.4	15.4	22.2	30.7	31.7	34.9	36.9	50.1	69.2
Liquor	3.8	6.3	8.1	11.1	16.1	21.7	27.7	28.1	34.0	50.8
Monopoly profits	0.0	7.5	10.0	16.4	24.3	30.1	45.4	42.9	57.0	69.0
Transport	1.2	2.8	4.9	6.7	9.8	13.4	17.1	14.6	21.8	15.7
Other	4.9	7.9	11.8	14.6	20.2	36.3	39.8	50.2	60.7	104.7
Total central	54.6	95.1	139.2	210.7	287.1	364.8	453.1	476.3	578.5	913.7[a]
Local government taxes										
On income and wealth	1.5	3.9	2.7	2.5	3.0	4.0	4.9	7.9	9.3	11.0
On domestic goods	9.9	12.3	11.4	16.9	23.6	29.2	34.9	38.6	42.7	48.9
Total local	11.4	16.2	14.1	19.4	26.6	33.2	39.8	46.6	74.1	108.0[a]
Total taxes	66.0	111.3	153.3	230.1	313.7	398.0	492.9	522.9	652.6	1,021.7[a]
Ratio of taxes to GNP (percent)										
Central government	6.8	9.2	9.9	12.2	13.8	14.1	14.3	12.3	11.8	13.5
Local government	1.4	1.6	1.1	1.2	1.3	1.3	1.3	1.2	1.4	1.6
Total	8.2	10.8	12.0	14.4	15.1	15.4	15.6	13.5	13.2	15.1

a. Totals may not add up because a full breakdown of revised totals is not available.

Table SA31. Public Investment Program (Development Budget), 1974–75
(billion won)

Sector	1974				1975			
	General budget	Special accounts	National Investment Fund	Total	General budget	Special accounts	National Investment Fund	Total
Agriculture	56.4	12.2	11.0	79.6	100.3[a]	4.5	11.4	116.2
Environment improvement	5.4	...	n.a.	n.a.	8.2	...	n.a.	n.a.
Fisheries	2.2	0.2	n.a.	n.a.	3.4	0.1	n.a.	n.a.
Forestry	5.2	1.1	n.a.	n.a.	6.8	1.0	n.a.	n.a.
Irrigation	18.2	8.6	n.a.	n.a.	29.0	1.2	n.a.	n.a.
Modernization	6.5	...	n.a.	n.a.	6.1	...	n.a.	n.a.
Self-help guidance	1.1	...	n.a.	n.a.	20.2	...	n.a.	n.a.
Support program	3.7	0.2	n.a.	n.a.	9.7	...	n.a.	n.a.
Other	14.1	2.1	n.a.	n.a.	16.9	2.3	n.a.	n.a.
Communication	...	45.6	...	45.6	...	75.5	...	75.5
Education	20.0	1.6	...	21.6	24.9	0.1	...	25.0
Housing	1.1	...	...	1.1	6.4[a]	...	...	6.4
Manufacturing	13.5	11.6	54.5	79.6	14.1[a]	15.8	60.6	90.5
Korea Development Bank	9.1	...	n.a.	n.a.	1.5	...	n.a.	n.a.
Monopoly Facilities	...	11.6	n.a.	n.a.	...	15.8	n.a.	n.a.
Sae Maeul	...	...	4.0	4.0	...	...	4.8	4.8
Steel Mill	2.6	...	n.a.	n.a.	...	...	n.a.	n.a.
Other	1.8	...	n.a.	n.a.	12.6	...	n.a.	n.a.

Mining	9.8	. . .	0.5	10.3	17.2	. . .	17.2
Power	27.8	. . .	17.0	44.8	19.7	35.0	54.7
Interest Subsidy	4.3	. . .	:	4.3	3.6	:	3.6
Korea Electric Company	23.5	. . .	17.0	40.5	16.1	35.0	51.1
Public Health	2.1	. . .	. . .	2.1	2.8	. . .	2.8
Public Works	17.7	. . .	. . .	17.7	11.1	. . .	11.1
Multipurpose dam	13.6	. . .	. . .	13.0	6.6	. . .	6.6
Other	4.7	. .	. . .	4.7	4.5	. . .	4.5
Science and Technology	10.4	1.4	. . .	11.8	14.5	2.1	16.6
Transport	69.8	21.0	. . .	90.8	92.0	34.1	126.1
Highway	28.4	5.6	. . .	34.0	39.8[a]	7.4	47.2
Railway	18.8	15.4	. . .	34.2	20.3	26.6	46.9
Other	22.6	. . .	. . .	22.6	31.9	. . .	32.0
Other	23.8	1.4	7.0	32.2	32.7	9.6	45.3
Export promotion	4.9	. . .	n.a.	n.a.	4.3	. . .	n.a.
Interest subsidies	12.8	. . .	n.a.	n.a.	18.8	. . .	n.a.
Stock market promotion	. .	. .	n.a.	n.a.	3.0	. .	n.a.
Other	6.1	1.4	n.a.	n.a.	6.6	9.6	n.a.
Total	263.4	95.2	90.0	448.6	355.4	141.6	607.0

. . . Zero or negligible.
n.a.: Not available.
a. Does not include W20 billion of employment-creating investment added to budget as follows:

Agriculture	12.8
Housing	2.0
Road maintenance	2.0
Textile machinery	2.0
Water works	1.2

Source: Economic Planning Board.

Table SA32. Selected Annual Interest Rates on Loans and Discounts of the Bank of Korea, 1965–72
(percent)

Item	Nov. 16, 1965	Dec. 1, 1965	Mar. 1, 1968	Oct. 1, 1968	June 1, 1969	June 18, 1970	June 28, 1971	Jan. 17, 1972	Aug. 3, 1972
Export on UN supply loans	3.5	3.5	3.5	3.5	3.5	3.5	3.5	3.5	3.5
Rice lien loans	4.0	4.0	4.0	4.0	4.0	4.0	4.0	4.0	4.0
Commercial bills	21.0	28.0	21.0	23.0	22.0	21.0	16.0	13.0	11.0
Other bills	23.0	28.0	28.0	28.0	26.0	26.0	24.0	19.0	14.0
Purchase of aid goods	23.0	26.0	26.0	25.2	24.0	24.0	. . .	. . .	. . .

. . . Zero or negligible.
Source: Bank of Korea, *Monthly Economic Statistics.*

Table SA33. Selected Annual Interest Rates on Loans and Discounts of Commercial Banks, 1965–74
(percent)

Item	Prior to Sept. 30, 1965	June 1, 1969	June 18, 1970	June 28, 1971	June 17, 1972	Aug. 3, 1972	May 14, 1973	Jan. 24, 1974	Nov. 12, 1974
Export bills	6.5	6.0[a]	6.0[a]	6.0	6.0	6.0	7.0	9.0	9.0
Import bills	. . .	6.0	6.0	6.0	6.0	6.0	7.0	9.0	9.0
Commercial bills	14.0	24.6	24.0	22.0	19.0	15.5	15.5	15.5	15.5
Other bills	16.0	24.0	24.0	23.0[b]	20.0[b]	16.5	15.5	15.5	15.5
Overdraft	8.5	26.0	26.0	24.0	22.0	17.5	17.5	17.5	17.5
Overdue loans	20.0	36.5	36.5	36.5	31.2	25.0	25.0	25.0	25.0
Loans for machinery and industry promotion	. . .	12.0	12.0	12.0	12.0	10.0	10.0	10.0	10.0

. . . Zero or negligible.
a. Commercial bank loans for raw materials imports for export production carry an interest rate of 6 percent; interest rate on loans for imports of raw materials for other purposes is 24 percent.
b. Other bills applied to 3–5 years.
Source: Bank of Korea, *Monthly Economic Statistics.*

Table SA34. Deposit Interest Rates of Banking Institutions, 1965–74

Deposits	1965 Prior to Sept. 30	1965 Sept. 30	1968 April 1	1968 Oct. 1	1969 June 1	1971 June 28	1972 Jan. 17	1972 Aug. 3	1973 Aug. 16	1974 Jan. 24	1974 Dec. 9
Time deposits											
Over 18 months	15.0	30.0	27.6	—	—	21.3	17.4	12.6	12.6	15.0	15.0
Over 12 months	15.0	26.4	26.4	25.2	22.8	20.4	16.8	12.0	12.0	15.0	15.0
Over 6 months	12.0	24.0	20.4	19.2	16.8	14.4	11.4	8.4	8.4	13.2	13.2
Over 3 months	9.0	18.0	15.6	14.4	12.0	10.2	8.4	6.0	6.0	12.0	12.0
Short-term savings											
Notice	3.65	5.00	5.00	5.00	5.00	5.00	5.00	3.65	3.65[c]	3.65	3.65
Savings[a]	3.60	7.20	—	—	—	—	—	—	—	—	—
New household deposits[b]	—	—	12.0	12.0	9.6	8.7	6.6	4.8	4.8[c]	4.8	4.8
Installment savings	10.0	30.0	28.0	25.0	23.0	21.0	17.0	12.0	12.0[c]	13.2	13.2
National Savings Association	16.8	30.0	28.0	25.2	22.8	21.0	17.4	12.6	12.6[c]	12.6	12.6
Demand deposits											
Passbook	1.80	1.80	1.80	1.80	1.80	1.80	1.80	1.80	1.80[c]	1.80	1.80
Temporary	1.00	1.00	1.00	1.00	1.00	1.00	1.00	1.00	1.00[c]	1.00	1.00

— Not applicable.

Note: Time deposit rates are actual rates agreed upon by the Korea Banking Association; others are maximum rates decided by the Monetary Board.

a. Abolished in November 1967.

b. Maximum balance per account is 5 million won; depositors must be individuals or nonprofit organizations, and 30 days' notice is required for withdrawal.

c. May 1, 1973.

Source: Bank of Korea, *Monthly Economic Statistics.*

Table SA35. Production of Agricultural Crops, 1965–74
(*thousand metric tons*)

Crop	1965	1966	1967	1968	1969	1970	1971	1972	1973	1974
Cereals										
Barley	1,807	2,018	1,916	2,084	2,066	1,974	1,857	1,965	1,778	1,705
Corn	40	34	60	63	63	68	64	54	61	58
Millets	61	58	42	78	60	44	34	31	30	29
Rice	3,501	3,919	3,603	3,195	4,090	3,939	3,998	3,957	4,212	4,445
Rye	29	41	27	25	27	22	17	16	12	11
Wheat	300	315	310	345	366	357	322	241	162	136
Other	19	15	12	21	14	12	12	9	13	10
Total	5,757	6,400	5,970	5,811	6,686	6,416	6,304	6,273	6,268	6,394
Cocoons	7.8	9.6	10.9	16.6	20.7	21.4	24.7	26.8	31.0	37.0
Fruits										
Apples	167	174	190	199	219	212	221	261	291	297
Grapes	19	23	25	28	37	34	34	48	57	59
Peaches	54	63	71	72	68	78	66	80	84	89
Pears	40	41	41	48	46	52	48	50	52	57
Persimmons	24	22	24	35	34	30	23	31	32	42
Other	6	8	8	10	13	17	12	19	34	38
Total	310	331	359	392	417	423	404	489	550	582
Potatoes										
Sweet	929	834	518	635	658	662	589	582	517	449
White	116	138	113	123	120	121	118	92	94	94
Total	1,045	972	631	758	778	783	707	674	611	543
Pulses										
Soybeans	174	161	201	245	229	232	222	224	246	319
Other	29	34	34	43	44	45	41	37	37	49
Total	203	195	235	288	273	277	263	261	283	368
Tobacco	56	72	66	70	59	56	63	116	112	95
Vegetables										
Chinese cabbage	480	520	609	700	791	797	989	826	782	908
Radishes	587	597	580	690	722	765	874	821	797	915
Red peppers	46	67	67	84	62	53	74	73	77	71
Other	463	533	613	676	853	905	980	997	956	1,082
Total	1,576	1,717	1,869	2,150	2,428	2,520	2,917	2,717	2,612	2,976
Special crops										
Cotton	12	14	12	13	14	13	12	11	12	9
Other	29	43	50	54	69	60	71	55	55	79
Total	41	57	62	67	83	73	83	66	67	88

Source: Ministry of Agriculture and Fisheries.

Table SA36. Yield per Hectare of Major Crops, 1965–74
(*kilograms per hectare*)

Crop	1965	1966	1967	1968	1969	1970	1971	1972	1973	1974
Apples	8,780	8,930	9,580	9,840	10,550	10,080	10,950	12,550	12,590	10,800
Barley (polished)	1,750	1,960	1,850	1,760	2,050	1,930	1,940	2,070	1,920	1,760
Barley, naked (polished)	1,760	2,210	2,070	2,450	2,290	2,360	2,440	2,370	2,340	2,130
Cabbage	18,120	19,150	22,300	21,110	22,130	17,760	23,590	23,370	21,330	20,930
Corn	800	790	1,180	1,490	1,400	1,440	1,600	1,510	1,680	1,640
Peaches	5,120	5,830	6,200	6,150	5,910	6,600	7,340	8,400	8,220	7,490
Pears	7,640	7,370	6,930	7,750	7,380	7,770	7,090	6,800	6,740	6,020
Potatoes, sweet	19,500	18,040	12,110	14,900	15,540	16,700	16,950	17,860	17,270	n.a.
Potatoes, white	9,570	11,290	9,670	10,180	10,610	11,210	11,220	10,530	11,290	n.a.
Radishes	14,110	14,130	13,010	13,980	13,260	11,520	13,940	13,400	12,790	13,590
Rice (polished)	2,830	3,160	2,890	2,750	3,330	3,250	3,330	3,290	3,530	3,660
Soybeans	560	580	640	780	740	780	800	790	780	1,110
Wheat	1,960	2,040	2,030	2,170	2,370	2,240	2,240	2,350	2,290	2,010

n.a.: Not available.
Source: Ministry of Agriculture and Fisheries.

Table SA37. Utilization of Cultivated Land, 1965–74
(thousand chungbo)[a]

Year	Area of cultivated land	Planted crop area	Planted area of major crops								
			Rice	Barley and wheat	Miscellaneous grain	Pulses	Potatoes	Fruits	Vegetables	Sericulture and tobacco	Other
1965	2,275	3,586	1,238	1,211	216	368	214	43	151	84	61
1966	2,312	3,482	1,242	1,148	171	345	210	45	154	99	68
1967	2,331	3,541	1,246	1,151	162	380	196	48	177	107	74
1968	2,338	3,552	1,160	1,161	200	384	198	51	193	133	72
1969	2,330	3,575	1,230	1,120	144	379	193	56	226	138	89
1970	2,321	3,504	1,213	1,085	124	368	182	60	255	128	89
1971	2,294	3,325	1,200	993	101	341	165	55	257	122	91
1972	2,265	3,292	1,201	987	86	343	149	59	248	137	82
1973	2,264	3,246	1,192	893	92	373	140	64	254	136	102
1974	2,261	3,325	1,217	936	82	353	125	73	274	142	123
Percentage of the total planted area											
1965–68[b]		100.0	34.5	33.0	5.3	10.4	5.8	1.3	4.8	3.0	1.9
1969		100.0	34.4	31.3	4.0	10.6	5.4	1.6	6.3	3.9	2.5
1970		100.0	34.6	31.0	3.5	10.5	5.2	1.7	7.3	3.7	2.5
1971		100.0	36.0	29.9	3.0	10.3	5.0	1.7	7.7	3.7	2.7
1972		100.0	36.5	30.0	2.6	10.4	4.5	1.8	7.5	4.2	2.5
1973		100.0	36.7	27.5	2.8	11.5	4.3	2.0	7.8	4.2	3.1
1974		100.0	36.6	28.2	2.5	10.1	3.8	2.2	8.2	4.3	3.7

a. A chungbo = 0.99 hectares.
b. Average.
Source: Ministry of Agriculture and Fisheries.

Table SA38. Number of Livestock and Output of Livestock Products, 1965–74

Livestock and products	1965	1966	1967	1968	1969	1970	1971	1972	1973	1974
Number (thousands)										
Cattle										
Beef	1	1	2	3	4	3	2.9	4.8	6.3	n.a.
Dairy	7	9	10	14	19	24	30	36	52	73
Draft	1,314	1,290	1,243	1,193	1,202	1,284	1,247	1,333	1,486	1,778
Goats	178	161	133	109	99	131	128	152	194	253
Pigs	1,382	1,457	1,296	1,396	1,339	1,126	1,333	1,248	1,595	1,818
Poultry										
Chickens	11,893	14,008	17,079	25,968	22,651	23,633	25,903	24,537	29,071	18,814
Ducks	210	233	227	319	200	. . .	252	224	483	491
Turkeys	2	2	2	2	2	. . .	2	2	4	12
Rabbits	763	908	833	651	489	469	364	421	587	848
Sheep	1	2	2	2	3	7	3	4	4	5
Output										
Meat (thousand metric tons)										
Beef	27.3	29.4	31.9	35.8	33.1	37.3	39.4	40.2	46.5	n.a.
Pork	55.9	95.8	72.2	61.8	76.1	82.5	80.9	90.2	103.3	n.a.
Poultry	14.6	18.7	24.0	35.8	42.2	45.2	50.0	54.3	59.2	n.a.
Other meat	1.9	2.2	2.5	3.0	3.6	2.4	. . .	. . .	. . .	n.a.
Total	99.7	146.1	130.6	136.4	155.0	167.4	170.3	184.7	209.0	n.a.
Eggs (million)	856.0	1,298.0	1,349.0	1,585.0	2,430.0	2,456.0	2,536.0	2,790.0	3,079.0	n.a.
Milk (thousand metric tons)	10.6	14.6	19.2	23.4	35.5	51.9	65.3	79.9	103.3	n.a.

. . . Zero or negligible.
n.a.: Not available.
Source: Livestock Bureau, Ministry of Agriculture and Fisheries.

Table SA39. Paddy Area Classified by Irrigation Facilities, 1965–74
(thousand hectares)

Area	1965	1966	1967	1968	1969	1970	1971	1972	1973	1974
Facilities provided by										
irrigation associations	281	286	293	283	296	304	310	314	320	309
Fully irrigated with										
other facilities	421	445	456	448	515	544	558	562	556	584
Subtotal	702	731	749	731	811	848	868	877	876	893
Percentage of total	59	61	62	65	68	72	74	74	75	70
Partially irrigated paddy	299	289	279	252	248	223	210	213	210	289
Rain-fed paddy	198	180	177	144	140	113	100	89	83	88
Total	1,199	1,200	1,205	1,127	1,199	1,184	1,178	1,178	1,169	1,270

Source: *Yearbook of Agriculture and Fisheries Statistics, 1975.*

Table SA40. Growth of Industrial Production, 1967–74
(annual growth rates, seasonally adjusted, in percent)

Product	Index weight	1967-71	1972	1973	1974[a]
All industry	100.00	19.5	14.6	35.7	27.6
Electricity	5.63	21.1	12.4	25.1	13.6
Manufacturing	85.93	21.2	16.4	35.4[b]	29.2
Chemicals, petroleum, coal,					
rubber and plastics	20.60	25.1	7.9	25.4	11.4
Food, beverages, and tobacco	18.52	19.5	13.4	11.3	6.1
Metal, basic	4.97	23.8	19.1	54.6	87.2
Metal products (fabricated),					
machinery, equipment	15.31	16.9	11.4	82.6[b]	89.6
Nonmetallic mineral products	6.52	12.6	−1.0	35.4	9.4
Paper and paper products,					
printing, publishing	6.22	16.8	9.1	17.9	16.2
Textiles, wearing apparel,					
and leather	20.28	28.5	36.2	39.9	16.4
Wood and wood products	4.04	19.2	13.0	18.4	11.2
Miscellaneous	3.54	9.9	25.7	13.2	16.3
Mining	8.44	2.7	−4.6	16.2	9.2
Special classification					
Consumer goods	42.55	20.8	21.0	28.6	27.8
Consumable	24.82	16.8	9.8	16.0	15.3
Durable	4.08	19.0	19.5	84.2	46.5
Semidurable	13.65	30.7	39.7	32.3	36.2
Producer goods	57.45	23.5	12.8	45.4	54.6
Construction materials	13.58	20.0	4.3	32.3	11.3
Durables	7.99	13.8	4.8	115.4	150.0
Raw materials	35.88	27.7	17.8	36.7	40.7

a. 1974 data under "Special classification" for first six months only.
b. Revised figure (March 1975).
Source: EPB, *Monthly Statistics of Korea,* 1973–74, and Bank of Korea, March 1975.

Table SA41. Number and Tonnage of Fishing Vessels, 1965–74

Year	Nonpowered			Powered			Total		
	Number	Gross tonnage	Average tonnage	Number	Gross tonnage	Average tonnage	Number	Gross tonnage	Average tonnage
1965	43,500	83,600	1.9	7,600	119,500	15.7	51,100	203,100	4.0
1966	44,400	85,500	1.9	8,900	160,500	18.0	53,300	246,000	4.6
1967	46,300	83,000	1.8	11,000	179,000	16.3	57,300	262,000	4.6
1968	50,558	86,600	1.7	11,444	206,362	18.0	62,002	292,962	4.7
1969	53,263	91,215	1.6	12,852	251,065	19.5	66,115	342,280	5.2
1970	54,270	90,184	1.6	14,085	268,182	19.1	68,355	358,365	5.2
1971	53,612	85,393	1.6	14,657	307,256	21.0	68,269	392,649	5.8
1972	52,938	84,923	1.6	14,741	366,843	24.9	67,679	451,767	6.7
1973	52,125	78,994	1.5	16,742	432,118	25.8	68,597	511,112	7.5
1974	50,030	76,188	1.5	18,001	526,183	29.2	68,031	602,371	8.9

Source: Office of Fisheries.

Table SA42. Index of Industrial Production, 1962–74

(*1970 = 100*)

Product	Weight	1962	1963	1964	1965
1. *Totals*	100.0	28.1	31.7	34.3	36.8
2. Electricity	5.6	21.4	24.1	29.5	35.4
3. Manufacturing	85.9	26.2	29.6	31.8	33.9
4. Mining	8.4	62.8	71.6	78.8	82.8
Mining	100.0				
5. Coal	52.9	59.6	71.7	77.7	82.8
6. Metal	24.3	82.5	73.6	82.7	88.3
7. Nonmetal	22.8	46.3	64.6	85.6	71.5
Manufacturing	100.0				
8. Apparel	3.4	. . .	. . .	. . .	46.2
9. Chemicals, industrial	5.6	11.8	14.4	18.4	20.0
10. Other	6.0	18.5	23.6	19.8	21.6
11. Food, beverages, tobacco	18.5	37.8	40.0	35.5	40.4
12. Footwear	0.4	. . .	. . .	. . .	. . .
13. Furniture	0.4	. . .	. . .	. . .	62.8
14. Leather products	0.2	95.8	86.5	99.1	95.1
15. Machinery	4.1	95.5	69.7	63.7	54.4
16. Electrical	4.1	20.8	27.2	30.3	28.8
17. Metal, basic	5.0	26.9	37.0	29.4	33.4
18. Metal products, fabricated	2.8	40.9	74.2	39.8	48.0
19. Nonmetallic mineral products	6.5	25.9	27.7	38.4	51.4
20. Paper products	2.8	42.3	50.4	51.8	55.2
21. Petroleum refineries	4.0	. . .	. . .	12.3	25.0
22. Printing and publishing	3.5	32.4	34.5	42.9	50.3
23. Rubber products	2.4	54.2	63.6	73.7	87.7
24. Textiles	16.3	20.0	20.8	24.1	28.1
25. Transport equipment	5.7	9.9	18.3	19.0	29.4
26. Wood products	3.6	20.6	24.5	20.1	21.4
27. Other	3.5	33.3	49.5	38.1	39.9

. . . Zero or negligible.
Source: Bank of Korea, *Monthly Economic Statistics*, March 1975.

	1966	1967	1968	1969	1970	1971	1972	1973	1974
1.	45.1	57.1	74.8	89.7	100.0	115.4	132.2	176.4	225.0
2.	42.4	53.6	65.8	84.0	100.0	115.0	129.2	161.7	183.7
3.	42.2	54.7	74.3	89.6	100.0	116.6	135.7	183.8	237.5
4.	91.0	93.6	88.3	89.6	100.0	103.3	98.5	114.5	125.1
5.	93.8	100.4	82.7	82.9	100.0	103.2	100.1	109.5	123.4
6.	97.6	91.0	107.0	105.1	100.0	94.9	89.7	101.9	106.4
7.	66.7	67.7	75.4	84.6	100.0	112.3	104.1	139.6	148.9
8.	46.4	58.4	76.4	81.8	100.0	141.9	210.2	389.1	510.3
9.	21.1	30.2	68.6	86.9	100.0	102.6	110.1	135.3	152.4
10.	29.1	49.5	60.1	61.2	100.0	113.2	120.6	154.2	184.5
11.	47.4	59.6	72.9	89.6	100.0	121.3	137.5	153.1	162.5
12.	. . .	. . .	. . .	. . .	100.0	141.5	134.7	162.2	262.7
13.	84.8	113.3	91.2	101.4	100.0	86.8	87.8	74.2	90.7
14.	109.1	123.0	124.0	109.5	100.0	200.3	378.7	852.7	2,000.8
15.	55.8	103.7	114.8	96.5	100.0	124.8	157.0	243.7	232.0
16.	51.1	50.5	58.9	93.5	100.0	126.1	165.6	337.8	648.8
17.	47.1	48.8	77.5	95.9	100.0	108.5	129.2	199.8	374.0
18.	64.8	81.6	98.3	100.0	100.0	115.2	112.9	168.8	201.2
19.	61.6	74.3	84.2	102.3	100.0	117.7	116.5	157.7	172.6
20.	62.3	68.5	108.2	108.2	100.0	134.4	152.6	201.4	243.8
21.	30.7	40.0	59.7	81.1	100.0	113.5	118.4	138.7	137.7
22.	62.1	68.0	89.1	91.0	100.0	105.4	111.6	114.6	125.2
23.	89.1	87.7	116.1	130.1	100.0	123.1	141.4	199.8	235.1
24.	33.3	44.1	63.6	86.2	100.0	120.5	160.5	201.1	207.5
25.	39.8	53.3	70.0	97.9	100.0	102.1	96.7	184.3	453.7
26.	29.3	54.3	87.7	90.3	100.0	116.4	132.9	160.8	139.7
27.	55.1	64.8	59.7	78.5	100.0	88.6	111.4	126.1	146.6

Table SA43. Gross Output and Value Added of the Manufacturing Sector by Economic Activity, 1973
(million won)

Industry	Output				Value added				Value added (constant) as percent of output (constant)
	Current price	Constant price (1970)	Percent		Current price	Constant price (1970)	Percent		
Beverages	149,843	126,778	3.9		81,010	63,009	6.3		49.7
Chemicals and chemical products	260,734	223,153	6.9		96,565	76,072	7.6		34.1
Fertilizer	42,906	37,818	1.2		18,339	17,321	1.7		45.8
Other	217,828	185,335	5.7		78,226	58,751	5.9		31.7
Clay, glass, and stone products	138,382	118,728	3.7		51,602	44,286	4.5		37.3
Coal and petroleum products	329,969	195,106	6.0		96,208	74,346	7.4		38.1
Petroleum products	245,886	132,286	4.1		83,926	65,614	6.5		49.6
Other	84,083	62,820	1.9		12,282	8,732	0.9		14.0
Food	574,899	415,852	12.9		105,297	102,373	10.3		24.6
Ricemill products	41,393	24,111	0.8		23,679	13,840	1.4		57.4
Other	533,506	391,741	12.1		81,618	88,533	8.9		22.6
Footwear, wearing apparel, and made-up textile goods	622,721	514,452	15.9		153,357	130,671	13.1		25.4
Furniture and fixtures	13,150	9,745	0.3		3,843	3,323	0.3		34.1

Leather and leather products	87,234	50,202	1.6	17,287	12,952	1.3	25.8
Machinery	52,562	43,611	1.3	13,996	13,782	1.4	31.6
Machinery, electrical	247,625	214,317	6.6	75,696	70,296	7.0	32.8
Machinery, transport	154,031	124,085	3.8	44,165	42,566	4.3	34.3
Railway equipment	13,038	9,951	0.3	6,931	5,244	0.5	52.7
Other	140,993	114,134	3.5	37,234	37,322	3.8	32.7
Metal, basic	235,262	173,629	5.4	56,457	27,260	2.7	15.7
Metal products	49,946	40,450	1.2	14,575	10,355	1.0	25.6
Paper and paper products	94,487	69,837	2.2	30,336	20,183	2.0	28.9
Printing and publishing	51,454	39,719	1.2	18,969	16,642	1.7	41.9
Rubber products	72,466	52,020	1.6	17,823	13,889	1.4	26.7
Textiles	677,672	508,926	15.7	232,423	152,169	15.2	29.9
Tobacco	134,859	89,150	2.8	92,641	61,781	6.2	69.3
Wood and cork products	163,422	101,247	3.1	37,557	22,274	2.2	22.0
Miscellaneous	174,330	125,766	3.9	50,310	40,522	4.1	32.2
Plastic products	39,157	33,313	1.0	10,557	10,660	1.1	32.0
Other	135,173	92,453	2.9	39,753	29,862	3.0	32.3
Grand Total	4,285,048	3,236,773	100.0	1,290,117	998,750	100.0	30.9
Light industries	2,722,050	2,033,857	62.8	810,517	619,605	62.0	30.5
Heavy and chemical industries	1,562,998	1,202,916	37.2	479,600	379,145	38.0	31.5

Source: Bank of Korea, Industrial Statistics Division.

247

Table SA44. Structure of the Manufacturing Sector, 1970–72

Industry	Number of establishments (units)			Number of workers (persons)			Value added (million won)		
	1970	1971	1972	1970	1971	1972	1970	1971	1972
Chemicals, petroleum, coal, rubber and plastic products	1,723	1,542	1,705	101,628	104,298	112,198	121,032	162,305	188,068
Food, beverages, and tobacco	5,156	5,011	4,937	117,327	114,806	136,929	141,135	170,213	224,938
Metal, basic	344	321	362	31,528	25,872	27,628	21,978	25,680	35,138
Metal products and machinery	3,889	3,719	3,860	149,896	144,362	172,364	76,117	83,354	115,022
Nonmetallic minerals	2,278	2,221	2,019	50,366	48,406	45,241	32,695	41,403	47,209
Paper and paper products, printing, publishing	1,738	1,732	1,761	49,360	51,461	56,970	27,819	38,900	45,187
Textiles, wearing apparel, and leather	6,393	6,287	6,216	267,479	274,734	317,471	93,750	120,804	185,687
Wood, wood products, furniture	2,008	2,023	2,177	45,230	41,660	45,080	19,487	31,697	39,453
Other	575	556	692	48,227	42,595	59,534	15,779	16,178	19,706
Total manufacturing	24,114	23,412	23,729	861,041	848,194	973,415	549,793	690,535	899,408
Light industries	18,598	13,321	14,022	619,873	431,200	559,014	348,540	322,714	458,784
Heavy and chemical industries	5,516	10,091	9,707	241,168	416,994	414,401	201,254	367,820	431,624

Note: Covers only establishments with five or more workers.
Source: Ministry of Commerce and Industry, Statistics Yearbook, 1974, tables 35, 36, and 38.

248

Table SA45. Summary of Mining and Manufacturing Survey, 1972

(billion won)

Industry	Number of establishments (units)	Number of workers (numbers)	Employees' salaries	Production costs	Value of shipments	Gross output	Value added	Change of inventories	Tangible fixed assets Investments	Tangible fixed assets Disposals
Mining, quarrying, and manufacturing	25,248	1,045,201	230.9	1,360.0	2,288.2	2,302.4	942.4	34.8	262.9	33.9
Mining and quarrying	1,519	71,786	19.5	17.8	60.3	60.8	43.0	0.6	7.7	0.8
Manufacturing	23,729	973,415	211.5	1,342.2	2,227.9	2,241.6	899.4	34.3	255.2	33.1
Joint stock companies	2,739	604,564	153.3	1,084.9	1,754.9	1,767.8	682.9	31.4	236.7	31.6
Other corporations	344	35,617	9.7	57.4	135.5	136.3	78.9	1.8	4.3	0.6
Individuals	20,646	333,234	48.4	199.9	337.4	337.6	137.7	1.1	14.3	0.9
Chemicals, petroleum, coal, rubber and plastic products	1,705	112,198	33.4	275.5	463.0	463.6	188.1	1.5	81.5	1.7
Food, beverages, and tobacco	4,937	136,929	29.5	285.8	509.4	510.7	224.9	5.1	28.0	2.1
Metal, basic	362	27,628	8.3	102.2	135.6	137.3	35.1	2.5	54.9	0.2
Metal products (fabricated), machinery, equipment	3,860	172,364	40.7	172.9	283.5	287.9	115.0	7.8	25.1	7.5
Nonmetallic minerals except products of petroleum and coal	2,019	45,241	10.5	44.1	90.3	91.3	47.2	1.6	17.6	1.0
Paper and paper products, printing, publishing	1,761	56,970	16.8	64.0	108.7	109.2	45.2	0.8	7.7	0.5
Textiles, wearing apparel, and leather	6,216	317,471	55.2	303.7	482.8	489.4	185.7	17.2	30.2	19.4
Wood and wood products, furniture	2,177	45,080	8.8	70.6	112.1	109.0	38.5	-3.0	6.5	0.5
Other	692	59,534	8.3	23.4	42.6	43.1	19.7	0.8	3.6	0.2

Note: The Manufacturing Survey does not cover the self-employed or establishments with less than five workers.
Source: Bureau of Statistics, EPB.

Table SA46. Financial Indicators of the Manufacturing Sector, 1968–73
(*ratios*)

Item	1968	1969	1970	1971	1972	1973
Net profit to gross capital	5.33	3.67	2.49	0.99	3.77	7.90
Net profit to net sales	5.96	4.31	3.27	1.18	3.94	7.49
Net profit to net worth	16.05	13.57	10.67	4.50	16.73	30.04
Interest expenses to net sales	5.90	7.81	9.15	9.86	7.08	4.61
Fixed assets to net worth	78.00	79.80	81.00	87.40	76.10	73.60
Current ratio	129.70	120.50	117.10	108.10	128.20	134.20
Fixed assets to total assets	48.70	46.40	45.60	49.20	47.10	45.60
Personnel expenses to total expenses	9.68	10.75	10.89	10.17	9.71	9.06
Debt ratio	201.3	270.0	328.4	394.2	313.4	272.7

Source: Financial Statements Analysis for 1973, Bank of Korea, 1974. This survey analyzed 1,026 enterprises employing 478,396 persons in 1973. Of these, 590 firms employing 444,886 were classified as "large" and 436 employing 33,510 people, as "medium."

Table SA47. Foreign Investment, 1962–June 30, 1973
(*million U.S. dollars*)

Approvals	Number of projects	Amount	Arrivals (amount)
By sector			
Ceramics	20	17.4	15.9
Electric and electronics	127	84.5	58.2
Food processing	16	8.3	4.3
Hotels and tourism	9	52.2	9.3
Machinery	74	20.4	10.1
Oil refining	4	33.0	32.9
Petrochemicals	62	24.0	20.3
Steel and metals	50	31.7	14.6
Textiles and apparel	61	126.1	57.7
Transport equipment	6	27.6	25.6
Transport and storage	8	6.0	2.2
Other manufacturing	142	46.5	34.5
Other services	8	27.8	12.9
Total	633	512.8	301.2
By country			
United States	119	169.6	
Japan	476	305.3	
Other	38	47.9	
Total	633	512.8	

Source: EPB.

Table SA48. Imports of Raw Materials for Manufactures, 1966–74: Dollar Value
(million U.S. dollars)

Industry	1966	1968	1969	1970	1971	1972	1973	1974
Chemicals, inorganic	7.0	13.0	14.8	16.0	20.0	19.1	36.1	54.2
Chemicals, organic	14.0	35.0	45.9	62.0	81.0	92.1	137.2	294.8
Copper	0.6	2.6	3.7	8.4	7.7	6.4	16.9	37.9
Cotton, raw	42.7	49.0	52.0	62.7	84.2	85.5	112.4	189.5
Iron and steel ingots	4.9	17.5	29.6	35.5	58.7	101.1	197.0	236.5
Plates and sheets	15.7	19.0	16.6	21.7	22.0	22.9	43.5	81.5
Scrap	12.4	22.9	40.3	61.8	53.5	27.7	74.3	56.1
Tubes and pipes	3.6	12.2	12.9	12.9	20.1	14.4	10.4	23.6
Plastic materials	7.9	18.1	25.2	37.0	44.8	45.2	60.7	92.8
Pulp	12.3	21.5	24.4	31.2	35.1	35.0	64.9	111.1
Rubber, crude	9.4	11.8	17.6	17.6	20.2	22.5	46.7	75.5
Synthetic fibers	12.7	20.9	22.0	37.5	37.2	47.1	83.5	74.4
Textile fabrics	8.7	75.9	36.4	57.2	77.0	64.9	152.3	141.2
Textile yarn and thread	32.7	69.3	63.9	59.4	47.3	43.6	108.1	78.6
Wood	43.1	191.5	108.4	125.3	153.7	140.8	311.6	343.5
Wool and other animal hair	6.7	14.3	13.9	14.7	10.8	22.7	54.4	36.8
Total imports of raw materials	234	595	528	661	773	791	1,510	1,928
Total imports	716	1,463	1,823	1,984	2,394	2,522	4,240	6,894

Source: Bank of Korea, *Monthly Economic Statistics,* and unpublished government documents.

252

Table SA49. Imports of Raw Materials for Manufactures, 1966–74: Percentage Distribution

Industry	1966	1968	1969	1970	1971	1972	1973	1974
Chemicals, inorganic	3.0	2.2	2.8	2.4	2.6	2.4	2.4	2.8
Chemicals, organic	6.0	5.9	8.7	9.4	10.5	11.6	9.1	15.3
Copper	0.3	0.4	0.7	1.3	1.0	0.8	1.1	2.0
Cotton, raw	18.2	8.2	9.8	9.5	10.9	10.8	7.4	9.8
Iron and steel ingots	2.1	2.9	5.6	5.4	7.6	12.8	13.0	12.3
Plates and sheets	6.7	3.2	3.2	3.3	2.8	2.9	2.9	4.2
Scrap	5.3	3.8	7.6	9.3	6.9	3.5	4.9	2.9
Tubes and pipes	1.5	2.1	2.4	2.0	2.6	1.8	0.7	1.2
Plastic materials	3.4	3.0	4.8	5.6	5.8	5.7	4.0	4.8
Pulp	5.3	3.6	4.6	4.7	4.5	4.4	4.3	5.8
Rubber, crude	4.0	2.0	3.4	2.7	2.6	2.8	3.1	3.9
Synthetic fibers	5.4	3.5	4.2	5.7	4.8	6.0	5.5	3.9
Textile fabrics	3.7	12.8	6.9	8.7	10.0	8.2	10.1	7.3
Textile yarn and thread	14.0	11.6	12.1	9.0	6.1	5.5	7.2	4.1
Wood	18.4	32.5	20.5	19.0	19.9	17.8	20.6	17.8
Wool and other animal hair	2.9	2.4	2.6	2.2	1.4	2.9	3.6	1.9
Total imports of raw materials	100.0	100.0	100.0	100.0	100.0	100.0	100.0	100.0

Source: Based on Table SA48.

Table SA50. Average Monthly Earnings of Regular Employees in Mining and Manufacturing, 1970–74

(won)

Industry	1970	1971	1972	1973	1974[a]
Total Average	15,432	18,389	21,229	23,267	n.a.
Electricity	44,482	54,060	59,354	61,326	n.a.
Manufacturing	14,561	17,349	20,104	22,330	30,215
Chemicals, petroleum, rubber, and plastic products	16,749	20,121	23,525	28,578	n.a.
Food, beverages, and tobacco	16,155	20,334	23,512	24,881	32,265
Metal, basic	18,679	22,609	27,083	38,250	48,765
Metal products, machinery, equipment	15,332	18,578	20,623	22,046	n.a.
Nonmetallic mineral products	16,311	19,649	22,677	25,590	n.a.
Paper and paper products, printing, publishing	17,939	21,481	25,057	27,495	n.a.
Textiles, wearing apparel, and leather	11,223	13,124	15,837	18,322	25,150
Wood and wood products	14,085	16,543	19,583	22,383	n.a.
Miscellaneous	13,633	13,993	14,791	15,970	n.a.
Mining	17,921	21,564	25,586	30,415	n.a.

n.a.: Not available.
a. Estimated.
Source: Bank of Korea, *Monthly Economic Statistics,* March 1975.

Table SA51. Annual Changes in Price Deflators, 1954–74
(*percent*)

Year	GDP	Gross domestic fixed capital formation	Consumption expenditures	
			Government	Private
1954	31.5	38.2	84.0	29.5
1955	64.0	69.1	43.5	63.3
1956	31.7	25.8	31.8	34.9
1957	20.4	15.0	54.0	13.2
1958	−0.5	3.5	19.4	−1.5
1959	3.1	8.4	18.8	1.0
1960	9.0	6.2	13.7	12.2
1961	14.7	19.7	13.4	17.3
1962	14.0	11.3	21.2	12.0
1963	28.8	11.2	5.7	32.2
1964	32.2	29.3	14.7	36.6
1965	8.2	16.2	16.4	6.7
1966	13.9	16.2	24.8	12.8
1967	14.2	7.3	15.9	12.4
1968	11.9	8.5	20.1	10.3
1969	13.4	4.7	15.8	12.5
1970	15.5	15.6	18.6	14.2
1971	11.5	7.2	14.1	12.4
1972	14.5	10.4	18.0	13.7
1973	9.6	16.0	5.8	8.8
1974	26.8	36.1	34.6	33.7
Annual averages				
1954–57	36.90	37.03	53.33	35.23
1958–62	8.06	9.82	17.30	8.20
1963–67	19.46	16.04	15.50	20.14
1968–72	13.36	9.28	17.32	12.94
1973–74	18.20	26.05	20.20	21.25

Table SA52. Changes in the Price of Food Grains, 1969–73

Item	1969	1970	1971	1972	1973
Producer's price support policy in food					
Rice (80 kilograms)					
Price (won)	5,510	7,000	8,750	9,888	11,377
Percent increase	22.6	35.9	25.0	13.0	15.1
Barley (76.5 kilograms)					
Price (won)	3,348	3,850	4,890	6,357	6,993
Percent increase	26.8	15.0	27.0	30.0	10.0
Soybeans (75 kilograms)					
Price (won)	4,125	5,060	6,328	8,750	9,625
Percent increase	19.7	22.7	25.0	38.3	10.0
Status of rice price level					
Highest fluctuation in the year (percent)	n.a.	11.2	7.2	10.3	n.a.
Sales price (won)	n.a.	5,000	5,400	6,500	9,500
Amount sold (thousand metric tons)[a]	n.a.	749	1,181	589	605
Dual price system of barley (won)					
Procurement price	3,348	3,850	4,890	6,357	6,993
Prime cost[b]	3,787	4,398	5,562	7,152	n.a.
Sales price[c]	2,750	3,100	4,300	4,800	n.a.
Deficit per 76.5 kilograms	1,037	1,298	1,262	2,712	n.a.

n.a.: Not available.
a. Throughout the year.
b. Procurement price plus handling cost.
c. Government releasing price.

Table SA53. Family Income Distribution in All Cities, 1965–71

1965		1969		1970		1971	
Income (won)	Percent of total	Income (won)	Percent of total	Income (won)	Percent of total	Income (won)	Percent of total
0–2,000	0.6	0–7,999	3.0	0–11,999	6.2	0–19,999	16.7
2–4,000	10.8	8–11,999	10.4	12–19,999	24.8	20–27,999	29.4
4–6,000	24.0	12–15,999	16.5	20–27,999	28.7	28–35,999	25.1
6–8,000	21.5	16–19,999	15.1	28–35,999	19.2	36–43,999	12.1
8–10,000	14.2	20–23,999	14.1	36–43,999	8.6	44–51,999	7.3
10–12,000	10.4	24–27,999	9.7	44–51,999	6.1	52–59,999	2.6
12–14,000	6.8	28–31,999	9.9	52,000 and over	6.4	60,000 and over	6.8
14,000 and over	11.7	32–35,999	4.7				
		36–39,999	2.9				
		40,000 and over	13.7				

Source: *Annual Report on the Family Income and Expenditure Survey*, EPB.

257

Table SA54. Price Trends, 1966–74

Index	Weight	1966	1967	1968	1969	1970	1971	1972	1973	1974
Wholesale price index, (1970 = 100)										
All commodities	1,000.0	74.6	79.4	85.8	90.6	100.0	108.6	123.8	132.4	188.2
Producer Goods	395.9	81.9	84.0	88.0	91.2	100.0	106.3	120.7	135.6	219.2
Building Materials	106.6	75.1	76.5	83.5	87.1	100.0	101.1	110.2	124.2	172.1
Raw Materials	182.3	89.6	89.5	90.7	93.1	100.0	106.3	120.0	136.3	192.0
Consumer Goods	551.5	70.6	77.0	84.6	92.0	100.0	110.5	126.5	130.9	169.7
Grains	99.9	62.1	68.7	77.6	91.4	100.0	125.2	169.0	166.9	208.7
All commodities excluding foods	687.0	79.8	84.1	89.3	93.0	100.0	105.7	117.5	127.3	186.5
Wholesale price index of imported goods (1970 = 100)										
All commodities	1,000.0	88.5	86.9	88.8	92.6	100.0	107.1	121.6	139.0	209.8
Chemicals, industrial	185.8	91.2	95.1	93.5	93.9	100.0	109.1	117.3	145.9	315.6
Lumber	107.5	95.0	89.4	88.7	91.5	100.0	107.1	128.4	175.2	253.1
Machinery and parts	191.4	75.0	78.2	86.7	89.9	100.0	105.1	109.4	119.5	163.2
Medicines and pesticides	143.2	104.6	99.9	100.0	94.8	100.0	111.2	132.5	137.2	163.2
Metals and metal products	64.9	67.9	73.4	80.9	86.4	100.0	100.1	118.5	129.4	174.2
Miscellaneous	151.7	83.9	83.9	84.6	89.2	100.0	108.7	138.8	154.5	219.1
All-urban consumer price index (1970 = 100)										
All items	1,000.0	62.5	69.1	76.6	86.2	100.0	113.5	126.8	130.8	171.8[a]
Food and beverages	461.3	59.5	64.5	70.9	82.3	100.0	118.9	134.7	138.2	160.4[a]
Seoul consumer price index (1970 = 100)										
All items	1,000.0	65.4	72.5	80.6	88.7	100.0	112.3	125.6	129.5	160.1[a]
Food and beverages	443.8	63.9	68.9	76.5	85.5	100.0	117.0	132.4	136.3	172.6[a]

a. Provisional.
Sources: Bank of Korea, Monthly Economic Statistics, August 1973, January 1975; EPB, Major Economic Indicators, 1962–72, July 1973.

Table SA55. Pattern of Consumption of Electric Power, 1965–74
(million kilowatt hours)

Consumer	1965	Per-cent	1970	Per-cent	1971	Per-cent	1972	Per-cent	1973	Per-cent	1974	Per-cent
Agriculture and forestry	33.11	1.34	42.88	0.55	48.70	0.55	59.95	0.60	54.0[c]	0.53	66.0[c]	0.55
Fisheries	4.17	0.17	7.35	0.09	5.73	0.06	6.10	0.06	n.a.	n.a.	n.a.	n.a.
Mining	194.63	7.90	401.91	5.19	441.03	4.96	398.38	3.99	368.0	3.55	424.0	3.54
Canneries	173.60	7.05	742.22	9.59	852.94	9.60	869.09	8.70	n.a.	n.a.	n.a.	n.a.
Chemicals	141.11	5.73	1,145.75	14.80	1,237.84	13.93	1,329.10	13.30	1,902.0	18.35	2,061.0	17.20
Coal and petroleum products	21.22	0.86	95.96	1.24	135.90	1.53	145.55	1.46	n.a.	n.a.	n.a.	n.a.
Food	208.35	8.46	433.69	5.60	528.80	5.95	594.55	5.95	711.0	6.86	802.0	6.69
Lumber mills	34.83	1.41	153.38	1.98	197.73	2.23	226.73	2.27	262.0	2.53	240.0	2.00
Machinery and tools	56.17	2.28	177.64	2.30	167.31	1.88	200.29	2.00	n.a.	n.a.	n.a.	n.a.
Metal products	130.64	5.30	839.04	10.84	750.21	8.44	862.73	8.63	693.0	6.69	814.0	6.79
Paper mills	142.90	5.80	341.50	4.41	393.02	4.42	437.49	4.38	615.0	5.93	754.0	6.29
Rubber products	61.90	2.51	109.23	1.41	126.16	1.42	136.50	1.37	n.a.	n.a.	n.a.	n.a.
Textiles	300.45	12.19	787.69	10.18	966.36	10.88	1,223.00	12.24	1,571.0	15.16	1,810.0	15.10
Other manufacturing	31.69	1.29	150.94	1.95	143.93	1.62	170.26	1.70	46.0	0.44	65.0	0.54
Other industry[a]	244.40	9.91	642.09	8.30	817.40	9.20	1,139.08	11.40	1,784.0	17.21	2,018.0	16.84
Total industrial use	1,778.97	72.21	6,071.22	78.44	6,813.08	76.69	7,798.77	78.05	8,006.0	77.25	9,054.0	75.54
Other consumers[b]	684.72	27.79	1,668.46	21.56	2,070.51	23.31	2,193.58	21.95	2,358.0	22.75	2,932.0	24.46
Total	2,463.69	100.00	7,739.68	100.00	8,883.59	100.00	9,992.35	100.00	10,364.0	100.00	11,986.0	100.00

n.a.: Not available.
a. Includes construction, transportation, communication, water, community and business services.
b. Includes government, Army, UN Forces, KECO use and residential use.
c. Includes fisheries.

Table SA56. Growth of Power Demand by Industry, 1968–74
(gigawatt hours)

Demand	1968 Consumption	1968 Growth rate (percent)	1969 Consumption	1969 Growth rate (percent)	1970 Consumption	1970 Growth rate (percent)
1. Agriculture, forestry, and fisheries	51	21.4	51	. . .	51	. . .
2. Manufacturing	3,123	31.9	4,203	34.6	4,983	18.6
3. Chemicals	1,079	49.2	1,365	26.5	1,487	8.9
4. Food and beverages	327	12.0	385	17.7	433	12.5
5. Pulp and paper	91	40.0	119	30.8	153	28.6
6. Textiles	509	16.2	679	33.4	787	16.0
7. Ceramics	428	48.6	616	43.7	742	20.6
8. Machinery	117	23.0	139	19.1	177	27.1
9. Metallurgy	356	23.2	619	73.9	839	35.4
10. Petroleum and coal products	43	30.3	59	37.2	96	62.7
11. Miscellaneous	170	18.9	220	29.4	260	18.2
12. Mining	259	. . .	297	14.3	402	35.6
13. Residential	656	14.7	827	26.1	1,009	22.0
14. Services	761	14.8	980	28.8	1,296	32.2
15. Total power demand	4,850	24.3	6,358	31.1	7,740	21.7
16. Peak demand (megawatts)	1,079	38.7	1,340	24.1	1,555	16.0

. . . Zero or negligible.
n.a. Not available.
Source: Korea Electric Company.

	1971 Consumption	1971 Growth rate (percent)	1972 Consumption	1972 Growth Rate (percent)	1973 Consumption	1973 Growth rate (percent)	1974 Consumption	1974 Growth rate (percent)
1.	54	5.8	66	22.2	54	−18.2	66	22.2
2.	5,500	10.4	6,195	12.6	8,158	31.7	9,479	16.2
3.	1,631	9.7	1,766	8.3	1,902	7.7	2,061	8.4
4.	528	21.9	594	12.5	711	19.7	802	12.8
5.	198	29.4	227	14.7	877	286.3	994	13.3
6.	966	22.7	1,221	26.4	1,571	28.7	1,810	15.2
7.	853	15.1	869	1.9				
8.	167	−5.6	200	19.8				
9.	750	−10.6	863	15.1	3,097	29.9	3,812	23.1
10.	136	41.7	146	7.4				
11.	230	−11.5	307	33.5				
12.	441	9.7	395	−10.4	368	−6.8	424	15.2
13.	1,204	19.3	1,442	19.8	1,547	7.0	n.a.	n.a.
14.	1,657	27.9	1,896	14.4	1,784	−5.9	2,018	13.1
15.	8,884	14.8	9,992	12.5	10,364	3.7	11,987	15.7
16.	1,777	14.3	2,097	18.0	2,542	21.2	n.a.	n.a.

Table SA57. Power Generation and Fuel Use, 1965–74

Category	1965	1966	1967	1968	1969	1970	1971	1972	1973	1974
Total power generation (gigawatt hours)	3,250	3,886	4,911	6,026	7,700	9,167	10,540	11,839	14,826	16,835
Hydropower	710	985	953	929	1,427	1,219	1,319	1,367	1,221	1,492
Thermal power	2,540	2,901	3,958	5,097	6,273	7,948	9,221	10,472	13,605	15,343
Total fuel consumption Anthracite coal (thousand metric tons)	1,610	1,464	1,415	1,347	1,047	676	555	587	n.a.	n.a.
Fuel oil (kiloliters)	132,811	354,971	771,787	1,136,503	1,460,166	1,934,375	1,917,101	1,819,878	n.a.	n.a.
Bunker C (kiloliters)	128,155	349,254	677,061	860,995	1,247,898	1,836,473	1,882,142	1,802,699	n.a.	n.a.
Diesel oil (kiloliters)	4,656	5,717	94,726	275,508	212,268	97,902	34,959	17,179	n.a.	n.a.
Impact of imports[a]	15.5	35.0	54.8	65.2	75.6	98.4	98.7	87.6	n.a.	n.a.

n.a.: Not available.
a. Ratio of imported fuel to total use of power fuel on calorie basis.
Source: Ministry of Commerce and Industry.

Table SA58. Number of Registered Vehicles at Year's End, 1964–74

Vehicle	1964	1965	1966	1967	1968	1969	1970	1971	1972	1973	1974
Cars	11,409	13,001	17,502	23,235	33,112	50,229	60,677	67,582	70,244	78,334	76,462
Trucks	14,951	16,015	19,432	22,995	31,582	40,134	48,901	53,405	55,116	64,584	76,833
Buses	8,617	9,316	10,888	11,499	12,786	14,237	15,831	17,411	17,550	18,871[a]	19,583[a]
Microbuses	2,160	2,385	295	536	810	856	154	166	182}		
Special vehicles	678	794	2,043	2,472	2,661	3,143	3,808	5,773	6,943	8,925	10,666
Total	37,815	41,511	50,160	60,697	80,951	108,669	129,371	144,337	150,035	170,714	183,544

a. Includes microbuses.
Source: Ministry of Construction and Ministry of Transportation.

Table SA59. Korean National Railroads: Equipment and Revenues, 1964–74

Item	1964	1965	1966	1967	1968	1969	1970	1971	1972	1973	1974
Equipment											
Track (kilometers)[a]	4,780	4,897	5,049	5,103	5,381	5,381	5,500	5,582	5,507	5,541	5,664
Engines (number)											
Steam	272	272	261	203	115	115	109	95	95	93	88
Diesel	125	125	173	252	252	282	277	337	336	336	336
Railcar	80	77	163	163	159	163	158	158	157	133	126
Electric	—	—	—	—	—	—	—	—	30	57	66
Passenger cars	1,260	1,390	1,418	1,363	1,531	1,662	1,681	1,621	1,597	1,577	1,660
Freight cars	10,764	10,587	11,454	12,617	13,239	13,994	14,407	15,189	16,808	16,269	16,117
Tank cars	664	793	952	1,307	1,826	2,097	2,107	2,313	2,301	2,253	2,228
Revenues (billion won)											
Passenger fares	5.84	7.19	9.23	11.86	15.58	18.23	19.47	17.37	20.81	22.96	n.a.
Freight charges	4.36	5.67	6.24	7.62	9.69	11.16	11.18	11.60	13.30	18.12	n.a.
Total	10.20	12.86	15.47	19.48	25.27	29.39	30.65	28.97	34.11	41.08[b]	n.a.

n.a.: Not available.
— Not applicable.
a. Including double track and sidings.
b. Estimated.
Source: Korean National Railroads.

Table SA60. Growth of Domestic Traffic, 1962–73

Year	Railways Million passenger kilometers	Railways Per-cent	Motor vehicles Million passenger kilometers	Motor vehicles Per-cent	Coastal shipping Million passenger kilometers	Coastal shipping Per-cent	Total[a] Million passenger kilometers	Total[a] Per-cent
Passenger traffic								
1962	5,869	51.1	5,461	47.5	154	1.3	11,499	100.0
1963	6,676	49.6	6,571	48.9	172	1.3	13,447	100.0
1964	7,353	51.8	6,459	46.4	195	1.4	14,061	100.0
1965	6,917	45.7	7,975	52.7	182	1.2	15,136	100.0
1966	8,665	42.5	11,463	56.2	197	1.0	20,379	100.0
1967	9,577	44.4	11,698	54.3	223	1.0	21,540	100.0
1968	10,590	42.6	13,930	56.1	218	0.9	24,829	100.0
1969	11,077	39.6	16,688	59.2	256	0.9	28,200	100.0
1970	9,819	32.3	20,045	66.0	241	0.8	30,362	100.0
1971	8,750	26.2	22,917	68.6	256	0.8	33,429	100.0
1972	10,062	27.2	26,258	71.1	301	0.8	36,944	100.0
1973[b]	10,708	25.1	31,190	73.0	435	1.1	42,711	100.0

264

Freight traffic

	Million metric tons	Million kilometer tons	Per-cent	Million metric tons	Million kilometer tons	Per-cent	Million metric tons	Million kilometer tons	Per-cent	Million metric tons	Million kilometer tons	Per-cent
1962	17.9	3,977	87.2	16.9	388	8.5	2.0	194	4.3	36.8	4,561	100.0
1963	18.0	4,067	87.5	18.1	429	8.6	2.0	194	3.9	39.9	4,981	100.0
1964	18.9	4,296	86.2	18.7	510	9.7	2.2	213	4.5	41.2	5,246	100.0
1965	21.0	4,815	86.8	24.0	503	8.7	2.3	263	4.5	49.1	5,810	100.0
1966	22.4	5,158	81.6	24.5	558	8.4	2.2	672	10.0	51.3	6,680	100.0
1967	26.1	5,960	78.4	28.6	660	8.4	4.2	1,043	13.2	60.2	7,881	100.0
1968	27.6	6,672	73.6	46.1	1,065	11.4	5.6	1,401	15.0	80.6	9,331	100.0
1969	29.2	7,117	62.2	56.6	1,307	12.2	8.2	2,107	19.5	95.3	10,742	100.0
1970	30.3	7,488	57.7	61.8	1,441	10.7	10.5	4,232	31.7	103.8	13,384	100.0
1971	30.7	7,643	50.4	73.9	3,302	20.4	11.3	4,652	29.2	117.2	15,796	100.0
1972	30.5	7,085	53.1	58.7	2,494	18.3	8.7	3,905	28.6	99.0	13,640	100.0
1973	36.4	8,394	52.7	71.0	3,112	19.1	9.8	4,574	28.2	119.3	16,240	100.0

a. Including domestic aviation whose contribution is still very small.
b. Provisional.
Source: Ministry of Transportation.

Table SA61. Mode of Transport of Major Commodities, 1967–74
(thousand metric tons)

Year	Anthracite coal	Oil	Grains	Fertilizer	Cement	Other	Total
Railroads							
1967	11,044	1,335	1,328	1,190	2,223	8,982	26,102
1968	9,676	1,693	1,562	1,469	3,173	10,007	27,580
1969	10,343	2,053	1,375	1,194	4,358	9,830	29,153
1970	11,989	2,420	1,299	1,052	4,858	8,680	30,298
1971	12,113	2,468	1,393	1,135	5,780	7,807	30,696
1972	11,287	2,161	1,649	1,259	5,986	8,160	30,502
1973	13,606	2,708	1,599	1,533	7,546	9,430	36,422
1974	15,017	n.a.	1,264	1,878	7,831	12,335	38,325
Highways							
1967	4,179	1,507	4,507	1,406	2,200	14,817	28,616
1968	6,208	2,125	6,124	1,983	2,647	27,006	46,093
1969	4,700	2,672	7,362	1,873	2,512	37,456	56,575
1970	5,037	2,872	7,239	1,815	3,739	41,073	61,775
1971	5,827	4,451	9,174	2,029	4,160	48,293	73,934
1972	4,570	4,275	8,860	1,847	3,650	35,471	58,673
1973	4,890	3,881	7,990	2,329	3,990	47,946	71,026
Marine							
1967	1,717	1,431	64	110	92	1,037	5,945
1968	1,249	2,740	98	217	342	1,174	7,801
1969	1,182	4,679	117	351	1,256	1,278	11,055
1970	1,681	6,786	117	322	1,736	1,062	14,133
1971	1,477	7,654	120	237	2,492	970	15,453
1972	1,049	6,814	47	369	2,289	538	14,667
1973	1,089	7,340	121	194	2,935	1,150	17,711
1974	1,455	7,021	56	105	3,355	n.a.	19,085
Total							
1967	16,883	4,236	5,915	2,697	4,522	25,946	60,229
1968	16,984	6,549	7,790	3,635	6,211	39,383	80,552
1969	16,033	9,134	8,850	3,325	8,010	49,980	95,332
1970	18,476	11,679	8,661	3,051	9,980	51,989	103,836
1971	19,101	14,199	10,692	3,326	11,516	58,318	117,125
1972	16,718	12,382	10,555	3,181	10,987	45,183	99,006
1973	19,354	13,506	9,742	3,999	13,228	59,489	119,318

n.a.: Not available.
Source: Ministry of Transportation; Korean National Railroads.

Table SA62. Status of Harbor Facilities, December 31, 1973
(*meters*)

Port	Quay	Lighter's wharf	Breakwater	Cargo handled in 1973 (thousand metric tons)
Inchon	4,635	3,621	1,371	11,932
Janghang	. . .	255	. . .	319
Gunsan	. . .	606	700	772
Mogpo	168	365	. . .	500
Yeosu	995	1,916	1,698	9,517
Jeju	375	361	1,384	627
Masan	1,155	1,236	240	1,034
Pusan	5,033	6,320	3,417	13,344
Samcheog	240	920	1,048	. . .
Mukho	790	671	1,298	3,613
Pohang	1,620	. . .	3,287	2,302
Ulsan	1,264	220	620	12,735
Jinhae	202	120	. . .	873
Others	318	9,691	14,112	787
Total[a]	16,875	26,302	29,175	58,355

. . . Zero or negligible.
a. Provisional.
Source: Ministry of Construction.

Table SA63. Public Roads, 1962–73
(*thousand kilometers*)

Year	Paved	Unpaved	Unrepaired	Total
1962	1.26	23.03	3.86	28.15
1963	1.39	22.92	3.83	28.15
1964	1.51	22.81	3.82	28.15
1965	1.63	22.72	3.80	28.42
1966	1.93	28.25	4.30	34.48
1967	2.09	28.51	4.20	34.80
1968	2.20	29.96	2.80	35.00
1969	2.97	30.36	3.84	37.17
1970	3.43	30.13	3.68	37.25
1971	5.79	31.68	3.17	40.64
1972	6.77	32.70	3.40	42.87
1973[a]	7.43	n.a.	n.a.	43.23

n.a.: Not available.
a. Provisional.
Source: EPB, *Major Economic Indicators,* July 1973.

Table SA64. Hospital Beds per Population Unit, 1960–72

Item	1960	1965	1970	1971	1972
Population (thousands)	24,989	28,754	31,317	31,849	32,359
Beds	9,951	11,413	15,900	17,391	19,934
Number of beds per 100,000 population	39.7	39.7	50.8	54.6	61.6

Source: Ministry of Health and Social Affairs.

Index

(Page references in italics indicate tables.)

Acrylics, 129, 170, 172, 175
Agricultural employment, 47, 139, 154; growth in, 4; labor shortages in, 110; trends in, 155
Agricultural productivity, 140–41; compared with industry, 55; diversification of, 141; expansion of, 110
Agricultural terms of trade, 12, 18, 23, *46*, 76, 108, 110, 141
Agriculture: adverse natural conditions for, 140; drainage systems in, 142; exports in, *146*; gross value added in, 155, *156*; growth in, 139–40, 143; growth rate of principal subsectors in, *142*; import-substitution in, 149; investment in, 120, 148–49, 150; irrigation in, 142; land-labor ratio in, 143; long-term program for, 141–43; marketing in, 150; output per worker in, 142; parity price ratio in, 148; reclamation in, 142; share of, in GNP, 40; shift to industry from, 4, 40; use of fertilizers and pesticides in, 142; wages in, 47. *See also under* Farm

Aluminum industry: need for low-cost electricity in, 137; plans for, 19, 121; expansion of, 137
Asian Development Bank, 16, 106
Association of West European Shipbuilders, 190
Automobile companies, 125, 135; suppliers, 133. *See also* Motor vehicle industry; Passenger cars

Balance of payments, 60, 66, 98, 103, 121n; deficits in, 7, 9, 11, 12, 15, 59, 60, 78, 79, 88, 101; estimates for 1976–81, 103–06; measures to improve, 43
Balassa, Bela, 88n
Barley, 22, 44, *46*, 53, 149; import substitution in, 92; self-sufficiency in, 144;
Belgium, 13, 88
Beverages, 67, *68*, 95
Budgets, government, 108, 159; (1973), 45

Calculators, 180, 181, 184
Canada, 170
Canned food, export of, 146
Capital goods, 20, 21, 85, 92, 95, 103, 107, 122, 124

Capital requirements, external, 15–17
Capital-intensive industry, 136, 137
Capital-intensive investments, 11, 96, 103, 121
Capital-intensive projects, 102, 125
Cement industry, 67, 68, 137–38
Central Vocational Training Institute (CVTI), 35
Chang Won, machinery complex at, 133, 136
Chemical industry, 19, 20, 115, 116, 121–23; exports of, *119*; growth of, 67, 68, 69
China, 4, 25
Chosun, 25
Clothing, 4, 5, 38, 39, 67, *68*, 89, 91, 93, 127, 156, 164–65, 167, 170–71
Coal, 28, 70, 92
Commodity concentration, 5, 89
Communications, 32, *33*, 39; research in, 127; and the Sae Maeul movement, 163. *See also* Telecommunications
Components (electronic), 58, 130–31, 179–80, 184
Concessionary loans, 105
Consumer electronics, 177, 179, 180, 184–86
Consumer goods, 85, 130, 131, 177, 179, 181, 182, 184–86
Copper industry: plans for, 19, 121; expansion of, 137
Cotton textiles, 127–28; exports of, 167, 168, 170; improved quality of, 169; production of, 167; supply and demand, 169
Cotton yarn: capacity increase in, 116; productivity in, 167, *169*, 170; supply and demand, 169
County *(gun)* government, 161, 162, 164
Credit: for distressed industries, 75–76; long-term, 124

Credit Union Law (1972), 162
Crops and livestock: exports of, 146; growth of, 142, 143
Cultivated land, increase in, 146–47
Current account: deficit, 78, 105; surplus, 17

Daeduk, science town at, 127
Debt service, 7, 15, 16, 41, 47, 65, 66, 67, 105, 106
Defense spending, 99
Democratic Republican Party, 28, 45
Devaluation (of *won*), 43, 61, 76, 94, 95, 169, 174
Distribution of growth benefits, 11, 83
Domestic market, 118, 129, 134, 135, 179
Domestic savings, 6, 11–13, 17, 18, 41–43, 60, 83, 97–98, 100–03, 124
Double cropping, 140
Drainage, 142, 143, 147, 150
Duties. *See* Tariffs

Economic growth, 27, 37, 40–41, 59, 60, 69, 82–83
Economic Planning Board (EPB), 10, 62, 81, 95, 97
Education, 33–35; expenditures in, 34
Electric power, 31, 32, 39, 56, 70, 124, 137, 177
Electrification, rural, 108, 163, 164
Electronics industry, 38, 181–82; capacity of, 116; composition of, 180; concentration on, 4, 5, 89; consumer goods in, 180–81, 184–85; employment trends in, 157; exports in, 14, *119*, 130, 178, 184, 186; industrial equipment in, 181; foreign investment in, 177, 179; growth of, 67, *68*, 69, 82, 130, 177–79; labor-intensive nature of, 182; long-term

plan for, 182; marketing development in, 186; production of components, 131, 179–80; research for, 127; and semiconductor technology, 131; supply and demand in, 182–83
Electronics Industry Promotion Law, 179
Employment: in agriculture, 17, 47, 139, 154–56; estimates for 1972–81, 152; in industry and mining, 154–55, 156; long-term projections for, 152–57; nonagricultural, 22, 23, 55, 82, 109–11, 159; opportunities for, 83; and population, 151–52; rural and urban, 47; and school attendance, 152, 154–55; in service sector, 47, 155, *156*, 157; trends in, 22, 46–51, 155, *156*, 157; and unemployment, 22–23, 47
Employment Sample Survey, 152
Energy, 11, 19, 91, 102, 120, 191; demand and supply, *71*; import substitution in, 13, 14, *71*, 92
Engineering industries, 125
Ericson (electronics company), 181
Europe, 62, 85, 89, 135, 171
European Economic Community (EEC), 62, 89, 170, 171
Exchange rate, 21, 43, 56–58, 62, 93–94
Export incentives and subsidies, 8, 21, 41, 56–58, 93–95, 124, 174
Export markets, 128, 162, 170, 171, 174
Exports, 5–6, 13, 30, 38; of agricultural products, 146; diversification of, 14, 128–29; of electronic products, 184, 186; geographic dispersal of, 89; growth in, 13, 15, 59, 60, 61, 62, 63, *64*, 65, 70, 73, 79, 86, 97; long-term framework for, 84–87, 119; of manufactured goods, 86–87; ratio of, to GNP, 4, 13, 40, 88; and Sae Maeul factories, 164; of ships,

189–91; and small- and medium-size factories, 164; of textiles, 167–68; value added content of, 11
External resources, 6, 7, 9, 14, 15, 16, 17, 41, 60, 79–80, 98, 102

Fabrics, 58, 170, 174; production of, 166. *See also* Textile industry
Fairchild Semiconductor, 182
Farm households, *54*, 111; incomes of, 108–10
Farm income, 110
Farm labor, 54, 147
Farm mechanization, 93, 110, 142, 147–48, 150
Farm population, 45, 56, 111–12, 143
Farm sector, 51, 53
Feed grains, 92, 144–46
Fertilizers, 18, 74, 110, 140–42, 144, 148; increased use of, 150; prices of, 53, 149; subsidies on, 18, 75, 100
Fibers. *See* Synthetic fibers
Firewood, 142, 144, 163
Fisheries, 22, 110, 141, 150; employment in, 4; exports of, 146; growth rate, 142–44; investment in, 148–49; production of, 142, 148; value added in, 139
Five-year plans: first (1962–66), 8; second (1967–71), 8, 115; third (1972–76), 8, 81, 82, 83, 116, 148; fourth (1977–81), 10, 13, 19, 81, 83, 87, 88, 91, 101, 102, 120, 141, 148
Flood: control, 147, 150; damage, 140
Food grains, 8, 11, 19, 46, 69, 71, 88, 96, 102–03, 110, 120, 144–46; import substitution in, 13–14, 92–93; prices of, 59–60, 74; production of, 139–40
Footwear, 38, 89, 93, 164
Foreign exchange, 83, 98; earnings, 66, 79, 120; loans, 94, 123; re-

serves, 15, 105, 107; shortage of, 11; uses and sources of, 101–03

Foreign inflows, 63, 65, 106

Foreign investments, 19, 85, 106, 121, 137, 177

Foreign markets, 19, 88, 121

Foreign savings, 6, 9; elimination of dependence on by 1981, 10, 12, 82, 101, 103; reliance on, 41, 97–98; trends in, 60, 79–80

Foreign trade, 106, 132. *See also* Foreign markets

Forest Development Law, 144

Forestry, 110, 150; employment growth in, 4; growth rate in, 142–44; investment projection for, 148–49; value added in, 139

Garment industry, 38, 39, 127–28, 171–72; exports of, 171; production of, 171; prospects of, 172

Garments. *See* Clothing

Germany, 135, 175, 181

Gold Star Company, 180, 181

Grain, 54, 74–75; deficits, 141; imports, 140, *145*–46; production of, 144, 148; subsidies of, 18, 100. *See also* Feed grains; Food grains

Handicrafts, 164

Highways, 31

Hong Kong, 171

Housing, 11, 19, 32, *33*, 55, 96, 124

Hydroelectric power, 26, 32, 70

Hyundai Shipyard, 125, 187, 188

Import substitution: and balance of payments, 13; and capital goods production, 122; in energy, 92; and export growth, 13–14, 30, 88–89, 93; in food grains, 92; in machinery, 92; in raw materials, 14, 92; in intermediate products, 92

Imports: dependence on, 5, 14; of food, 9; growth of, 15, 60, 103, 146; of fuels, 9, 70, 120, 191; pat-

tern of, *72*; ratio of, to GNP, 14, 88, 93; of raw materials, 9, 19, 88, 99, 121

Incentives: for domestic production, 95; for exports, 21; for investment, 174–75; trade, 124

Inchon, 23, 35, 55

Income distribution, 22

Incomes, urban and rural, 22–24, 41, 45–47, 51–56, 82, 108–13, 141

India, 4, 141

Indonesia, 89, 141

Industrial capacity, utilization of, 67

Industrial exports, 38, 56

Industrial financial needs, 122–24

Industrial growth, 3–6, 19–21, 28, 29–30, 37, 44, 78, 79, 118, 124, 125, 135

Industrial machinery, 13, 20, 121, 135–37. *See also* Machinery

Industrial planning framework, 124–25

Industries: heavy, 14, 19, 20, 90–91, 115, 117, 120, 121, 156; heavy and chemical, 12, 115, 116, 121, 123, 124, 125; labor-intensive, 4; light, 20, 67, *68*, 116, 121, 156–57; Sae Maeul, 163–64

Industry: decentralization of, 55; diversification of, 11; rural, 163–64

Inflation: 7, 8, 18, 44–45, 61, 74, 76, 79, 100, 101; international, 13, 15, 16, 102, 105, 122

Infrastructure, 11, 19, 30–32, 96, 177

Interest rates, 18; and inflationary pressures, 101; policy on, 7, 43, 100–01; reduction in, 45

Intermediate goods, 20–21, 92–93, 95, 117, 119, 121

International Labour Organisation, 35

International Monetary Fund, 78

Investment: fixed, 39, 40, 60; gross, 97; in heavy and chemical industries, 19; increases in, 43; industrial, 120–21, 125; in light manufacturing, 20; need for, 11, 95, 96, 97; public sector, 75; rate of, 43, 79; ratio of, to GNP, 6, 7
Iran, 89
Iron and steel industry, 133–35; exports of, 5; growth of, 67, 68, 69
Irrigation, 93, 140–43, 147, 149, 150

Japan: as a market, 4–5, 14, 38, 59, 63, 64, 78, 120; economic growth in, 85–86; loans from, 105; participation ratio of, 154; recession in, 70, 73; overseas investments by, 106
Japan Shipbuilders' Association, 190

Kim, Kwang, 58n
Knit goods, 128, 165, 167, 170–72
Knitting industry, 129, 170–71
Koje Island, 187
Korea, historical background of, 25–29
Korea Development Institute, 57
Korea Electric Company, 163
Korea Institute of Science and Technology (KIST), 125, 126, 135
Korea–U.S. Joint Economic Committee for Economic Rehabilitation and Stability, 27
Korean Productivity Center, 130
Korean Shipbuilding and Engineering Company (KSEC), 132, 187
Korean Traders' Association (KOTRA), 129, 172
Korean War, 26, 30, 151

Labor force, 29, 153, 155, 177, 180
Labor productivity, 22, 47, 67, 82, 140, 141, 156
Labor-intensive: activities, 4, 141, 164, 167, 184; exports, 13; products, 5, 128, 129, 182; services, 157
Land consolidation, 147, 148
Land reclamation, 142, 163
Land reform program, 26, 53n
Land resources, development of, 146–47, 150
Large-scale integrated (LSI) technology, 181, 184
Lead, 19, 121
Leather industry, 67, 68
Light industry, 20, 118, 121, 136, 156–57
Light manufactures, 14, 38, 90, 91, 122, 126
Livestock, 54, 139, 141, 144–45, 148, 150, 163. *See also* Crops and livestock
Long-term framework, 10, 81, 82, 95; and agricultural development, 141; and entrepreneurial skills, 84; and energy, 83; and electronics, 115; and exports, 84–87, 89; and foreign exchange, 102; and foreign investment, 85; and the fourth five-year plan, 120; and heavy industry, 91, 115–16; and incomes of households, 108; and manufacturing investment, 116–17, 121n; and manufacturing output, 115–16; and pollution in other countries, 85; and world trade, 85
Long Term Agreement (LTA), 169

Machine tools, 135–37
Machinery, 67, 91, 156; imports of, 94; import substitution in, 92, 93; and parts, 192. *See also* Industrial machinery
Machinery industry, 76, 93, 124, 134, 135–37; employment trends in, 156; growth of, 67, 68, 135; export targets of, 90, 119
Malaysia, 13, 85, 88

Manufactured goods, world trade in, 86–87
Manufactured exports, 3–5, 8, 37–39, 120, 167
Manufactures: heavy, 14, 90–91, 117–20; light, 14, 38, 90, 91
Manufacturing: capacity expansion of, *118*; capital-output ratios of, 4, 39; concentration of, 69; debt-equity ratio for, 123; employment growth in, 4; in GNP, 4; growth in, 19, 45, *66*, *67*, *68*; investment in, 39, *117*, 120, 121, 122, 145; output of, 40, 115, 116; wages in, 47
Marginal saving, 17; rate of, 12, 42, 44, 60, 98, 103
Market: concentration, 4–5, 14; diversification, 14, 73, 128; research, 129, 172, 185–86
Mechanical engineering, 125, 127
Medical facilities, 108, 163
Metals: exports of, *119*; growth of fabricated, 67, *68*; smelting of, 85
Migration, rural-urban, 22, 23, 24, 55, 107, 139, 159
Minerals, 26, 28, 29, 106
Mining, 154
Ministry of Commerce and Industry, 125
Ministry of Education, 34
Ministry of Finance, 123
Ministry of Health and Social Affairs, 151
Ministry of Home Affairs, 159, 163
Monetary survey (1970–74), 77
Motor vehicle industry, 14, 90, 137, 138. *See also* Automobile companies
Mukho, limestone deposits at, 137

Naphtha production, 69, 115
National Agricultural Cooperative Federation (NACF), 162
National Investment Fund (NIF), 123, 124

National Service Law (1973), 163
Natural resources, 28
Netherlands, 13, 88, 136
Neutral Nations Inspection Committee, 27
Nippon Electric Company, 181
Nonferrous metals industry, 19, 123; plans for, 121; proposed expansion of, 137
Norway, 13, 88
Nuclear power, 32
Nylon, 129, 172, 175

Ocean research, 127
Office of Labor Affairs, 34, 35
Oil, 5, 8; crisis, 70, 132, 138, 190; effect of price rise of, 59, 71, 74, 88, 190; refining capacity, 132
Okpo, proposed shipyard at, 132, 187
Organisation for Economic Cooperation and Development (OECD), 13, 78, 87, 103
Organization of Petroleum Exporting Countries (OPEC), 16, 106
Oriental Precision Company, 181

Paddy area, 142, 146, 147, 188
Pakistan, 149
Park Chung Hee, 10, 23, 28, 45, 46, 81, 107, 159
Passenger cars, 14, 71, 90, 138
Pesticides, 141, 142, 144, 149, 150
Petrochemical industry, 5, 85, 115, 123, 125; plans for, 19, 82, 121; research in, 127
Petroleum. *See* Oil
Petroleum industry: growth of, 67, *68*, 69; investment in, 123; technical assistance in, 125
Philippines, 34, 85, 141, 149
Plastics, 69
Plywood: concentration on, 4, 5, 89; exports of, 38, 58, 67, 69
Pohang, steel plant in, 69, 115, 117

Pohang Iron and Steel Company (POSCO), 133–34

Pollution, industrial, 85, 106, 121

Population: and age distribution, 151–52; and participation rate, *153*, 154; trends in, 37, 47n, 111, 151–52; urban and rural, 45, 111

Pork, 146

Port facilities, 31

Products: design and promotion of, 171, 185–86; diversification of, 14

Provincial government, 161

Public finances, weakness in, 17, 98, 99

Pusan, 22, 23, 26, 35, 55; shipyard in, 187, 188

Radios, 131, 177, 180, 181, 185

Railroads, 31, 70

Raw materials: decline in price of, 103; import substitution in, 92, 93; rise in price of, 9, 60, 73; stockpiling of, 76, 78; for textile industry, 165, 170, 172–74

Recession in Japan and U.S., 59, 60

Reforestation, 162–63

Research and development, 124, 126–27

Research institutes, 127

Resource requirements, 11–13

Revenues and expenditures, government, 17, 42–43, 58, 100

Rhee regime, 28

Rice: crop yields of, 141; imports of, 53, 92, 100; price of, 22, 44, 45, 46, 53, 74, 76, 110, 149; production of, 140, 143, 144; self-sufficiency in, 144

Roads, 31, 108, 162–63

Roof improvement program, 108, 162

Russo-Japanese War, 28

Sae Maeul (New Community), 23, 46, 107–08; and communications, 163; investment in, 159–61; and land reclamation, 163; and medical facilities, 163; objectives of, 107, 159; physical achievements of, *160*; and rural industries, 163–64; and village improvement, 162–63; and women, 161

Sam Sung, 180

Saudi Arabia, 89

Savings, 6, 12, 59, 60, *61*; domestic, 6, 13, 17, 18, 41–43, 97–98, 101, 103; government, 6, 42; and investment, 75; private, 7, 8, 43; public, 17, 42, 43, 74, 75, 98; rural, 162

Savings-investment gap, 41, 102

School attendance, 152, 154, *155*

Semiconductor products: assembly of, 180, 182; technology for, 131

Seoul, 22, 23, 45; concentration of industry in, 55; subway system in, 138

Sericulture, 141, 142, 144, 146, 150

Sewing machines, 135

Ships: export of, 5, 14, 90, 91, *119*, 132, 189–90; launchings by other countries, *188*; orders for, 188–89

Shipbuilding industry: capacity of, 116, 121, 132, 187, 190; credit in, 133; domestic market of, 132, 191; employment trends in, 156; expansion of, 82, 193; and oil crisis, 190; plans for, 121; and research, 127; and second-hand vessels, 191–92; and ship components, 192; and Suez Canal, 132, 191; and U.S. policy, 191

Shipyards, 19, 69, 117, 121, 132, 187–88, 191

Siemens AG, 181

Signetics, 182

Silk: looms for, 135; exports of, 128, 146; raw, 54, 139. *See also* Sericulture

Social overhead capital, 31, 96, 120
Soybeans, 144, 145, 149
Spinning, 129, 167; machinery, 136
Steel industry, 5, 14, 133–35; export targets of, 90, 91; plans for, 82, 121; plan for second plant, 19, 117, 121, 134; projected capacity, 116–17
Subsidies, grain and fertilizer, 18, 75, 100
Suez Canal, 132, 191
Sugar, raw, 146
Switzerland, 135
Synthetic fiber industry, 129; capacity of, 116; growth of, 69, 128, 129; and oil prices, 175; prospects for, 174–75; structural weaknesses in, 174
Synthetic fibers: consumption of, 128, 173; export of, 91; import substitution in, 69, 174; production of, 165, 167, 172–73, 175

Taehan Aluminum Refinery Company, 137
Tai-Han Electric, 180, 181
Taiwan, 23, 37, 39, 55, 57, 140, 141, 145, 148, 149, 154n, 169, 171
Tamura Electric Works, 181
Tankers, 132, 187–88, 190–91
Tape recorders, 131, 180
Tariffs: exemptions, 56–57; rates, 95, 174; reduction, 45, 60
Tax: effort, 42–43; exemptions, 56–57; incentives and penalties, 159; relief, 76; structure, 99–100
Technical training, 34–35, 154
Telecommunications: development of, 108, 163; equipment, 177, 181
Telephone: facilities, 32; sets, 181
Television sets, 131, 180, 181, 184, 185
Terms of trade, 5, 9, 69, 71, 73, 79–80, 83, 97, 103; agricultural, 12, 18, 23, 46, 76, 108, 110, 141

Textile industry, 38, 127–30, 165–75; concentration on, 4, 5, 89; and cotton textiles, 166, 169–70; and economies of scale, 167; employment trends in, 156; exports, 14, 91, *119*, 128, 167, *168*; growth of, 67, 68, 69, 170; import substitution in, 128; labor-intensive and capital-intensive segments of, 128–29; linkages in, 165; market research in, 129; shift toward synthetics in, 127; structure of, 166, 170; world, 128
Textile machinery, 135–36
Thailand, 34, 85
Thermal power, 32
Timber, 144, 163
Tobacco, 67, 141, 142, 143
Tourism, 63, 65, 66
Trade policies and incentives, 93, 124
Transport, 31, *32*, 71, 138, 177; equipment, 5, 65. *See also* Railroads; Roads
Turkey, 34

Ulsan: oil refinery at, 69, 115; shipyard at, 69, 187
United Nations Development Programme, 35, 125
United Nations Korean Relief Agreement on Economic Matters, 27
United States: assistance from, 6, 16, 26, 42, 105; as market for exports, 4, 5, 14, 38, 44, 59, 61, 62, 63, *64*, 78, 89; and electronics, 179–80, 186; oil imports, 190–91; recession in, 59–60, 70, 73; and textiles, 128, 170, 171
Urbanization, 30, 45, 55–56, 139

Vegetables, 53, 54, 139, 141, 142, 144
Villages, 107, 108, 159–62

Vocational training, 34, 154, 164

Wage trends, 23, 47, *50*, 51, 85, 154, 157
Wastage allowance, 56, 56n, 57
Water resources, 110, 140, 145, 147, 150
Water supply, 108, 162
Weaving, 167, 169
Westphal, Larry, 58n
Wheat, 74, 92, 144, 145, 149

Wigs: concentration on, 4, 5; exports of, 38, 39, 89, 93
Wood products, 67, *68*, 69
World Bank: estimates, 82n, 86, 111; and future borrowing, 16, 106; survey of agriculture by, 143

Yarn, 166, 167, 170

Zinc, 137

The Rural Population of Korea by Province, 1973
A Computer-Generated Map

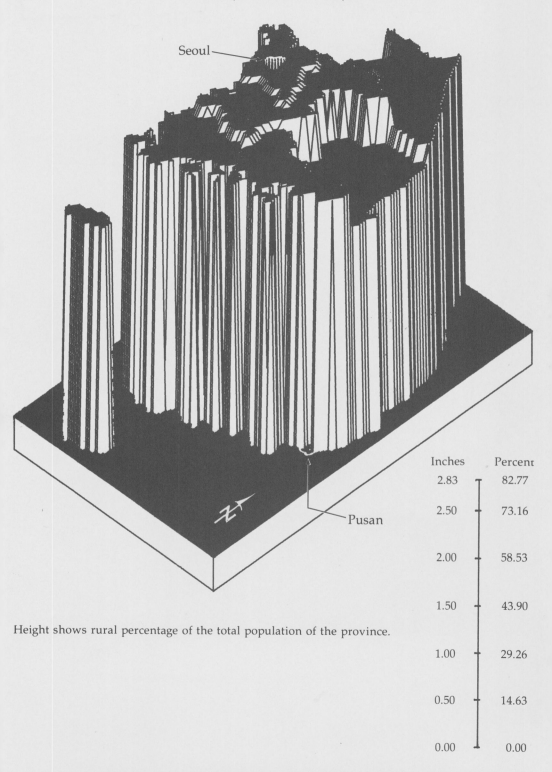

Seoul

Pusan

Height shows rural percentage of the total population of the province.

Inches	Percent
2.83	82.77
2.50	73.16
2.00	58.53
1.50	43.90
1.00	29.26
0.50	14.63
0.00	0.00